"The purpose of Proverbs is to make a person wise, able to navigate life well, be good, and fear the Lord. Preaching on the book of Proverbs is essential to the development of spiritually mature Christians. Jared Alcántara is an excellent guide to the book and to its exposition and proclamation. I am very happy to enthusiastically recommend this book to everyone, but especially to those who preach."
  Tremper Longman III, Distinguished Scholar and Professor Emeritus of Biblical Studies, Westmont College

"For many preachers, the scriptural nuggets called proverbs seem too small to generate full sermons. Not for Jared Alcántara who, skillfully using the razor-sharp tools of exegesis, reaches again and again into the depths of biblical proverbs to find provocative images, fascinating characters, profound theological themes, and more. Preachers who read this stimulating, engagingly written book will be transformed from a reluctance to preach on proverbs to enthusiasm."
  Thomas G. Long, Bandy Professor Emeritus of Preaching, Candler School of Theology

"*How to Preach Proverbs* by Jared Alcántara is an exegetically profound, homiletically practical look at a neglected portion of Scripture. Focusing primarily on proverbs from the Old Testament, Alcántara counters the common preacherly misconception that proverbs are harmless sound bites to embroider on pillows. On the contrary, he convincingly argues, they have prophetic bite. He connects the literary features of proverbs to ethical goals and theological affirmations related to justice and integrity, showing how we can convey a prophetic message through the ethical and theological emphases of Proverbs. Not only is *How to Preach Proverbs* a substantive, exegetically profound work, it is also highly practical for homiletical use. Each chapter ends with a "conclusion," "for further study," "talk about it," "dig deeper" and "practice." I highly recommend this practical, profound contribution to the preaching of proverbs."
  Alyce M. McKenzie, Le Van Professor of Preaching and Worship, Altshuler Distinguished Teaching Professor, Perkins School of Theology

"Preaching Proverbs is notoriously difficult and tends to be avoided, even in the most distinguished pulpits. Yet, the modern church needs contextualized wisdom from Proverbs more than ever! Jared Alcántara provides an accessible resource that is sure to be an asset to contemporary preachers for generations to come. Alcántara's helpful book supplies the tools to facilitate faithful, non-moralistic preaching of the proverbs, along with constructive advice that can immediately be put into practice. Readers will lay aside their misconceptions about preaching Proverbs when they pick up Alcántara's outstanding resource. This book is a must-read for those who desire to have a God-centered approach to preaching the book of Proverbs!"

Dominick S. Hernández, Associate Professor of Old Testament and Semitics, Talbot School of Theology, Biola University

"Jared Alcántara digs deep into the book of Proverbs to explore its rich resources of wisdom to assist preachers in preparing and presenting fresh perspectives on a book long overlooked in the pulpit. Alcántara offers strategies and concrete examples for preaching the major themes, images, and characters found throughout the book. Preachers will discover a treasure trove of fresh insights and creative ideas for developing challenging sermons. Alcántara's work couldn't be timelier and more practical for preachers."

Dave Bland, Professor Emeritus, Harding School of Theology, Memphis, TN

"Jared Alcántara's *How to Preach Proverbs* fills a gap in the field of homiletics as well as hermeneutics. This well-written handbook provides the preacher with the information and tools needed to approach a sometimes daunting biblical book. In each chapter, Alcántara offers thoughtful strategies—genre, imagery, characters, themes, timing, integrity, and justice—that serve as keys to interpreting and preaching this biblical book. Alcántara is to be commended for writing a rich, clear, and accessible source for preaching Proverbs that every pastor will want to use."

Scott M. Gibson, David E. Garland Chair of Preaching, Truett Seminary

How to Preach Proverbs

*For Tío (Uncle) Jesús Alcántara (1937-2021) y (and)
Tía (Aunt) Francisca Matamoros de Alcántara (1936-2020)
en (in) Honduras*

*Su amor y generosidad perduran en
las generaciones que les siguen*

*Their love and generosity endure
in the generations that follow after them*

How to Preach Proverbs

Jared E. Alcántara

Fontes

How to Preach Proverbs

Copyright © 2022 by Jared E. Alcántara

ISBN-13: 978-1-948048-78-1 (paperback)

All rights reserved. No part of this publication may be reproduced, stored in a retrieval system, or transmitted in any form or by any means—electronic, mechanical, photocopy, recording, or any other—except for brief quotations in printed reviews, without the prior permission of the publisher.

All Scripture quotations, unless otherwise indicated, are taken from the Holy Bible, New International Version®, NIV®. Copyright ©1973, 1978, 1984, 2011 by Biblica, Inc.™ Used by permission of Zondervan. All rights reserved worldwide. www.zondervan.com. The "NIV" and "New International Version" are trademarks registered in the United States Patent and Trademark Office by Biblica, Inc.™

Typeset by Monolateral™ in Minion 3 and Museo Sans.

FONTES PRESS
DALLAS, TX
www.fontespress.com

Contents

Acknowledgments xv

Preface xvii

1. Genre 1
   Strategy 1: Do What the Genre Does 2
   - Use Genre-Specific Tools: Know What a Proverb Is 3
   - Do in Your Context What (You Believe) It Did in Its Context .. 9
   - Remember the Point 16
   - Conclusion 21
   - For Further Study 22

2. Imagery 25
   Strategy 2: Bring Images to the Center 27
   - Identifying Imagery in the Book of Proverbs 27
   - Bringing Images to the Center of a Sermon on Proverbs 33
   - Conclusion 41
   - For Further Study 42

3. Characters 45
   Strategy 3: Use Characterization 46
   - Animals 46
   - Woman Wisdom Versus Woman Folly 50
   - The Sluggard 55
   - The Wife of Noble Character 58
   - Conclusion 65
   - For Further Study 66

4. Themes 69
   Strategy 4: Use a Thematic Approach 70
   - Preaching a Thematic Sermon or a Thematic Series 75
   - Conclusion 88
   - For Further Study 89

5. Timing 91
   Strategy 5: Associate Timing with Wisdom 92
   - Knowing Roads and Seeing Signs 92
   - Connect the Appearance of Contradictions with the
     Importance of Timing 93

- Help People Make Well-Timed Choices in Context-Specific Situations 98
- Translate Timing's Importance for Modern Listeners 102
- Conclusion 104
- For Further Study 104

6. **INTEGRITY** 107
   Strategy 6: Tie Wisdom to Integrity 108
   - The Purpose of Proverbs 109
   - Protecting the Inner Life that Others Do Not See 112
   - Pursuing Uprightness Before Others 118
   - Living with "the Dash" in Mind 123
   - Conclusion 126
   - For Further Study 127

7. **JUSTICE** 129
   Strategy 7: Adopt a Prophetic Tone 131
   - Why (Some) Preachers Avoid Preaching about Justice from the Book of Proverbs 132
   - Proverbs in Three Dimensions 135
   - A Closer Reading of Proverbs' Purpose Statement 139
   - Preach the Purpose Statement 141
   - God Makes Promises to Those Who Reach Out 144
   - Conclusion 148
   - For Further Study 148

8. **CONCLUSION** 151

APPENDIX 1: UNDERSTANDING AND PREACHING PROVERBS 31:10–31
   Rebecca W. Poe Hays 155
   - The Hebrew Text of Proverbs 31:10–31 156
   - Personification in the Ancient Near East 157
   - The Organizing Structure of Proverbs 161
   - So How Should We Preach it? 162

APPENDIX 2: SERMONS 165
   "STREET SMARTS" – PROVERBS 3:21–35 165
       Jared E. Alcántara 165
   "WISDOM FOR TIMES OF UNCERTAINTY" – PROVERBS 30:24–28 .. 176
       Ralph Douglas West 176
   "PROVERBS 31" – PROVERBS 31:1–31 191
       Ingrid Faro 191

BIBLIOGRAPHY 203

SCRIPTURE INDEX. 209

SUBJECT INDEX 219

Acknowledgments

The list of people to whom I am indebted gets longer every year. The book you are about to read would not have been possible without the support and guidance of a cadre of friends, professional colleagues, and family members.

At the outset, I want to offer my thanks and appreciation to Todd Scacewater and the people at Fontes Press for publishing *How to Preach Proverbs* and for believing in the larger vision of the Preaching Biblical Literature series. Thank you to the series editors, Jeffrey D. Arthurs and Kenneth J. Langley, with particular appreciation given to Jeffrey D. Arthurs who was my primary editor for this book. I appreciated your keen eye for detail and your helpful ideas for how to improve the manuscript.

I am grateful to the many people who provided me with feedback as this project was taking shape: M. Daniel Carroll Rodas, W. Dennis Tucker, Stephen F. Reid, and the PhD in Preaching students who participated in my doctoral seminar on Psalms and Proverbs. Thank you to my research assistant, Todd Hilkemann, who was diligent and effective at finding resources, scanning books, transcribing one of the sermons in the appendices, proofreading chapters, and generating chapter discussions among many other things.

I am also appreciative toward those who came alongside later in the process to offer me feedback on the rough draft: Alyce McKenzie, Ingrid Faro, Greg Scharf, Scott Gibson, Paul Koptak, and Dave Bland. I know that you are busy, and I appreciate you for being generous with your time.

Thank you to the three people who made contributions to this volume in the appendices whether through writing an article or providing a sermon: Rebecca Poe Hayes, Ralph Douglas West, and Ingrid Faro. This book is better because of your contributions to it.

Thank you to my seminary and university colleagues for granting me the time and the space to complete this project. I could not have completed this book by the deadline without the blessings of a research leave granted to me by the administration at Baylor University's Truett Theological Seminary. Thanks to my dean, Todd Still.

Most importantly, I want to thank my family for providing me with constant support, encouragement, cheerleading, and sacrifice, especially around an imminent book deadline. In particular, I want to thank my wife Jennifer whose love, generosity, and friendship blesses me in more ways than I can fully comprehend.

This book is dedicated to two family members in Honduras whom I have lost in recent years: my Tía (Aunt) Panchita (her given name was Francisca) who died of kidney-complications and other health problems in 2020 and my Tío (Uncle) Jesús who died of complications from COVID-19 in 2021. They were married for 62 years before she preceded him in death. One of the only things that competed with their love for each other was their love for others. Those whose lives they touched are proof of it.

Preface

This year marks 25 years since I preached my first sermon. Years ago, somewhere around the 20-year mark, I started to file my sermons alphabetically by books of the Bible in one of those 5-foot-high metal filing cabinets so that I could archive them. Up until then, my filing system consisted of papers thrown in boxes with no order or sequence.

I learned a lot through a process that felt at times like a grueling ordeal. Some of my earliest sermons should remain under lock and key in the cabinet never to see daylight again. Some of my sermons from 10 years ago read with the flow and coherence of a preacher with young children at home. The Letter L folder revealed that I love preaching from the gospel of Luke. I needed extra room in the Letter J folder: Joshua, Judges, Job, Jonah, Jeremiah, John, James, 1–3 John, Jude. I guess I have a secret love for books of the Bible that start with J.

But I also noticed a gap in my files. The Letter P folder looked thin. I had a nice sampling of sermons from Philippians and some from Psalms, actually, more than I expected from Psalms. That was not the issue. The problem was, I could hardly find any sermons from the book of Proverbs. Where were they? I had less than 10 sermons in files that spanned 20 years. Were they lost somehow? I could remember leading lots of Bible Studies on Proverbs, and I thought that I had preached from the book, but my files told a different story. I was embarrassed, and I knew I needed to close the gap somehow.

Over the last five years especially, I have made it a point to preach as much as possible from the book of Proverbs while striving to hold in tension a concern to honor its message and genre in its ancient context, and a desire to contextualize its message and genre in a modern context. Easier said than done. I also chose to study the book in-depth, to conduct research on it, and to teach courses on it at the Masters- and PhD-level. I decided that I might as well lean into an area where I knew I needed to grow. It stretched me as a preacher and teacher but in the right ways. It will be a long journey to catch up for the years that I missed. Yet the window remains open to fill the Letter P folder with more sermons from Proverbs.

My commitment to closing this gap in my preaching gives you some context for the book that you are about to read: *How to Preach Proverbs*. You can trace this project's conception to a metal-filing-cabinet-epiphany in my garage. I wanted to publish a preaching resource that I wished I would have had years ago. If I had read it, I could have appreciated Proverbs earlier and preached from it more often. Perhaps you find yourself in a similar predicament. If so, I hope this resource will close a gap in your preaching as well.

This book is part of the *Preaching Biblical Literature* series edited by Jeffrey D. Arthurs and Kenneth J. Langley, a detail that will also provide some context for what you are about to read. The purpose of the series is to expose preachers to different genres in the Bible, in most instances, the ones that are preached less often (e.g., psalms or apocalyptic literature), and to equip them with genre-conscious strategies for preaching from these books. No need to be scared off or intimidated by the phrase "genre-conscious strategies." It simply means that we want to equip you in such a way that you will honor the content and genre in its ancient context and contextualize it well in your own context.

Think of it is as giving a builder the right tools for a job. Builders have tools that they bring with them to every job, but they also benefit from having particular tools for particular jobs. The same goes for preachers. We have exegetical, theological, and homiletical tools that we can bring with us to every text and every genre in the Bible, no doubt tools that will help us, but we can also benefit from having specific tools for specific genres. Builders who lack the right tools for the job do not know where to start. They feel stuck.

Builders who have the right tools for the job enjoy their work. Others get to benefit.

A genre-conscious approach to preaching proverbs, first and foremost, requires a willingness to study what the writers are saying *and* what the writers are doing with what they are saying. We already know that a proverb is different from an epistle, which is different from a narrative text. The genres are different. When we pay attention to what the writers are doing with what they are saying, we show that we care about *how* they are different.

In short, biblical proverbs are mini-poems that communicate powerful truths in memorable ways (often in eight words or less) using poetic parallelism and figures of speech. You can find these mini-poems in other books of the Bible (e.g., Ezek 12:22; Luke 4:23), but the main place to find them is the book of Proverbs, a book in which nearly every verse is a biblical proverb. The book of Proverbs is an anthology of biblical proverbs that spans several centuries. Sometimes the poems come in a string-like format that is successive (e.g., Chapters 1–9, 30–31) and other times they come in a single-sentence format that seems detached from the sentence that comes before and after it (e.g., Chapters 10–22). A preacher who is invested in understanding this genre will be able to identify its distinctive qualities such as its poetics and rhetorical effects, and consequently have a good sense of what the writers were doing with what they were saying.

Also, a genre-conscious approach to preaching proverbs requires a commitment to take what the writers were doing with what they were saying in *their* context and emulate it when we preach in our context. In *Preaching and the Literary Forms of the Bible*, Thomas G. Long poses the question well when he asks: "How may the sermon in a new setting, say and do what the text says and does in its setting?" a question I will answer more in-depth in Chapter 1.[1] For instance, if the proverb in its context uses figurative language such as similes or metaphors, how might you preach the similes or metaphors in your context? If the desired

---

[1] Thomas G. Long, *Preaching and the Literary Forms of the Bible* (Fortress, 1989), 61.

rhetorical effect of the proverb is humor, how might you use humor when you preach it?

Finally, a genre-conscious approach to preaching proverbs requires an openness to preaching differently than we might have in the past. Preachers avoid the book of Proverbs for a number of reasons. Perhaps it is too intimidating to preach a different kind of genre in a different kind of way. In this book, I will give you tools for identifying proverbs so that you can appreciate them better than you do now, and I will give you concrete strategies to help you preach them better than you do now.

In *How to Preach Proverbs,* I will commend seven integral aspects of biblical proverbs: genre, imagery, characters, themes, timing, integrity, and justice. My focus will be on biblical proverbs in the book of Proverbs. In each chapter, I will propose one specific strategy connected to the particular pattern under consideration, and I will offer concrete ideas for how to actualize that strategy in your sermon. You know your context best, which means that you know which ideas will work better in your congregation. That stated, just about every preacher I know likes to have something specific to aim at when trying new things. You never know what could happen. It may well be that, as a result of reading this book, your Letter P folder will get thicker and the sermons you put in it will be better.

Jared E. Alcántara
March 2022
Waco, TX

1

Genre

If you ask most movie buffs what types of movies they like to watch, they will know how to answer your question right away. They will say, "Action movies," "Romantic comedies," "Superhero films," "Horror films," or perhaps another category. Now, if you ask them for an academic answer on what movie genres are and how they function, they might look at you sideways. They might have a tacit understanding of what a movie genre is and perhaps choose the right answer if you put a multiple-choice test in front of them, but the word and the question would sound too academic. If you used another word like "type" or "category" of movie, then they would probably get your meaning. You would likely have a similar conversation and result if you talked to most music lovers, foodies, or car enthusiasts.

Perhaps the word "genre" sounds less peculiar if you use it with people who love to read since the word is more common in literature. Ask them to name their favorite genre of novel, they might say "thrillers," "mysteries," or "romance." Although genre is not a common, every-day word, many people already have a sense of what it means: some kind of category.

It makes sense, then, that the word comes up in conversations about the Bible, as it is a book that has many different genres and sub-genres. The books of the Hebrew Bible are divided into large macro-sections as a way to separate them: the Torah, the Writings, and the Prophets. Within one of these larger sections, a person studying a chapter or book could ask: "Am I reading poetry, prophecy, or narrative right now?" They could also ask sub-genre questions: "Is this a praise psalm, an enthronement psalm, or a lament psalm?" You get the point.

The book of Proverbs belongs to the genre of Wisdom Literature, a genre that includes two other major books: the book of Ecclesiastes and the book of Job.[1] Ecclesiastes uses prose as its primary mode of communication, Proverbs uses poetry, and Job uses both. A biblical proverb has a particular form, style, content, pattern, and structure that make it a distinct genre.[2] Incidentally, the book of Proverbs joins ten other books in that its title and its genre are the same (Chronicles, Psalms, Song of Songs, Lamentations, the four Gospels, Acts, and Revelation).[3]

When preaching from the book of Proverbs, we face a generic challenge of sorts. How will we use the knowledge we acquire about genre in order to preach from this book better than we do right now? In this chapter, we will formulate an answer. As I mentioned in the Preface, this book is organized around strategies. Let's turn our attention to the first one.

Strategy 1:
Do What the Genre Does

To get at what is meant by this strategy, I will focus on three areas

---

1 The word "major" here is intentional so that the focus is placed on the three books in the Wisdom Literature that are not debated by scholars. Some count Song of Songs as a Wisdom Book while others do not. Others include select psalms within the Psalter as a Wisdom Book. Thus, under a broad definition of Wisdom Literature, the list expands to five books: Job, Ecclesiastes, select psalms within the Psalter, Proverbs, and Song of Songs. When we go beyond the 39 books in the Protestant version of the Hebrew Bible, the list expands to seven books: Job, Ecclesiastes, Psalms, Proverbs, Song of Songs, Wisdom of Solomon, and Ecclesiasticus (Wisdom of Sirach).

2 OT scholar John Barton defines genre in the Bible as "a conventional pattern, recognizable by certain formal criteria (style, shape, tone, particular syntactic or even grammatical structures, recurring formulaic patterns), which is used in a particular society in social contexts which are governed by certain formal conventions." See John Barton, *Reading the Old Testament: Method in Biblical Study* (Westminster, 1984), 32, as cited in Thomas G. Long, *Preaching and the Literary Forms of the Bible* (Fortress, 1989), 24.

3 Longman makes a similar claim, but he does not include the Gospels in his examples. See Tremper Longman III, *Proverbs*, Baker Commentary on the Old Testament: Wisdom and Psalms (Baker Academic, 2015), 29–30.

in succession: know what a proverb is, do what a proverb does, and remember the point of a proverb.

Use Genre-Specific Tools: Know What a Proverb Is

Find Something Better than a Hammer

As preachers, we tend to use the same homiletical tools with unfamiliar biblical genres that have worked for us in the past. It turns out that other people do this, too. We have a modern proverb to describe this tendency: "When all you have is a hammer, everything looks like a nail." A close friend and mentor said this to me early in my ministry. He liked to speak in proverbs and still does. The saying did not originate with him.[4] Regardless, it contained enough wisdom and memorability that my friend heard it, remembered it, and passed it along. What does it mean? Put simply, if you apply the same solution to every problem or answer to every question, then you will fail to realize that different solutions are needed for different problems and different answers for different questions. Give a hammer to a five-year-old, and she will use it on everything from pounding a nail to baking a cookie.

Too often, we use a similar strategy when we preach from the book of Proverbs. We hammer away with a one-size-fits-all approach, when a genre-sensitive approach is what is needed. So, how do we use genre-specific tools? How do we trade in our hammer for something better? It starts with knowing the genre.

The Hebrew word for "proverb," *mashal*, has more than one meaning in the Wisdom Literature and in the rest of the Hebrew Scriptures. The biblical writers use the word to talk about allegories, parables, riddles, taunts, comparisons, contrasts, and other types of sayings.[5] The word occurs numerous times in Proverbs,

---

4 A version of this proverb appeared in 1966 in Abraham Maslow's *The Psychology of Science*. We do not know if the saying originated with Maslow or if he repeated something he heard. Maslow writes: "If the only tool you have is a hammer, it is tempting to treat everything as if it were a nail. In a word, I had either to give up my questions or else to invent new ways of answering them. I preferred the latter course." Abraham Harold Maslow, *The Psychology of Science: A Reconnaissance* (Harper & Row, 1966), 15–16.

5 According to Curtis, the Hebrew word *mashal* "has a broad range of

beginning at 1:1: "The proverbs [*mishle*] of Solomon, son of David, king of Israel." *Mashal* also occurs with reference to individual proverbs (Prov 1:6; 26:7, 9) and as a section header to announce three of the seven collections in the larger anthology (1:1; 10:1; 25:1). In its verb form, *mashal* means "to be like," a definition that shows how a wisdom saying often does the work of comparison and analogy. Although *mashal* is used often, the writers of Proverbs also use other terms such as "sayings" (*dabar*, lit.: "words") to announce the other four collections in the anthology (22:17; 24:23; 30:1; 31:1).[6]

The book starts with a general introduction or preface (1:1–7), and it concludes with an acrostic poem (31:10–31). Usually, the word "proverb" or "saying" signals to the reader that a new section has begun:

1:1	The proverbs of Solomon son of David, King of Israel
10:1	The proverbs of Solomon
22:17	Thirty Sayings of the Wise
24:23	These also are sayings of the wise
25:1	These are more proverbs of Solomon, compiled by…
30:1	The Sayings of Agur
31:1	The Sayings of King Lemuel

The structure of the book reveals that Proverbs is in fact a collection of collections.[7] Most of the wisdom that you find in the book originates in Israel, but there is evidence to indicate an indebtedness in some sections to wisdom traditions outside of Israel, mostly Egyptian.[8] In total, the book contains 915 proverbs.

---

meanings that includes literary forms such as allegories, parables, and taunts. The short aphorisms that we call proverbs are very common throughout the wisdom literature." See Edward M. Curtis, *Interpreting the Wisdom Books: An Exegetical Handbook* (Kregel, 2017), 48. For a similar statement about *mashal*'s broad range of meaning in Proverbs, see Longman, *Proverbs*, 30.

6 In Proverbs 24:23, the word "sayings" (*dabar*) does not appear. The writers use a common practice known as gapping to imply the word without actually writing it in the verse.

7 As Lucas observes, "The study of the structure of Proverbs shows that it is a collection of collections, some of which are attributed to named or unnamed authors other than Solomon." Ernest C. Lucas, *Proverbs* (Eerdmans, 2015), 6.

8 According to Witherington, "the degree of indebtedness of early Israelite

Many of the proverbs in the book are attributed to King Solomon, which makes sense given the rich tradition of Solomonic wisdom in Israel. According to 1 Kings 4:29–32, Solomon spoke 3,000 proverbs (even if he did not write them down, someone else did) and he composed over 1,000 songs. Even so, the titles of the collections reveal that the book is an anthology spanning several centuries and composed by several authors, named and unnamed. In every culture, proverbs are the property of a community that passes wisdom along from one generation to the next. As Ellen F. Davis reminds us, "Proverbs do not belong to an author so much as to a whole people. Sayings become proverbial when they have passed indiscriminately through many mouths."[9]

With that background in place, let me also provide some parameters around what I mean by a biblical proverb.[10] Although no definition is perfect, let me propose that a proverb is a brief, poetic, and memorable saying designed to help those who fear the Lord to know what is wise and to do what is right—in particular, those who are young, naïve, and new on their journey (1:4).

A Wisdom Saying that is Brief, Poetic, and Memorable

A biblical proverb has three main features that are related: brevity, poetic devices, and memorability. It prizes brevity even more than traditional poetry does. Every word counts, and with this genre in particular there are fewer words with which to count. Sometimes the writers use brevity to craft short, stand-alone wisdom sayings that are like pearls on a string. These usually come in a descriptive

---

Wisdom to international Wisdom and particularly Egyptian Wisdom is notable. This is so not only in the proverbs, but also in the instructions, and possibly also in the personification of Woman Wisdom." Benjamin Witherington III, *Jesus the Sage: The Pilgrimage of Wisdom* (Fortress, 2000), 49–50. Also, Longman writes: "It is always dicey to be dogmatic about specific borrowings, but there is little doubt that Israel's wise teachers read, understood, adapted, and appropriated the wisdom of their (pagan!) neighbors." Longman, *How to Read Proverbs*, 77.

9 Ellen F. Davis, *Proverbs, Ecclesiastes, and the Song of Songs*, Westminster Bible Companion (Westminster John Knox, 2000), 14.

10 As was stated in the Preface, you can find biblical proverbs outside of the book of Proverbs. Our focus in *How to Preach Proverbs* will be on biblical proverbs within the book.

and indicative mode and are found in Collection II (10:1–21:31) and Collection V (25:1–29:27). Other times the authors use brevity in a series of wisdom sayings that are like links in a chain. These "chains" will include some descriptive proverbs, but the majority are prescriptive (e.g., exhortations and direct commands). These proverbs are found in Collections I (1:1–9:18) and III–IV (22:17–24:34). Whether the proverb is a pearl on a string or a link in a chain, the larger purpose is to provide instruction for those in pursuit of wisdom.

According to Ernest Lucas, we lose some of the terseness in a proverb when we translate it into English. In Hebrew, the writers do one of two things to create an economical style. They omit "various Hebrew particles that are common in prose," or they omit key words (such as verbs) often in the second half of the verse through a practice known as "gapping."[11] The typical proverb in Hebrew contains only six to eight words.[12] Most of the time, the version in English uses more words, and it does not reveal the level of artistic brevity in the original language.[13]

A proverb also has poetic devices. Think of a proverb as a mini-poem. Sometimes, it occurs in a single sentence.[14] Other times, it occurs in a purposeful sequence, as is the case with a chain of proverbs.[15] Still other times, it comes as an extended poem, such as the acrostic poem found at the end of the book (31:10–31). To state that a proverb is a mini-poem does not mean that it only has a poetic layer. It also has a narrative layer in that it arises from narrative vignettes that have shaped the wisdom itself (remember that

---

11 Lucas, *Proverbs*, 24.

12 Ibid., 230–31.

13 For more on terseness as one of the three distinctive elements of proverbs specifically and biblical poetry more broadly (with the other two being imagery and parallelism), see Bruce K. Waltke and Ivan D. V. De Silva, *Proverbs: A Shorter Commentary* (Eerdmans, 2021), 10–11. On the matter of terseness, poetics, and translation, Ogden Bellis writes: "They [proverbs] are almost impossible to translate well into English, because of the interplay in the Hebrew between the sounds, rhythm, and meaning of the few words in each line. Additionally, double meanings and complex wordplays add to the translation problems." Alice Ogden Bellis, *Proverbs*, ed. Sarah Tanzer, vol. 23, Wisdom Commentary (Liturgical, 2018), xlv.

14 10:1–21:31; 25:1–29:27.

15 1:1–9:18; 22:17–24:34; 30:1–33; 31:1–9.

the Hebrew word for proverb can also be translated as parable). There is also a practical layer in that a proverb contains partial generalizations aimed at enhancing the common good. My larger point is this: although multi-layered, a biblical proverb contains the same elements as biblical poetry in an even more compact form. It consists of brevity, figurative language, and parallelism.[16] Since I have already mentioned brevity, I will touch briefly on figurative language and parallelism.

The writers of the book of Proverbs use figurative language with regularity. By figurative language, I mean language that uses figures of speech such as similes or metaphors to expand literal meaning. Some figures of speech are readily apparent in English translation, but others are obscured. According to Tremper Longman III, so many figures of speech get lost in the translation from Hebrew to English that a "systematic survey of the devices used in proverbs would be fruitless … most of them are hidden from the eyes of those who read the book."[17] I will say more about figurative language in Chapter 2.

As a sub-genre of poetry, proverbs also contain parallelism. A proverb or string of proverbs usually follows one of three major patterns: antithesis, elaboration, or answer.[18] In antithetical parallelism, the second half of the proverb contrasts with the first half.

---

16 Waltke and De Silva write: "Apart from the prose headings, Proverbs is written in poetry. Three elements characterize biblical poetry: terseness, imagery, and parallelism." See Waltke and De Silva, *Proverbs: A Shorter Commentary*, 10–11.

17 Longman, *How to Read Proverbs*, 44–45.

18 Alter divides the parallelism in the same way with a slightly different term for the final category; antithesis, elaboration, and the "riddle form." However, the third form can also be classified as answer in the sense that verset A implies a question which functions like a riddle and verset B answers it. See Robert Alter, *The Art of Biblical Poetry* (Basic, 2011), 212. Longman III argues for a fourth form of parallelism, what he refers to as "better-than parallelism" (e.g., 12:9; 15:16–17; 16: 8, 16, 19, 32; 17:1, 12; 19:1, 22; 21:9, 19, 25:24; 27:5; 28:6). These proverbs usually have a construction where one half of the verse is lifted up as better than the second half as in, "Better a little with the fear of the Lord than great wealth with turmoil" (15:16). Although this construction is unique when compared to other proverbs, the case could be made that it is a sub-genre of antithetical parallelism in terms of its construction: "better to have or be X *than* to have or be the antithesis of X." See Longman, *How to Read Proverbs*, 42.

For instance: "Whoever loves disciplines loves knowledge, but whoever hates correction is stupid" (12:1). In elaboration parallelism, the second half "intensifies the thought of the first or extends it in time."[19] For instance: "A friend loves at all times, and a brother is born for adversity" (17:17). In answer parallelism, the proverb appears as a sentence in two parts: an implied question and its answer. For instance, the following proverb uses vivid imagery to imply a question in Verset A that is answered in Verset B: "Like a broken tooth or a lame foot is reliance on the unfaithful in a time of trouble" (25:19).

Finally, a proverb is memorable. Of course, the other two characteristics—brevity and poetics—assist in making the proverb memorable, which is why the three are interrelated. Leland Ryken uses the language of "memorable conciseness" to refer to the relationship between brevity and memorability.[20] Imagery also helps us remember. A learner is more likely to remember, "For this command is a lamp, and this teaching is a light ..." (6:23a) than, "For this command will direct you toward what is right, and this teaching will show you the direction you should go."

Although there are strong connections between memorability and the other two features of the genre, memorability still stands on its own as a separate feature.[21] The proverb's memorability accomplishes an important pedagogical function in much the same way that a mnemonic device helps us remember what we have studied. It teaches those in the next generation by helping them remember the collective wisdom of others who have walked the path before them—especially since, in concrete situations, they will be called upon to remember the right proverb at the right time. The

---

19 Long, *Preaching and the Literary Forms of the Bible*, 60.

20 Ryken writes: "A proverb is always a brief utterance. This is part of the key to its memorability. Even the first time we encounter a proverb we know that it is worthy of memory. Its very conciseness makes it striking and attention-getting." See Leland Ryken, *Words of Delight: A Literary Introduction to the Bible* (Baker Academic, 1993), 314.

21 For examples of scholars who treat memorability as a separate category from conciseness or poetics, see Curtis, *Interpreting the Wisdom Books*, 49; Dave Bland, *Proverbs and the Formation of Character* (Cascade, 2015), 71–74; Lucas, *Proverbs*, 205.

goal in memorability for the learner, Dave Bland writes, is for the proverb to be "easily tucked away in the corners of the mind ready for active duty when the occasion demands it."[22]

Designed to Serve a Particular Audience

The audience matters here: the young, the simple, and the naïve are being instructed to know what is wise and to do what is right. Popular modern proverbs often diverge from biblical proverbs because of audience. A popular proverb might say to you, "He who dies with the most toys wins," whereas Proverbs 27:24 tells you, "Riches do not endure forever, and a crown is not secure for all generations." That is not to say that every popular proverb today encourages sinful revelry. Many proverbs lift up the value of friendship, family, or purposeful living. Rather, the contrast shows that biblical wisdom often diverges from popular wisdom in important ways. It also shows how the writers' aspirations for their hearers matter so much in this genre. According to Bruce J. Waltke, "Wisdom restricts the acceptance of her words 'to the upright,' 'to those who find knowledge' (8:9). Were they popular with the masses, Wisdom would not have to stand at the gate of the city pleading a hearing for her sayings (1:20–21; 8:1–3)."[23]

Now that we have discussed what the proverb is, we will turn our attention to doing what the proverb does.

Do in Your Context What (You Believe) It Did in Its Context

So, how do we take what we have learned about what a biblical proverb is and use it to shape how we prepare and preach sermons? To adopt a genre-conscious approach, we will need to go beyond understanding and identifying generic features. The challenge before us is not simply to say what the proverb says, but also to do what the proverb does. A genre-conscious approach, Tom Long

---

22 Bland, *Proverbs and the Formation of Character*, 74.
23 Bruce K. Waltke, *The Book of Proverbs: Chapters 1–15* NICOT (Eerdmans, 2004), 56.

writes, "is based upon the relatively simple idea that the literary form and dynamics of a biblical text can and should be important factors in the preacher's navigation of the distance between text and sermon."[24]

Think of it this way. If what the text says in its context is God's Word to us through the Holy Spirit, then is it not also possible that the Spirit inspired what the text does in its context? Not only can we pay attention to what the text does, but we can also take it one extra step: we can strive to do what the text does when we preach it. Long asks preachers this question: "How may the sermon in a new setting, say and do what the text says and does in its setting?"[25] To answer this question, we will connect preaching to the three elements of biblical poetry: brevity, poetics, and memorability.

Brevity

How do we prioritize brevity so that our sermons feature it in much the same way that a proverb does? We already have a sense of what we should *not* do: create our own long chain of proverbial sayings for the entire sermon. The genre of a sermon is different than the genre of a proverb so it would likely sound a bit peculiar.

To prioritize brevity, let me suggest that you interrogate the bones of your sermon, that is, your main idea along with your points or "moves."[26] For the main idea, work to develop a sentence that is twelve words or less, a complete sentence that is short enough for listeners to write down and be able to say back to you. The twelve-word count forces us to remove the words that are peripheral, and it gives more focus to the central idea. With the points or "moves" in a sermon, write a complete sentence in bold font that starts at the left-hand margin and ends at the right-hand margin without the sentence continuing to the next line. You have a few

---

24 Long, *Preaching and the Literary Forms of the Bible*, 11.
25 Ibid., 61.
26 Buttrick proposes that preachers sequence their sermons in "moves" rather than "points" which puts the sermonic focus on language modules, movement, sequencing, and narrative development. See David G. Buttrick, *Homiletic: Moves and Structures* (Fortress, 1987).

more words to work with, usually about 15 to 16 words instead of 12 words. I know a pastor who abides by this sentence length when he prepares a sermon manuscript, but here is the twist: he practices this rule with *every* sentence. He refuses to let the sentence length pass to the next line. If it runs too long, he re-casts the sentence. After writing from left to right, he hits "return," and starts a new sentence. The practice of writing brief sentences helps him be more succinct, and he also sounds more conversational to listeners.[27]

Also, find a way to mirror the brevity in the text through concise sentences that make similar claims, even if in subtle ways. Take Proverbs 3:35 as an example, a verse that is nine words in English and only six words in Hebrew: "The wise inherit honor, but fools get only shame." I would likely *not* build a sermon around this verse alone since it is part of the larger pericope of Proverbs 3:21–35. Nevertheless, I would still find a way to communicate the claim of this verse in a way that mirrors its brevity. For instance,

> We want to be wise in the end. God has said here, "I will lift up the wise and bring down the foolish." God will honor the wise one and shame the foolish one. God has made a promise to both, but only one will be glad that God did. The wise will be rewarded. The fool will be punished. The wise will get honor. The fool will get disgrace. The wise: an inheritance. The fool: shame. It may not look that way right now. But God has said that it *will* be that way in the future. Only one life will count in the end.

Honor the brevity of a verse like this one by writing in a terse, oral, aural, relational style. Repeat and restate. In delivery, pay attention to meter, flow, pause, and emphasis. Make sure your sentences are concise. The longest sentence in this paragraph is 15 words.

---

27 On the matter of sounding conversational when we preach, Donald R. Sunukjian writes: "We talk in short sentences. Fragments. Easy-to-follow phrases. We don't use big words. We don't sound literary. We sound normal. We talk so that eleven-year-olds can understand us." Donald R. Sunukjian, *Invitation to Biblical Preaching* (Kregel, 2007), 258.

Poetics

Use parallelism and figures of speech. Examine what type of parallelism you find in the verse(s)—antithesis, elaboration, or answer—and how that parallelism might shape what you do in the sermon, such as your outline, structure, flow, or movement. For brevity's sake, I will offer just one example from each type of parallelism:

- Antithesis: "Wounds from a friend can be trusted, but an enemy multiplies kisses" (27:6). Idea 1: make your main idea antithetical so that it mirrors this verse. Idea 2: make the structure of the whole sermon antithetical. In the first part, focus on how to know a true friend, and in the second, how to know a false friend. Set up a contrast: one type of person *versus* another type of person. You also have the freedom to start with verset B and then turn to verset A since the good news is found in the first half of the verse rather than the second half. Idea 3: introduce a theological anthesis as an added layer to the horizontal antithesis, in order to keep yourself from sounding too moralistic. For instance, "We have not been a friend to God, *but* God in Christ has chosen to be a friend to us."
- Elaboration: "Perfume and incense bring joy to the heart, and the pleasantness of a friend springs from their heartfelt advice" (27:9). Idea: Introduce "how much more" language in the sermon. Many (not all) elaboration proverbs are structured as "how much more" claims, what rhetoricians call an *a fortiori* argument: "If X is the case, how much more is Y the case." Tremper Longman III claims that, with elaboration, verse B is not just a restatement of A, but a further extension and continuation of A as in, "A, what's more B."[28] A sermon on this verse or a section of a sermon on this verse could follow a similar movement. The preacher would focus on the simple things that bring "joy

---

28 Drawing from James Kugel's argument that the structure of elaboration is *A, what's more B*, Longman writes: "B not only continues the thought of A, it also adds something to the message of the colon, frequently by focusing it more narrowly." Longman, *How to Read Proverbs*, 40. See also James Kugel, *The Idea of Biblical Poetry: Parallelism and Its History* (Yale University Press, 1981).

to the heart" in much the same way that the writer does (in his case, perfume and incense), and the turn would be the same: "how much more" is true friendship marked by heartfelt advice a source of joy. Both statements are true, but remember the importance of reproducing the rhetorical effect: If A is true, how much more is B true when we put it next to A?

- Answer: "Like a bird that flees its nest is anyone who flees from home" (27:8). With an answer proverb, the second half answers the first half. Question: Who is like a bird that flees its nest? Answer: a person who flees from home. Structure a sermon or a section of a sermon inductively as a question in need of an answer. For instance, in the first part, you might ask, "What do wayward people have in common with wayward birds?" After proposing possible answers, point your listeners to the answer that the text provides: both disappear without regard for the consequences.

With all of these examples, the poetic structure of the proverb in its ancient context shapes how we decide to structure the sermon in the modern context.

Just as parallelism can shape the sermon, so also can figurative language. Let me offer some basic guidelines here. See my chapter on imagery for more ideas.

Idea 1: Mirror the imagery. If there is one controlling image in the text, use a controlling image in the sermon. For example, in Proverbs 30:5, God is called a "shield." You could build the sermon around the imagery of a shield: main idea, key points, etc. If there are several images in the text, consider turning a point-driven or move-driven sermon into an image-driven sermon.[29] For instance, in Proverbs 3:1–6, the father uses images to frame his teachings. Love and faithfulness should be bound around the son's neck, written as a tablet on his heart, with the promise that God will make his paths straight. These three images could frame the movement of a sermon on this text.

---

29 For more on how to build an image-driven sermon, see Thomas H. Troeger, *Imagining a Sermon* (Abingdon, 1990).

Idea 2: Mirror the poetic devices. In other words, if there are metaphors and similes in the verse or verses, then introduce metaphors and similes in the sermon. If there is personification in the passage, then use personification in the sermon.[30] Bear in mind that there are times when modern translation will be needed, such as when we encounter agrarian imagery, but we are preaching in an urban or suburban setting. Or take Proverbs 25:18 as an example: "Like a sword or a club or a sharp arrow is one who gives false testimony against a neighbor." Although they get the main idea, most of our listeners have not used a sword, a club, or a sharp arrow. We might want to give modern examples. Perhaps we could say, "Like a knife or a gun or a grenade."

Idea 3: Mirror the rhetorical effects of the figurative language. Mirror in our context what the figures of speech do in their context. Some proverbs use humor and hyperbole to get the point across such as, "A sluggard buries his hand in the dish; he will not even bring it back to his mouth" (19:24; cf. 26:15). The image is both comedic and tragic. Consider how you might use humor and hyperbole in your context to communicate both the comedy and tragedy of this proverb. Other proverbs use imagery to issue warnings such as, "Like a muddied spring or a polluted well are the righteous who give way to the wicked" (25:26). Bring a tone of warning to the sermon since the proverb itself strikes the same tone. If the imagery of springs or wells does not resonate with modern listeners, consider using more contemporary imagery designed to warn people such as, "Like a river filled with toxic waste or a water main tainted with lead is the righteous who gives way to the wicked."

Memorability

We help our listeners remember our sermon when we deploy the aforementioned strategies, that is when we prioritize brevity in our

---

[30] Personification is the ascription of human characteristics to non-human entities. In the case of the book of Proverbs, two major examples are Woman Wisdom and Woman Folly. I say more about personification in Chapter 2. See also Rebecca Poe Hayes' discussion of personification in Appendix I.

main idea, points, or moves, and when we bring out the poetics in the passage through the use of parallelism and figurative language. Here are some questions to consider when working toward memorability:

- How does the text(s) in its original setting help its community remember the proverb?
- How might I do something like what the text does in my sermon?
- When it comes to my main idea, what poetic strategies can I use besides brevity and imagery that will help people remember the primary idea? Such strategies could include alliteration, assonance, rhyme, parallelism, and meter.
- If the passage uses comparison or contrast to help people remember, how might I use comparison or contrast in the sermon?
- If the passage uses imagery to make people laugh so that they remember, what humorous imagery might I use? Likewise, if the point of the imagery is to shock us, how might I shock people so that they remember? If it is to warn us, how might I warn people so that they remember?

When we consider questions like these, it will help our ideas stick.[31] Our listeners will be more likely to remember what we have said.

Bear in mind that you also have access to other pedagogical tools that assist in the work of memory. For instance, you can repeat and restate the most important claims, especially your main idea, so that people hear what is most important in your sermon multiple times rather than a single time. Also, you can use visual aids. For instance, when you encounter the language of wisdom and instruction as a "garland to grace your head and a chain to adorn your neck," (1:9, cf. 4:9), it does not take much effort to use a garland or a chain as a visual aid.

Finally, some (not all) preachers have access to projectors and screens. These technologies can help people connect the image to the larger claim. For instance, Proverbs 29:25 reads: "Fear of man

---

31 For more on how to make ideas "stick" in public, oral communication, see Chip Heath and Dan Heath, *Made to Stick: Why Some Ideas Survive and Others Die* (Random House, 2007).

will prove to be a snare, but whoever trusts in the Lord is kept safe." We may not have an image of an ancient snare, but we can show people an image of a bear trap or a mouse trap on a screen (or as an insert in a bulletin if we do not use screens in our church). We can also show images of safety and security as an option even if the imagery is only implied in verset B of Proverbs 29:25. For instance, we could use the image of a bank vault. When we use the image of the trap, the goal would be for people to associate the bear trap or mouse trap with the painful mistake of fearing people—it is a trap! When we use the image of a bank vault, the goal would be for listeners to associate its safety and security with what they have in God. If you want, you can juxtapose the two images. Fear of others equals insecure living, like being stuck in a bear trap. Trusting in God and not in others equals secure living, like being protected in a bank vault.

Now that we have discussed the value of doing what a proverb does, we will turn our attention in the last section to remembering the main point when we preach. In so doing, we will best honor what a proverb says and does.

Remember the Point

Finding God in Proverbs

To be sure, we will get better as preachers when we know what the proverb is and do what the proverb does. That stated, if we lose sight of the larger point of the book, then we will say and do things that are out of step with the aims of the book. Remember: the proverb's main job is to point to God as the main actor in creation (past, present, and future) with fear of the Lord serving as the only fitting response. If we miss this, then we miss the ground of a genre-conscious approach.

It all begins with God. Sometimes, we make the mistake of believing that wisdom sayings have little or nothing to say to us about God, that they are more commonsense observations than theological explications.[32] As Derek Kidner puts it, we assume

---

32 According to Long, many preachers avoid Proverbs because of the appearance of a theological void along with what seems like overly moralistic content.

that "the explicitly religious material has to be hand-picked from a large mass of sayings in which religion is only implicit."[33] It can be a challenge to avoid a horizontal focus especially when there is so much about human relationships in the book. How do we keep from sounding overly moralistic? Too many sermons already sound too horizontal and moralistic.[34]

What if our first impressions are misguided? It happens all the time in life. We even have a proverb for it: "Never judge a book by its cover." Perhaps the book of Proverbs is more God-centered than we realize. If we train our eyes to keep the larger purpose of the book in view, then we will find more of a vertical emphasis than we think. Moreover, will be more faithful to the book's overall message.

God is the Main Actor

The writers of the book of Proverbs mention the name(s) of God 98 times. Since the book consists of 915 verses, this amounts to about 11 percent of the verses. The percentage may sound low, but consider that it is a much higher percentage than the book of Ruth or the book of Esther in the Old Testament or the Epistle of James, which is the New Testament equivalent to Proverbs. Consider also that if you and I mentioned God by name one out of every ten sentences, then we would probably talk more about God than we do now.

He writes: "[B]iblical proverbs appear to be largely devoid of theological content . . . . Even when a proverb mentions God, it often appears to do so in a sentimental and mechanical way . . . . Proverbs also seem excessively moralistic and, beyond that, overly concerned with maintaining the status quo." Long, *Preaching and the Literary Forms of the Bible*, 53.

33 Derek Kidner, *Proverbs*, Kidner Classic Commentaries (IVP Academic, 2008), 33.

34 Gibson and Kim have edited a volume that offers an overview on four schools of thought, mostly in Evangelicalism, for having a God-centered hermeneutic: redemptive-historic (Bryan Chapell), Christiconic (Abraham Kuruvilla), Theocentric (Kenneth J. Langley), and Law-Gospel (Paul Scott Wilson). See Scott M. Gibson and Matthew D. Kim, eds., *Homiletics and Hermeneutics: Four Views on Preaching Today* (Baker Academic, 2018).

God's covenant name, the "Lord" or "Yahweh," appears 88 times in the book. At least 19 references connect directly to a prevalent theme—the "fear of the Lord"—the ground and goal of wisdom, a theme we will return to below. In six of the references to the Lord, the writers call on human beings to "trust in the Lord" or to "honor the Lord with your wealth."[35] That still leaves 63 references in which God is the primary subject and initiator. *Elohim*, translated as "God" in English, appears 8 times in the book.[36] At least two times, the writers refer to God as "Maker."[37]

The writers contend that God creates and sustains all things including wisdom itself. Furthermore, God creates all people whether they are rich or poor, oppressor or oppressed, wicked or good.[38] God comes near to those whose way is upright and delights in them.[39] God defends the vulnerable in society.[40] God "detests" perversity (3:32; 11:20), wickedness (3:33; 15:8–9, 26), dishonesty (11:1; 12:22; 20:10, 23), pride (15:25; 16:5), acquitting the guilty and condemning the innocent (17:15), along with the "seven deadly sins" named in Proverbs 6:16–19. God disciplines those he loves and provides justice to those who need it in a far more foundational way than any ruler ever could (3:11–12; 29:26). Human beings (including kings and queens) make plans, arrive at decisions, and take actions, but the book of Proverbs makes clear that it is God and God alone whose plans are enacted for humanity, who directs the steps of those who make decisions, who weighs their hearts in the scales and knows the motives for their actions.[41] God's Word is flawless (the word is *torah* in chapters 28 and 29) and those who obey it through resisting wickedness (28:4) receive blessing on account

---

35 3:5; 16:20; 22:19; 28:25; 29:25. See 3:9 for an "honor" passage.

36 2:5, 17; 3:4; 25:2; 30:1 (2x), 5, 9. Some scholars argue that the name for God appears once in 30:1.

37 For instance, "Whoever oppresses the poor shows contempt for their Maker" (14:31a; cf. also 17:5a with the phrase "mocks the poor").

38 3:19–20; 8:22–31; 15:3; 20:12; 22:2; 29:13. Referring to the creation texts in Proverbs, Waltke writes: "All these texts refer to the Lord as the Creator—none speak of creation apart from his activity, and all assume that he is the sole, sovereign Creator." See Waltke, *The Book of Proverbs*, 1:68.

39 3:26, 32b; 10:29; 11:20; 12:2, 22; 15:8b, 9, 29; 18:10.

40 14:31; 15:25; 17:5; 19:17; 21:3; 22:22–23.

41 5:21; 15:11; 16:1–6, 9, 33; 17:3; 19:21; 20:24; 21:1–2, 30.

of their obedience.[42] God desires to bless those who fear the Lord, who seek wisdom, and who walk in righteousness. This blessing might look like God's favor on their homes and families (3:33), material blessing (3:9-10; 10:22), the provision of food (10:3), a long life (10:27), the gift of a loving and God-fearing spouse (18:22; 19:14), and enemies that live at peace with them (16:7).[43]

God does not serve the part of an "extra" in a movie, an actor without lines who has no meaningful role in the story. No. God speaks and acts in a central and decisive manner as the director and curator of human affairs. God does not work behind the scenes but takes center stage. Leo Perdue writes: "God stands at the center of the teaching of the sages. This means that God provides the wise their insight and ability to understand and know the world but also authenticates the validity of what is taught."[44]

If our homiletical goal is to do what the genre does, then another layer required of us is to connect what we say about our horizontal relationships like marriage, children, neighbors, and friends to our vertical relationship with God. In doing so, we break the chain of misguided first impressions of Proverbs.

Some biblical commentators split their books into sections of textual interpretation, practical application, and theological

---

42 29:15; 30:5.

43 The phrase "might look like" is intentional here since living in a fallen world reminds us that God does not always give material prosperity, long life, a God-loving spouse, or reconciliation with enemies. Drawing on Carol Newsom's language of "iconic narrative," Yoder contends that the writers, especially the parents in Proverbs 1-9, lift up a vision for how things are according to God's plans (an iconic narrative) even if they do not appear that way. This vision functions as "a community's expression of how it understands the foundational structures of reality and the nature and tendencies of the world—in short, how the world 'works' (*The Book of Job: A Contest of Moral Imaginations* [Oxford University Press, 2003], 122-23). Iconic narratives ring 'true' not as lawlike guarantees or failsafe formulas but as affirmations of deep structures at work even when particular circumstances may suggest otherwise.... For the parent, the wise prosper and the wicked perish because that is how God created and sustains the world. The world is not neutral. So if the wicked prosper from time to time, it is an exception—not the rule. The wise may take heart." See Christine Roy Yoder, *Proverbs*, Abingdon Old Testament Commentaries (Abingdon, 2009), 49.

44 Leo G. Perdue, *Proverbs*, Interpretation: A Bible Commentary for Teaching and Preaching (Westminster John Knox, 2000), 37.

implications. Think of this as the third section. As a preacher, ask: What are the theological implications, and how might I convey them? How does the vertical relate to the horizontal? The proverb teaches us about humankind, but it also reveals something to us about God as creator, redeemer, and sustainer of all things. Of course, deal with the human aspect, but remember to connect it to God in some way. In so doing so, you will do for your listeners what the text did for its listeners.

The Fear of the Lord is the Fitting Response

What is a fitting response to the God who creates, upholds, blesses, speaks, acts, and judges? The book of Proverbs answers the question in a way that is both simple and profound: "the fear of the Lord," a phrase that appears as a description and as a command (e.g., "Fear the Lord" in 3:7, 24:21) at least 19 times in the book. Those who understand and appreciate God's presence and power start here. They decide at the outset that the fear of the Lord will serve as both the beginning and end of their existence, especially since it grounds and guides the pursuit of wisdom.

What exactly is the "fear of the Lord"? To fear the Lord means more than deference or reverence, although deference and reverence are appropriate responses for people who reflect on God's glory and their creatureliness in relation to it. Neither does the phrase mean that one should be afraid all the time, although the word "fear" is often used that way in English.

In Proverbs, the fear of the Lord typically means knowing God as the source of all knowledge in an intimate, reverent, and awe-filled way, and it implies following after God in obedience.[45] People who fear the Lord relate to God through pursuing knowledge of him (e.g., 1:7; 2:5; 9:10) and blamelessness before him (e.g., 3:7; 8:13; 14:12). Remember the motto at the beginning of Proverbs: "The fear of the Lord is the beginning of knowledge, but fools despise

---

45 Perdue writes: "The fear of Yahweh in Proverbs refers not to terror but rather to wonderment before the all-wise Creator who originated and continued to maintain the orders of existence." See Perdue, *Proverbs*, 36–37.

wisdom and instruction" (1:7).[46] The fear of the Lord grounds all things, and it is also the goal of all things. According to Proverbs 2:5, the desired result for anyone who pursues wisdom is this: "then you will understand the fear of the Lord and find the knowledge of God."

With the fear of the Lord being such a major theme, bring out this theme in your sermons. Of course, all of us can take simple steps such as defining "the fear of the Lord" (since the phrase might be confusing for many of our listeners), reiterating that this is part of the larger message of the book regardless of whether or not the phrase appears in our primary text, and connecting knowledge of God to obedience. Also, with application, we can get practical with listeners on what reverent understanding and faithful obedience look like as fitting responses, since these two responses were expected from those who feared the Lord in the ancient world. Finally, we can use the language of ground and goal to remind people what matters most in life and eternity. Our listeners often ground their lives and reach for goals that are inconsistent with God's heart and God's ways. Remind people that those who begin the path of wisdom start with the fear of the Lord and those who finish well on the path of wisdom understand the fear of the Lord. Time and again, bring people back to a choice: the will and ways of God and the values of the kingdom of God over against the will and ways of an age that is passing away.

Conclusion

In this chapter, we explored how to use a genre-conscious approach when we study and preach from the book of Proverbs: know what a proverb is, do what a proverb does, and remember the point. Yes, a genre-conscious approach requires more work from preachers, but it does not have to be busy or exasperating work. Perhaps many of us avoid proverbs because our genre questions remain unanswered, so the move from text to sermon feels forced. If you ask

---

46 Longman writes: "The theme of the fear of the Lord reverberates through the whole book. After all, if wisdom depends on understanding the world correctly, how can that be achieved if one does not acknowledge that God himself is a fundamental part of the cosmos?" Longman, *How to Read Proverbs*, 55.

mechanics who do not have the right tools for the job, or painters who do not have the right brushes for the canvas how they are doing, they will probably be frustrated as well. When all you have is a hammer, everything looks like a nail.

Pay attention to what the genre is and what the genre does. A good literary-rhetorical study will help you know where to begin, guide you in the move from text to sermon, and provide you with the right tools for the task. Pay attention to the purpose to which the genre points. It draws us toward the God of all creation and calls upon us to fear the Lord.

Yes, it might feel like more work at the beginning, but you will not feel overwhelmed or frustrated for long. Ask mechanics with the right tools how they are doing or painters with the right brushes how they are faring, and they will tell you: "It is a joy to do the work when you have the tools you need!"

For Further Study

- Alter, Robert. *The Art of Biblical Poetry*. Basic, 2011.
- Arthurs, Jeffrey D. *Preaching with Variety: How to Re-Create the Dynamics of Biblical Genres*. Kregel, 2007.
- Blocher, Henri. "The Fear of the Lord as the 'Principle' of Wisdom." *Tyndale Bulletin* 28 (1977): 3–28.
- Camp, Claudia V., and Carole Fontaine. "The Words of the Wise and Their Riddles." Pages 127–59 in *Text and Tradition: The Hebrew Bible and Folklore*. Edited by Susan Niditch. Semeia Studies. Scholars, 1990.
- Estes, Daniel J. *Hear, My Son: Teaching and Learning in Proverbs 1–9*. New Studies in Biblical Theology. Eerdmans, 1997.

Talk about It

For various reasons, both pastors and laypeople have misconceptions about the book of Proverbs. In your judgment, what are some of those misconceptions, and why do you think they exist? What would you say as a rebuttal to someone who raised one of these misconceptions?

Dig Deeper

Read Proverbs 13, a chapter in which terms like "God," "Lord," or "fear of the Lord" do not appear. Even so, the chapter has much to say to you about God, God's heart, and reverent obedience. What do you learn about God in this chapter, and how do you learn it? Where does the fear of the Lord show up in this chapter as a theme even if the term does not appear?

Practice

Look through past sermons that you have preached from the book of Proverbs. Ask yourself how much or how little you followed the three proposals from this chapter: knowing what the proverb is, doing what the proverb does, and remembering the main point. If there were gaps in one or more area, write down what you would have to change for the gap to close.

2

Imagery

Twenty-plus years ago, insurance agencies figured out what many in the advertising industry already knew. If they wanted increased name recognition, they needed a creative strategy. Many good exemplars preceded them. McDonald's transformed the letter "M" into the Golden Arches. Dave Thomas used an image of an adorable girl with red hair, his daughter Wendy, as the logo for his restaurant. However, insurance companies had a competitive disadvantage. Most people do not wake up thinking about insurance or saying, "Friday is going to be my hard deadline for deciding on an insurance company. No exceptions. No excuses."

So, to increase name recognition, the insurance companies took a page out of a familiar playbook: beer commercials, in particular, those put out by Anheuser-Busch in the 1980s and 1990s in the Super Bowl. In past decades, Anheuser-Busch had used cute animals to market their products. They used Clydesdale horses, a promotional gimmick starting in the 1930s, a practice they still follow to this day. In 1987, the company aired a Super Bowl ad with a fictional dog named Spuds MacKenzie, a bull terrier, who served as an adorable mascot for Bud Light beer. The ads took off, and it seemed like everyone was referring to Spuds MacKenzie as "the Budweiser dog." Bud Light actually had to retire the Spuds campaign in 1989 because too many people were complaining (including senators and parents) that an adorable dog might make beer appealing to children. Undeterred, eight years later, in 1995, Anheuser-Busch hit another homerun (as they like to say in baseball).

In a Super Bowl ad, they used frogs who said the syllables of the company—"Bud ... Weis ... Er"—across from a bar with a Budweiser sign at night. After the commercial aired, everyone was talking about "the Budweiser frogs."

Why not do what works? So, on January 1, 2000, a relatively unknown insurance company named Aflac aired a commercial with a big white duck whose sole job was to say the name of the company over and over again in a humorous yet slightly annoying way. Just before this date, another unknown insurance company named Geico aired a commercial that featured an eloquent green gecko; this digital animal with a British accent somehow made insurance funny, cute, and charming. The rest, as they say, is history.

Strangely enough, advertisers have something in common with those who wrote the book of Proverbs. They know how the mind works. Most of us think in images, remember concepts through images, and frame our lives with images. We remember ducks and geckos. A duck or a gecko helps us remember insurance, which is why the ad campaigns worked. As W. Macneile Dixon observes, "The human mind is not, as philosophers would have you think, a debating hall, but a picture gallery."[1] Since Dixon first made this statement in the 1930s, we can adapt his claim to today by stating that the mind is not an operating system or data archive either.

As preachers, we lean heavily on imagery and metaphor perhaps in more ways than we realize. We take words like "transgression," "righteousness," "redemption," or "reconciliation" and use word pictures to describe what they mean. We also preach metaphorically about exodus and resurrection. We believe that the exodus was an event as was the resurrection, but we also preach about being set free from captivity and being raised with Christ (cf. Col 3:1–3). We make metaphorical appeals when we quote from 1 Corinthians 5:7–8 during the Lord's Supper: "For Christ, our Passover Lamb has been sacrificed. Therefore, let us keep the festival."

The biblical writers use images all the time to help us understand who God is and what God is like. The psalmists declare: "The Lord is my rock, my fortress, and my deliverer" (Ps 18:2), "The Lord is my shepherd" (Ps 23:1), and "The Lord is my light

---

1 W. Macneile Dixon, *The Human Situation* (Edward Arnold, 1954), 65.

and my salvation" (Ps 27:1), to name just three examples. When John the Baptist spotted Jesus by the Jordan River, he said, "Look, the Lamb of God who takes away the sins of the world" (John 1:29), an allusion to the Passover lamb. Jesus calls himself the "bread of life" (John 6:35) and "the gate for the sheep" (John 10:7–9). In Revelation 5, the writer calls Jesus the Lion of the tribe of Judah, the Root of David, and the lamb who was slain, all in two verses (Rev 5:5–6). Dixon writes: "Remove the metaphors from the Bible and its living spirit vanishes, its power over the heart melts utterly away."[2]

Like other biblical writers, the authors of the book of Proverbs believed that imagery was crucial to deeper theological, relational, and practical wisdom. We might surmise that the only book with more imagery than Proverbs is Psalms, a book that also uses concise, evocative, and poetic speech to communicate theologically and liturgically. Of course, the book of Psalms has 150 chapters and the book of Proverbs only has 31, so there is no way for it to compete.

Since the book of Proverbs is such an image-rich book, how might we as preachers learn to preach the imagery in a way that honors its evocative power and emulates its rhetorical function? This brings us to our second strategy.

Strategy 2: Bring Images to the Center

For the sake of clarity, I will break this strategy down into two parts: identify the imagery and preach the imagery. A wise preacher identifies the ways that imagery presents itself and functions while also striving to incorporate the imagery and emulate its function in the sermon.

Identifying Imagery in the Book of Proverbs

The writers of the book of Proverbs use figurative language throughout the book. By figurative language, I mean language that

---
2 Ibid., 66.

uses figures of speech such as simile or metaphor to expand literal meaning. In English, we often use figurative language without even knowing it. We might use a simile to talk about how we slept: "I slept like a rock," or to say how much we ate: "I ate like a horse." We might use metaphor to describe someone's character such as, "He is a pig," or metaphorical language to say we are too busy such as, "My plate is too full." We say, "My football team stinks," by which we mean that they are playing poorly, not that they smell bad.

Ernest C. Lucas contends that figurative language occurs so often that it is one the three "key rhetorical devices" in the book of Proverbs with the other two being parallelism and terseness. He writes:

> Hebrew poetry makes use of a wide range of figurative language. Figurative comparisons are particularly common in proverbs. They are a form of 'terseness' since they can enable a brief saying to convey a lot of meaning at several levels. The comparisons may be either explicit (simile, using the comparative terms 'like/as') or implicit (metaphor). In both cases the things compared are unlike in nature yet have something in common.[3]

Of course, a study of figurative language in Proverbs could merit a full book-length treatment. We could go off in all manner of directions, too many to explore here. I will cite the following examples of figurative speech, though I could mention more:

- Alliteration: the patterned use of consonants or vowels at the beginning of words that are closely connected (e.g., Prov 16:3)
- Consonance: the patterned use of consonants in closely connected words at any point in the word (e.g., Prov 11:2)
- Assonance: the patterned use of similar sounds in a rhythmic manner in a verse or verses (e.g., Prov 15:32)
- Word play: using similar words or sounds to draw a connection between ideas (e.g., Prov 20:16–19 with the Hebrew word *arab*)

---

3 Lucas, *Proverbs*, 24.

Imagery

- Irony: a statement of one thing in order to communicate its opposite (e.g., the mother of King Lemuel tells him to give beer to the perishing so they will forget their poverty only to tell him immediately afterward to defend the rights of the poor and needy in Prov 31:6)
- Metonymy: the use of an associated item to describe a larger concept (e.g., the "tongue of the wise" in Prov 12:18 refers to the words of the wise and "crown" refers to the king and kingship in Prov 27:24)
- Synecdoche: the use of one part to describe the whole, such as the verses that use "gray hair" to refer to those who have reached old age (Prov 16:31, 20:29)
- Personification: the ascription of human characteristics to non-human entities, such as the personification of wisdom and folly as Woman Wisdom and Woman Folly (Prov 7–9)
- Simile: the comparison of two different things using imagery in a manner that illustrates their commonalities usually using "like" or "as" (e.g., stating that a king's rage is *like* the roar of a lion and a king's favor is *like* fresh dew on the grass in Prov 19:12)
- Metaphor: the comparison of two different things using imagery that states the ways that they are similar, usually (but not always) through the use of the verb "to be" without "like" (e.g., the statement that the adulterous person *is* a deep pit and the wayward spouse *is* a narrow well in Prov 23:27; see 1:17 for an example of metaphorical language without "to be")

The first four figures of speech are difficult to detect in translation since we would need to study the sound and placements of the words and phrases in Hebrew to catch their usage.[4] Moreover, they fall in the category of figures of sound as opposed to figures of thought. However, we can detect the use of the last six figures of speech in English. They make appearances at various points in the book.

---

4 For instance, Witherington writes: "alliteration (repetition of consonants) is another device used to make a saying memorable and memorize-able. Unless one reads Hebrew one misses all this (e.g., 10:9a has '*holek battom yeke betah*' or 11:2a has '*ba zadon wayyabo qalon*')." Benjamin Witherington III, *Jesus the Sage: The Pilgrimage of Wisdom* (Fortress, 2000), 25.

Simile and metaphor occur most often. When it comes to detecting similes, look for words such as "like" or "as." Here are some examples among many in Proverbs:

> The Lord disciplines those he loves
> > *as* a father the son he delights in. (3:12)

> A little sleep, a little slumber,
> > a little folding of the hands
> and poverty will come on you *like* a thief
> > and scarcity *like* an unarmed man. (6:10–11)

> All at once he followed her
> > *like* an ox going to the slaughter,
> *like* a deer stepping into a noose
> > till an arrow pierces his liver,
> *like* a bird darting into a snare,
> > little knowing it will cost him his life." (7:22–23)

> An honest answer
> > is *like* a kiss on the lips. (24:26)

> *Like* apples of gold in settings of silver
> > is a ruling rightly given. (25:11, cf. 12–14)

> *As* a door turns on its hinges,
> > so a sluggard turns on his bed. (26:14)

If you study the text in Hebrew (or in its Greek translation), you might discover that there are more figures of speech or slightly different figures of speech in the original language than there are in the English translation. Good commentaries should point out these cases.

Do not be surprised if you find similes or metaphors that Stuart Weeks refers to as "bizarre and exaggerated" for the sake of being hyperbolic.[5] A classic and oft-quoted example of hyperbolic simile occurs in Proverbs 11:22: "Like a gold ring in a pig's snout

---

5 Stuart Weeks, *Instruction and Imagery in Proverbs 1–9* (Oxford University Press, 2009), 68.

is a beautiful woman who shows no discretion." Notice how the exaggeration proves the point. Just as no one wants to see a beautiful gold ring on a pig's snout, so also no one wants to see a beautiful man or woman who lacks discretion. The two should not go together.

Take note also of the hyperbolic imagery in Proverbs 21:9 and Proverbs 25:9. The writer states that it is better to live on the corner of a rooftop than to share a house with a quarrelsome spouse (cf. Prov 21:19). No one wants to live on a rooftop, but being married to a quarrelsome spouse might make you consider it! The exaggeration once again proves the point.

Sometimes, the writers use bizarre imagery to make a paradoxical or ironic statement designed to make us think, as in Proverbs 25:15 "Through patience a ruler can be persuaded, and a gentle tongue can break a bone." In what situation could a gentle tongue ever break a bone? "That could never happen!" we say to ourselves. Yet, the point comes in the apparent impossibility. If you are under the authority of a ruler and you remain patient for long enough, even what appears to be impossible becomes possible: namely, the ruler can be persuaded to see or do things in the way you have proposed.

When it comes to detecting how the writers use metaphors, pay close attention to whether the imagery is used to compare two different things in a manner that illustrates their similarities. The writers will often (but not always) use the verb "to be" to make the comparison. Sometimes, metaphors jump off the page. For instance, we read that the Lord *is* a "shield" for the blameless (Prov 2:7). Wisdom *is* a "tree of life to those who take hold of her" (3:18). The wife of one's youth *is* a "loving doe, a graceful deer" (5:19). The father says, "This command *is* a lamp, this teaching *is* a light" (6:23). Other times, the metaphors sneak up on us through indirect language. For instance, in the father-son dialogue, the father warns him not to set his feet on the "path" of the wicked, a word that has a literal and a metaphorical connotation (1:15, cf. 1:19). At the literal level, the son must refuse to go the same places where the wicked go. At the metaphorical level, the son must pursue the lifestyle of those who are righteous. Path imagery reminds him to walk on the road of righteousness rather than wickedness.[6] Just a few verses later, the father uses birds metaphorically to describe the cunning sinners that the son must avoid. He exclaims, "How useless to spread a net where every bird [i.e., sinner] can see it" (1:17). It makes no sense at all to believe that they will be trapped with ease.

Some common themes emerge with imagery in the book. For instance, the writers instruct us to wear wisdom as a garment or ornament, and to cherish it more than silver, gold, or rubies. Wisdom and instruction are a garland to grace our head, a chain around our neck, and a crown for our heads.[7] The parents tell their son: let love and faithfulness be a necklace bound around his neck, written on the tablet of his heart.[8] Cherish wisdom, for it is more precious than silver, gold, or rubies. Value it, for it is worth more than anything we might buy in place of it.[9]

The writers of Proverbs also use the negative imagery of traps and snares to remind us to break free from that which destroys us, and they use the positive imagery of water and fountains to remind us that in wisdom there is life, sustenance, and refreshment. For instance, in Proverbs 6:5, we read: "Free yourself like a gazelle from the hand of the hunter, like a bird from the snare of a fowler."[10] By contrast, the writers proclaim that the fear of the Lord and words of instruction are a "fountain of life" and a "fountain of wisdom."[11] Sometimes, negative and positive imagery occur in the same verse to indicate how one relates to the other or is contrasted with the other: "The teaching of the wise is a fountain of life,

---

6 According to Stuart Weeks, path imagery has a strategic function, especially in the first half of Proverbs 1–9. The path imagery, Weeks argues, "revolves around the idea of walking straight rather than following a predetermined route. Although wisdom and instruction can point one in the direction of life and happiness, the danger is presented as lying not in the pursuit of a specific different path, but in wandering or turning aside." Ibid., 77.

7 1:9; 3:3, 22; 4:9.

8 3:3; 6:21; 7:3.

9 3:14–15; 8:11, 19; 16:16; 20:15; 31:10.

10 For more example of the dangers of traps and snares see 1:17; 11:6; 12:13; 13:14; 14:27; 18:7; 21:6; 22:5; 28:10; 29:6, 25.

11 10:11; 13:14; 14:27; 16:22; 18:4.

turning a person from the snares of death" (Prov 13:14). Skillful communicators often use contrast to make their point clear.

Bringing Images to the Center of a Sermon on Proverbs

Now that we have laid out how to identify the imagery, we will turn our attention to how to incorporate it and emulate its function in our preaching. I will propose the following: build the sermon around an image, preach the contrast, and tell the story behind the proverb.

Build the Sermon around an Image

My first proposal for bringing images to the center of a sermon is to build the sermon around an image. I have an acquaintance at another seminary who likes to say, "If you put lipstick on a pig, it's still a pig." If she were to put it in a less proverbial way, she might say that you cannot get away with dressing up something that is ugly and pretending that it has changed its nature. My friend liked to say this proverb whenever I would point to inconsistencies in what we say and do at our seminaries; for instance, what we declare on our website versus what we value as a community, or how we tell the story of our history versus our actual history. With respect to the parts of our stories and communities that are "ugly," we could put lipstick on them, but in the end, they would still be ugly.

Imagine for a moment that someone asked you to build a sermon around this pig-and-lipstick proverb. I would not actually build a sermon around it since the proverb is a folk proverb from modern American culture and not a biblical proverb, but as an exercise, what would you do to build a sermon around that one proverb? Where would you begin?

If I were doing it, I would want to make sure that the dominant image throughout the sermon was the pig with lipstick. I would not introduce the image and abandon it after a few minutes, but I would keep returning to it in much the same way that a singer returns to the chorus after each verse in a song. I would highlight the comedy and even lunacy of such an image. After all, who puts lipstick on a pig? How would you do such a thing? Imagine how difficult it would be, how messy, and how other people would think you were crazy. Imagine leaning over a fence on a farm. You look down and see a pig staring back at you, and the pig is wearing Maybelline Color Sensational Matte Lipstick in plum. No doubt it would provoke a reaction.

To weave the image into the sermon, I might use repetition, storytelling, analogy, and tone so that people not only remembered the image, but also the comedy and absurdity of it. Lastly, I would explain why the proverb exists by linking the comedic image in the first part, "If you put lipstick on a pig," to the second part, "it's still a pig," and by providing examples from everyday life. When we dress up something that is ugly, such as hiding our sins from those closest to us, offering willfully naïve accounts of history, or acting toward others in passive aggressive ways, it is ugly in the end.

Now we will do the same with a biblical proverb. Take Proverbs 25:28 as an example: "Like a city whose walls are broken through is a person who lacks self-control." Unlike the modern example, this example is tragic rather than comical. Because this is a simile, we can ask why a person who lacks self-control is compared to a city whose walls are broken down. Perhaps it is because the person is left unprotected and vulnerable.

How do we build a sermon around the imagery of broken-down walls? In order to do justice to the text in its context, we would want to devote a section of the sermon to talking about why ancient cities relied on strong walls. We have plenty of examples in Scripture of why strong walls around cities were important, with the best-known being the fall of Jericho. As the Israelites carried the ark around the city, they blew the trumpet, the army shouted, and *as soon as the wall collapsed,* "everyone charged straight in and took the city" (Josh 6:20). Consider also the sadness and heartbreak that Nehemiah felt when delegates from Judah arrived in Susa and reported that "the wall of Jerusalem is broken down, and its gates have been burned with fire" (Neh 1:4).

As preachers, we have at least one rhetorical challenge: most cities are not surrounded by walls anymore. We need to think of modern equivalents. In modern cities, we have closed-circuit TV cameras everywhere that track movements, record events, catch robberies, and follow suspects. Banks and homes have high-security padded safes, panic rooms, high tech alarm systems, video surveillance, human security guards, gates, locks, cybersecurity software, and all kinds of other forms of protection.

In a sermon about broken down walls, consider asking rhetorical questions that will help listeners understand the imagery better: what would happen to a city if it had no security cameras, no police officers, no traffic lights, and no city jails? What would happen to a bank that left its money on the counters, that had no safe, no security system, no security guard, and no surveillance? What would happen to a house in a dangerous part of town that had no locks on its doors or windows, no alarm system, and no key to get in or out? We know the answer. The place and the people would be unprotected, defenseless, vulnerable to destruction and even devastation. The use of rhetorical questions prompts listeners to make the conclusion themselves, a sage-like communication strategy.

Also, find ways to link the topic of self-control to the imagery of walls. Remember that the proverb itself uses the imagery of walls as a figure of speech to talk about what happens when we lack self-control. Ask practical questions about self-control while at the same time keeping the imagery of walls in front of your listeners. How do you know that your "walls" are broken down? In what areas of our lives might our lack of self-control lead to broken down walls? How do we build good walls through developing more self-control?

Preach the Contrast

My second proposal for bringing images to the center is to preach the contrast. I like studying the etymology of words. The word "contrast" got its start with the medieval Latin word *contrastare* which means "stand" (*contra-*) "against" (*+stare*). Before it made its way into English, it showed up in 17th century France in the world of fine art. French painters would bring out the *contraste* (noun) of the forms and the colors in their paintings. Their goal was to *contraster* (verb) one color with another. In English, we still use the word this way from time to time, like when we try to edit a digital photo or adjust the color controls on a television or computer monitor. Just look for the contrast button. But we also use the word with reference to arguments or debates. Like painters who use contrasting colors as a way to communicate through art, so also in argument we make claims as a way to communicate through ideas. How does one idea "stand against" another idea?

The book of Proverbs uses contrast with antithetical parallelism. When writers use antithesis, they communicate "the same truth from opposite perspectives," to use Tremper Longman's phrase, usually through the use or implied use of the word "but" in the second half of the proverb.[12] Most of the occurrences of antithetical parallelism occur in Proverbs 10–15.[13] Ben Witherington observes: "of 183 verses in Proverbs 10–15, 163 use antithetical parallelism (e.g., 'a wise child is a father's joy [but] a foolish child is a mother's grief,' 10:1)."[14] Here are just four examples from the section. Notice that they occur in succession in Proverbs 11:

> The Lord detests dishonest scales,
>   *but* accurate weights find favor with him.
> When pride comes, then comes disgrace,
>   *but* with humility comes wisdom.
> The integrity of the upright guides them,
>   *but* the unfaithful are destroyed by their duplicity.
> Wealth is worthless in the day of wrath,
>   *but* righteousness delivers from death. (11:1–4)

---

12 Longman, *How to Read Proverbs*, 41. Not every proverb uses the word "but" to present a contrast. For instance, the better-than proverbs set up the contrast differently: better is way X than way Y, its contrast. The word "than" sets up the contrast in verset B as an opposite perspective to the way laid out in verset A. Here is one example of a better-than contrast: "*Better* a dry crust with peace and quiet *than* a house full of feasting with strife."

13 According to Perdue, "Antithetical proverbs govern the formal character of chs. 10–15." See Leo G. Perdue, *The Sword and the Stylus: An Introduction to Wisdom in the Age of Empires* (Eerdmans, 2008), 98.

14 Witherington, *Jesus the Sage*, 24.

Imagery

The antithetical proverbs present readers with "a fundamental choice in life, the choice between wisdom and folly. These antithetical proverbs are fleshing out the differences between the two."[15] Put differently, one rhetorical function of contrast is to limit options for readers, moving them to make a choice rather than remaining stuck between multiple options.

As an example, we will look at Proverbs 12:18: "The words of the reckless pierce like swords, but the tongue of the wise brings healing." At first, it appears as though the first half of the verse is the only part that has striking imagery. Not necessarily. It has a contrasting image–the tongue.[16] Thus, we have two contrasting images in the proverb, the sword and the tongue, described in two contrastive ways, reckless and healing. It also becomes clear, albeit in an implicit way, that those whose words are reckless (in the first half of the verse) are actually fools, since those whose words bring healing (in the second half of the verse) are called wise: "the tongue of the *wise* brings healing."

So, how do we preach the contrast? One of the hurdles to overcome is a lot like the hurdle we had with the city whose walls are broken down. Most modern soldiers do not use swords, and most people do not come into close proximity with swords. Most of our listeners are unfamiliar with the violence and destruction that swords bring upon people. They may have seen movies where warriors use swords, but they have not wielded swords themselves. Modern listeners will be more likely to resonate with the damage that a knife or gun could cause. Modern figures of speech can also help: "his words went through me," "his words killed me," "she tore me up," or "he cut me down."[17]

We have a decision to make about whether we will use the tongue as the contrasting image. While Waltke is right that the tongue was probably chosen because it looks like a sword, it also functions here as a metonymy to describe the speech of the wise

---

15 Longman, *How to Read Proverbs*, 42.

16 Waltke argues that, in addition to being a metonymy (the tongue describes the larger concept of speech), the tongue was "probably chosen because its shape resembles that of a sword." Waltke, *The Book of Proverbs*, 1:537.

17 Waltke mentions the first two modern examples in his commentary on this verse in Ibid., 1:537.

in the first half of verset B. To create a contrast with a knife, a gun, or another image, try choosing an image that symbolizes healing since that is the emphasis at the end of the verse. I might choose the image of a balm or an antidote. A balm brings healing to a wound. An antidote provides a remedy to someone who has suffered illness or who has been poisoned. The words we use can be like a knife that harms and even destroys or like a balm that restores and heals, like a gun that takes lives or an antidote that remedies ills.

Also, consider how you might emulate the rhetorical effect of the text. In the case of Proverbs 12:18, the intended effect is that the hearer will make a choice. Will you be like the first half of the verse or the second? Invite your listeners to make a choice between wisdom and folly in their speech in much the same way that the writers invite the young to make a similar choice.

Also, use the contrast in your main idea, points, or moves. With this verse, the first half of the sermon could be about sword-people, whose words are reckless, and the second half of the sermon could be about balm-people, whose words bring healing to those around them.

Another idea: use space to highlight the contrast when you preach. Is there a side of the pulpit or platform that you could go to when you talk about sword-people and an opposite side of the pulpit where you could go to talk about antidote-people? That way, you communicate at the non-verbal level in addition to the verbal through "blocking" the sermon.[18]

Tell the Story behind the Proverb

The Ashanti people in Ghana have a popular folk proverb about leadership, a wisdom saying that I have stuck on my bulletin board near my desk: "The responsibility of power is like holding an egg. Grasp it too tightly and it will drip through your fingers; hold it too loosely and it will drop and break."[19] The proverb made its way

---

18 Viola Spolin defines blocking as "the choreography of state movement" by the actors in a play. See Viola Spolin, *Theater Games for Rehearsal: A Director's Handbook* (Northwestern University Press, 1985), 37.

19 Ashanti proverb as cited in Willem Saayman, ed., *Embracing the*

into the popular imagination because of a story or stories behind it. My third proposal for bringing images to the center of a sermon on Proverbs is to tell the story behind the proverb.

Members of the Ashanti people likely watched some of their leaders wreak havoc because they refused to loosen their grip on power. Other leaders fell victim to the opposite extreme: they lost leadership because they refused to speak or act when the community needed it. Perhaps the proverb originated because older leaders wanted to find a memorable way to exhort younger leaders. They wanted to share all that they had learned about leadership through trial and error. The proverb exists and is true for a community because stories and experiences from the past demonstrate it to be true to life. It distills wisdom derived from "case studies."

The same holds true for biblical proverbs. They exist because stories demonstrate that they are true to life. In a sermon, consider how you might tell a story, fictional or non-fictional, to demonstrate why a biblical proverb is true to life. If the proverbs were memorized by a community and preserved in ancient manuscripts, then there are stories that illustrate why they are both wise and true. Although we cannot recover the stories that led to the original coining of the ancient proverb, we can look for stories that are available now in Scripture, tradition, culture, and our experience, stories that demonstrate that a saying is insightful and practical counsel for living wisely in the world today.

For instance, Proverbs 17:14 reads: "Starting a quarrel is like breaching a dam; so drop the matter before a dispute breaks out." With a verse like this one, we should put on our poetic hat. The word "like" indicates that this a simile. It compares the dangers of being quick to quarrel with the dangers of breaching a dam. Both scenarios lead to destruction, which is why the simile is used.

In addition, we should also put on our storyteller hat. Think through a story or stories you could tell that show why this proverb is consistent with lived experience. When have you started a quarrel with someone, perhaps a spouse, or a neighbor, or a member of your church, only to realize in the end that both of you lost, even

---

Baobab Tree: The African Proverb in the 21st Century (University of South Africa, 1997), 229.

if one of you technically won? You know you should have let it go; it caused a lot more harm than good. Also, when have you been on the receiving end of the damage caused by a quarrelsome person? Perhaps you have seen how much damage can be caused when a person is quick to quarrel and slow to let go of a dispute. Like a breached dam wreaking havoc on fields and villages, everywhere this person went, he or she caused damage and destruction. In addition to stories from your own life, you can draw from stories in Scripture, tradition, culture, and the lives of others.

Another idea to consider: tell a fictional story that illustrates why this proverb is true to life. For instance, you could tell a short apocryphal story about a pastor who was so quarrelsome that, one day he showed up at church, only to realize that there was no one left to pastor. He was ministering in a congregation of one. Not only did he destroy other people, he destroyed himself and his church. If you make up a fictional story, go to great efforts to make sure that your listeners know that you are telling a parable so that they do not confuse fiction for non-fiction.

In *Preaching and the Literary Forms of the Bible,* Thomas G. Long provides us with an example from Proverbs 15:17: "Better a small serving of vegetables with love than a fattened calf with hatred." He claims that the rhetorical point of a proverb like this one is to summon the reader backward *and* forward, backward to the stories in life that demonstrate the wisdom of the proverb and forward to the person that God would have us be in the future when we sit down at tables in our homes. In a sermon on this verse, he claims:

> Narratives, vignettes, story-like threads that the proverb tugs from the fabric of everyday life would be told, each thread punctuated by the proverb itself, quoted as an interpretive refrain. Now the proverb completes its task. Because of what it allows us to remember, we think of the next table where we will take our places.[20]

Long argues that preachers can devote an entire sermon to one proverb in instances like these because of the stories that brought

---

20 Long, *Preaching and the Literary Forms of the Bible,* 65.

the proverb into being and the potential stories that will come about as a result. Preachers have an opportunity to draw from a reservoir of experiences that illustrate the truth and the wisdom of this proverb, to summon the hearer backward and forward.

When we tell the story behind the proverb, we do more than illustrate abstract concepts in concrete ways (though that is part of what we do). Through storytelling, we help people understand why the proverb is true to lived experience, why the saying itself is wise, and how we can live differently from this point forward because we have heard it.

Conclusion

In this chapter, we discussed how to identify imagery, how to incorporate it when we preach, and how to emulate its rhetorical function. If the writers of the book of Proverbs prioritized figurative language, why would we not also highlight the various poetic devices and rhetorical effects in the book? With image-centered proverbs, why would we not construct an image-centered sermon, even if our best attempts are approximate?

When we bring images to the center of a sermon, it might seem awkward and disorienting, especially for those of us who tend to be analytical, propositional, and deductive in our approach. Even so, if we do not push past this discomfort, we will miss much of the power of the genre. Our sermon in its new setting will not "say and do what the text says and does in its setting."[21]

In everyday life, we think in imagery more than we know, even if we do not use imagery much in our preaching. Let your preaching sound more like the way you think in everyday life. Thomas Troeger claims: "If God communicates with you through an image, then that tells you something about how to let God speak through you to the congregation. Share the vision you received."[22]

Most of your listeners already know about the power of imagery to shape their lives. They know that the human mind is "not

---

21 Ibid., 61.
22 Thomas H. Troeger, *Creating Fresh Images for Preaching* (Judson, 1982), 1982.

a debating hall, but a picture gallery," to return to Dixon's phrase.[23] The real question is: Do you?

For Further Study

- Brown, William P. "The Didactic Power of Metaphor in the Aphoristic Sayings of Proverbs." *Journal for the Study of the Old Testament* 29, no. 2 (December 2004): 133–54.
- Jonker, Peter. *Preaching in Pictures: Using Images for Sermons That Connect.* Abingdon, 2015.
- Troeger, Thomas H. *Creating Fresh Images for Preaching.* Judson, 1982.
- Troeger, Thomas H. *Imagining a Sermon.* Abingdon, 1990.
- Wilson, Paul Scott. *Preaching as Poetry: Beauty, Goodness, and Truth in Every Sermon.* Abingdon, 2014.

Talk about It

Many preachers have a proclivity to exegete abstract ideas rather than concrete images. For instance, one preacher I trained told me that he knew how to write a sermon on Psalm 100:3a: "Know that the Lord is God," but he did not know how to talk about Psalm 100:3c: "we are his people, the sheep of his pasture." Why do you think this proclivity exists? What would you have to do in a sermon to offer a faithful exegesis of metaphors and similes?

Dig Deeper

Read Proverbs 3:1–20. Write down all the different images that are used in these verses for wisdom: its presence, purpose, function, and necessity. Write down how each image is used and what purpose it serves.

---

23 Dixon, *The Human Situation*, 65.

Practice

Prepare a sermon on a proverb or string of proverbs in which imagery is central to the text and to the sermon you write. Feature the imagery in the text in your main idea and your key points or moves. For instance, if the sermon is on Proverbs 13:14, "The teaching of the wise is a fountain of life, turning a person from the snares of death," then you would feature the images of a fountain and a snare. Avoid abstraction whenever possible in the outline of the sermon.

3

Characters

LIKE MOST PEOPLE, I enjoy watching good movies, and I detest sitting through bad ones. I know I am watching a good movie when two hours pass quickly. The plot makes sense and the story flows. The drama is entertaining. I am moved to think and feel deeply. I know I am watching a bad movie when none of this happens.

To assist my preaching, I try to learn as much as I can from movies, especially the art of good storytelling. In 2011, I attended a conference on preaching and filmmaking so I could expand my knowledge. I will never forget one of the sessions. I sat there in rapt attention as one of the plenary speakers told us about her experiences as a screenplay vetter and consultant in Hollywood. She said that Hollywood gets roughly 35,000 screenplays a year. After the vetting process, producers make about 100 movies. Only 10 are successful. About 1–2 will be remembered more than a year later. The odds are against you. Bear in mind that this was 2011 so the numbers have probably changed. Some of these statistics challenged me, but it was one of her offhanded comments that changed the way I watch movies. She said: "Pay attention to the characters. Watch them experience one of two things: redemption or transformation. They will not be the same person they were at the beginning." Ever since then, I have paid more attention to characters in films: who they are, what makes them complex, and how they change.

Pay attention to the characters in the book of Proverbs. We can study the book from many angles, and we can preach it using a number of different strategies. Even so, most homiletics texts do not encourage us to focus on the characters in the book. The most concise and compelling emphasis on characters comes in biblical studies: Derek Kidner's short *Proverbs* commentary, a text in which he conducts subject studies before doing verse-by-verse exegesis.[1]

In this chapter, I commend characterization as a homiletical tool. By characterization, I mean the description of attributes in a person or a type of person (e.g., when we say, "he or she is characterized by kindness") or the imaginative embodiment of characters so that they seem like real people speaking to us right now. The writers of Proverbs use characterization in both ways in order to convey wisdom, describe reality, and present us with a choice between wisdom and folly. As preachers, we can use characterization in both ways as well.

Strategy 3:
Use Characterization

In what follows, I describe five central characters in Proverbs and offer ideas for how to preach about them in genre-conscious ways. I will not provide an in-depth discussion of the fool or the neighbor here, since I will bring up these characters in other chapters. The five for this chapter are animals, Woman Wisdom, Woman Folly, the sluggard, and the wife of noble character.

Animals

Animals Teach Us Wisdom

What do animals teach us about wisdom? Many modern western Christians do not take the time to ask, especially if we live in cities

---

1 Kidner organizes his subjects into the following eight studies: God and man, wisdom, the fool, the sluggard, the friend, words, the family, life and death. Kidner, *Proverbs*, 29–52. For a later contribution organized around themes (the first edition of Kidner's commentary was published in 1964), see David Hubbard, *Mastering the Old Testament: Proverbs*, WBC 15a (Word, 1989).

or suburbs. If we do ask, our unfiltered answer quite often is, "Little to nothing at all. Maybe something about the value of creation." When we think like this, it puts us out of step with what Proverbs tells us about animals. The writers believed that animals had much to teach them and their children about wisdom. For instance, they state that an ant teaches the sluggard about the value of discipline, hard work, saving, and planning: "Consider the ant, you sluggard" (Prov 6:6–8). Likewise, a strong ox teaches the farmer about the connection between hard-working animals and the "abundant harvests" that come because of them (14:4).

Animals get the most attention in the Sayings of Agur in Proverbs 30. On two occasions, the writer uses a poetic formula highlighting three illustrations followed by a fourth that compares human behavior to what animals do. Question: What is amazing and beyond comprehension? Answer: "the way of an eagle in the sky … a snake on a rock … a ship on the high seas … [and] a man with a young woman." Question: Where do we observe those that are "stately in their stride?" Answer: when we see a lion that will not retreat, "a strutting rooster, a he-goat, and a king secure against revolt" (30:29–31).

Sometimes the writer does not adhere to the 3-plus-1 formula. He simply lifts animals up as wise and worthy of emulation. In Proverbs 30:24–28, he says that we should pay attention to four animals that are small "yet they are extremely wise" (30:24). Ants are small but they can build a whole storehouse of food. Hyraxes have a little power, but they have the capacity to live in crags. Locusts have no king, but they know how to advance like an army. A lizard can be caught in one's hand, but it has the cunning and resilience to find its way into kings' palaces.

Animal imagery also serves a poetic and rhetorical function. The writers use animal imagery in similes and metaphors to offer counsel to the young, to promote caution in concrete situations, and to convey the differences between wisdom and foolishness. For instance, to young men, the parents say to rejoice in the wife of their youth for she *is* a "loving doe, a graceful deer" (Prov 5:19) and to break free from folly's trap like a gazelle slips away from a hunter, like a bird breaks loose from "the snare of the fowler" (6:5).

Those who follow after folly remain as ignorant to its destructive outcome as an ox on its way to the slaughter, as a deer about to be caught in the noose, or as a bird about to be trapped in the snare (7:21-23). Examples abound of animal imagery used in this way as a poetic and rhetorical device.[2]

Sometimes animals teach us about foolishness. The fool who returns to his folly day after day can be compared to the dog that returns to its vomit (26:11-12). The verb "returns to" implies that the dog eats it rather than just smelling it or looking at it. Modern readers might engage this passage and say, "Disgusting! How idiotic to do such a thing day after day." Unlike in many modern Western settings, the ancients saw dogs as unclean animals. All 32 occurrences of the word "dog" (*keleb*) in the Hebrew Bible have a negative connotation. This proverb shows up with a similar connotation in 2 Peter 2:20-22 as a way to illustrate what happens when those who have initially "escaped the corruption of the world" through Jesus Christ are once again "entangled in it and are overcome" (2 Pet 2:20).

The Way We Treat Animals Reveals Our Character

Because animals have much to teach us about wisdom—how to act, what to pursue, and what to avoid—is it any wonder that the writers urge us to treat them with care? How we interact with animals reveals our character. Look at Proverbs 12:10 "The righteous care for the needs of their animals, but the kindest acts of the wicked are cruel." According to Bruce J. Waltke, the writer invokes an *a minores ad maiores* (lesser to greater) argument here. If a righteous person takes care of the "lesser" animals, then how much more the greater? "By contrast, if the wicked are cruel to the lesser, who can entrust them with the greater?"[3] Notice also the command in Proverbs 27:23-27 to know our flocks and watch after our herds. The writer warns that riches are never promised, thus the command to pay attention. He also offers reassurance: your herds will more than feed your household if you take care of them.

---

2 See also Proverbs 17:12; 19:12; 20:2; 26:1-2; 28:15.
3 Waltke, *The Book of Proverbs*, 1:526.

Characterizing Animals in Preaching

With all that is stated about animals, we have a challenge before us. How do we use characterization when we preach about them? For human characters, we might turn to imaginative embodiment characterization, that is, speaking as if the characters are speaking to us right now. For animals, though, this is rather difficult. Thus, the first form of characterization mentioned in my initial definition—the description of attributes in a person or a type of person—makes the most sense here.

As preachers, we can make simple gestures such as using visual or auditory aids, for instance, images of the animals on screens (or paper), a simple prop like an ant farm, or perhaps audio of the sounds they make. Help people see and hear the animals, especially since many people do not know what a hyrax is or what a locust looks like. Images and sounds can make them more familiar.

When the animal association is negative, assist people in making the same association. For instance, with the negative imagery of the dog, we can show images of wild dogs in packs as a way to shake people loose from the cuddly and cute way of thinking about dogs, or we can tell a story of someone being attacked by a wild dog.

When the animal association in the passage is positive, we have the same job, that is, to help listeners make the same associations. Through storytelling, statistics, or images, sounds, or video, we can help people to emulate the positive attributes mentioned. Notice how Ralph Douglas West does this in a short paragraph when talking about ants in the book of Proverbs. This sermon in its entirety is included in Appendix II.2:

> The ants teach us what time it is in life. The ant is small. It's weak. It's powerless in many ways. And yet, it can carry ten to fifty times its body weight. But these colonies of ants with their leaders that go out and explore the ground do more than that. They are really known according to verse 24, that they are extremely wise because they always have their eye on preparation.[4]

---

4   Ralph D. West, "Wisdom for Times of Uncertainty [Sermon]," Appendix II.2.

The challenge we face as communicators is to describe animals in such a way that listeners marvel at them *so that* they will experience the rhetorical effect the author intended. With a 3-plus-1 poetic formula, for instance—the example of the lion, the rooster, and the he-goat—we have a responsibility to show how each of these animals helps us marvel at the "king who is secure against revolt."

Woman Wisdom Versus Woman Folly

Characterizing Wisdom and Folly

Proverbs 1–9 culminates in the personifications of wisdom and folly. The two characters appear in Chapters 8–9. In Chapter 8, the parents offer a hymn of praise to Woman Wisdom (8:1–36). In chapter 9, they present two "invitations" to the son: the first from Woman Wisdom (9:1–12) and the second from Woman Folly (9:13–18).[5] These personifications serve a pedagogical and rhetorical purpose. Pedagogically, they teach the son about what wisdom is like and not like, where it originates, and why it matters. Rhetorically, they cast a compelling vision for why Woman Wisdom is the obvious choice, why we should "marry" her. Although the parents leave the decision to the son, they make it clear which is better. They devote 48 verses to praising Woman Wisdom (8:1–36; 9:1–12) and only six verses to describing Woman Folly (9:13–18). They have much to say about wisdom as the best option and little to say about folly.

What does the text say about Woman Wisdom? Much more than time and space permit in one section of one chapter. I will focus on just three themes. First, Woman Wisdom has a public ministry made available to all who hear and heed her. According to Proverbs 8:1–3, Wisdom calls out (1) in public: from the high point of the city (2), "beside the gate leading into the city," (3) and "at the entrance" to the city (3, cf. also 1:20–21). Carol Newsom

---

5 Old Testament scholars generally agree that the invitations in Chapter 9 serve as an epilogue to the prologue in Proverbs 1:8–8:36. Waltke writes: "Almost all scholars agree that it functions as an epilogue to the prologue." See Waltke, *The Book of Proverbs*, 1:11.

observes: "Where the father is the authoritative voice in the family, *Hokmot* (personified wisdom) is the corresponding public voice 'in the streets,' 'in the public squares' who occupies the places that are physically symbolic of collective authority and power ('at the entrance of the gates,' v. 21)."[6] Woman Wisdom cries out beyond the home and the family to the society at large; she makes her presence known to all who listen for her. Her offer extends to all people (4): to the simple for gaining prudence (5), the foolish so they can "set [their] hearts on it," and the discerning and knowledgeable (9).

Second, Woman Wisdom offers far more to us than money can buy or people can give. Proverbs 8:10-11 explains why it is far better to choose instruction over silver and knowledge over gold: "for wisdom is more precious than rubies, and nothing you desire can compare with her" (8:11, cf. 3:15, 8:19). In Proverbs 8:17, Woman Wisdom declares, "I love those who love me." She offers enduring riches, honor, wealth, and an inheritance (8:18-21). She promises blessing to all who "keep [her] ways" (8:32-34). Those who find her "find life and receive favor from the Lord" (8:35-36).

Third, Woman Wisdom existed before the universe existed, and she rejoiced in God's presence before the foundations of the world. The Lord brought wisdom forth (8:22) "at the very beginning" (23), before the watery depths (24), the mountains (25), or the dust of the earth (26) came into existence. Wisdom rejoiced in God's presence at the time of creation; she remained "constantly at his side" (30) as the foundations of the earth were laid. Woman Wisdom at creation offers a fascinating Christological echo to Christ himself, who is described as the Wisdom of God (1 Cor 1:24-30). That stated, our Christological correlations should be measured and nuanced so as to avoid confusion. "Woman wisdom is not a pre-incarnate form of the second person of the Trinity," Tremper Longman writes. "Jesus being the 'firstborn of creation' is not to be pressed literally as if Jesus were a created being. But—and this is crucial—the association between Jesus and Woman Wisdom in the New Testament is a powerful way of saying that Jesus is the

---

6 Carol A. Newsom, "Woman and the Discourse of Patriarchal Wisdom: A Study of Proverbs 1-9," in *Gender and Difference in Ancient Israel*, ed. Peggy L. Day (Fortress, 1989), 146.

embodiment of God's Wisdom."[7] Be careful not to put more into the biblical text than what is actually there, while at the same time pointing to and even celebrating the Christological echo.

When you preach about Woman Wisdom as a character, you can engage in both forms of characterization: elevation of attributes and imaginative embodiment. The latter can come in two forms: first person or third person. Through the preacher, Woman Wisdom can speak to listeners in the first person (e.g., "I rejoiced in God's presence as the watery depths came together") or we can narrate her words, actions, and attributes in the third person (e.g., "She stood at God's side as the foundations of the earth were set in place"). In both instances, we have an opportunity to maximize our creativity and imagination as storytellers and poets. Although we should leverage our creativity here, we should do so with at least some restraint. Remember that our goal is to help listeners hear and heed wisdom's call.

Although Woman Wisdom gets most of the attention in these chapters, another character—Woman Folly—arrives at the close to Chapter 9 (vv. 13–18). The writers use three words to describe her in Proverbs 9:13. She is unruly (or ESV has "noisy"), simple, and she "knows nothing." Each word is loaded. The writers use the word "unruly" elsewhere to describe the adulterous woman as "unruly and defiant" (7:11). "Simple" is used in various ways, but in Chapters 8–9, wisdom is available to the "simple" who want prudence (8:5) and to those who heed the call: "Leave your simple ways and you will live" (9:6). The phrase "knows nothing" does not appear elsewhere, but it is noteworthy that the wicked do not "know what makes them stumble" (4:19). The adulterous woman "gives no thought to the way of life; her paths wander aimlessly, but she does not know it" (5:6). The "simple" or the "youth who ha[s] no sense" (7:7) does not "know" that sexual infidelity "will cost him his life" (7:23).

On a parenthetical but important note, the personification of folly as a woman leaves many modern readers confused and uncomfortable with the way the Bible depicts women, especially since there is already so much in the preceding chapters about avoiding

---

[7] Longman, *How to Read Proverbs*, 110.

the adulterous woman, sometimes called the "Strange Woman" (5:1-22; 6:20-29; 7:1-27). Is this section on Woman Folly a swipe at women in general?

Although what I will propose does not resolve the tension fully, let me offer some reminders concerning the rhetorical challenge for any preacher who talks about Woman Folly or the Strange Woman. Remember that the parents warn the son that the most dangerous people, those who should be avoided at all costs, are "sinful men" (1:10-19; cf. also 2:12-15; 4:14-19; 6:12-15). Notice that some of the passages on avoiding sinful men occur immediately before warnings about the adulterous woman. More parity exists than one might initially suppose. No one is exempt.

Also, remember that the positive image of Woman Wisdom represents a rarity in the Ancient Near East; one is hard pressed to find such positive depictions of women elsewhere. Remember that the parents spend 48 verses talking about her. Ernest Lucas observes: "all that is good and life-giving is personified in a woman's form, Wisdom." The "problem" in the text, he writes, is not "in being a woman, but in being an untutored man who lacks insight."[8]

Invite Listeners to "Marry" Wisdom

Finally, remember that Woman Folly and the adulterous woman teach us more about why we should marry wisdom than they do about why wise people should avoid adultery or how young people can find a spouse. Yes, we receive counsel on how to avoid sexual predatory behavior, but we need not miss the larger implications for everyone. Alice Ogden Bellis writes,

> Today the strange woman may be seen as a sexual predator or pedophile, and these come in more than one gender, though they tend to be male. The ultimate point of Proverbs is not about finding the right mate, though for some demographics

---

8 Lucas, *Proverbs*, 271. Ogden Bellis writes: "Proverbs includes perhaps the most positive female imagery of the divine in the entire Jewish and Christian canons, reflecting high social status for at least some women at the time it was being brought into final form." See Ogden Bellis, *Proverbs*, l.

this is a significant quest, but about bonding with wisdom, which is a gender-neutral activity. Finding the right partner is an important element of happiness if we are inclined to mate, but it is only one element of life. Marriage with wisdom is universally necessary.[9]

Yes, these texts challenge preachers to speak out against sexual infidelity and to speak in favor of prioritizing godliness and wisdom while seeking out a marriage partner. Full stop. But they also have a larger point in their context. The broader message is this: marry wisdom over folly.

In Proverbs 9:13–18, Woman Folly tries to trick us into "marrying" her instead of Woman Wisdom. We are invited to a banquet, an invitation that sounds eerily similar to the same invitation given by Woman Wisdom in Proverbs 9:1–12. Like Woman Wisdom, Woman Folly calls out from her seat "at the highest point of the city" (9:13, 15; cf. 8:1–2; 9:3), she opens the door of her house (9:14, 17; cf. 9:1–3), and she makes the same invitation: "Let all who are simple come to my house" (9:16; cf. 9:4), but this time with the added caveat that the sweetest water is stolen water and the most delicious food is secret food (9:17). Verse 17 makes clear that she intends to deceive all who accept her invitation.

Through personification, the parents state without apology that only one path leads to life. Those who go to Woman Wisdom's banquet table will find life (9:6). Those who go to Woman Folly's banquet table will sit with those who live "deep in the realm of the dead (*Sheol*)" (9:18). The decision remains ours, but it is not merely a decision between wisdom and folly or life and death. Longman argues that terms like "high point" and "house" are allusions to God's temple. He writes: "Proverbs 1–9 culminates in a choice that the reader must make before proceeding in the book. With whom will you dine, Woman Wisdom or Woman Folly? We now know that the choice is really between Yahweh and the false gods of the nations."[10]

The contrast between Woman Wisdom and Woman Folly opens up several possibilities for preachers. As communicators, we

---

9 Ogden Bellis, *Proverbs*, xlix–l.
10 Longman, *How to Read Proverbs*, 34.

can use characterization in both ways: a description of attributes and an imaginative embodiment of the characters. Just as the writers use personification to make an abstract category concrete, we can do something similar through description: "A person who is wise is like, sounds like, acts like..." We can also frame our sermons as dialogues between two types of people: a wise person and a foolish person, each of whom calls out, inviting us to a banquet. Finally, through narration, we can transport people back in time so that they sit at a banquet table in one "person's" house and then in another "person's" house. Like the writers, imagine one banquet teeming with life and the other as a place of death. Present listeners with a choice.

The Sluggard

The Folly of Laziness

The image of the sluggard or lazy person reminds me of the recurring conversations that my mother-in-law would have with employees before she retired. She worked at a credit union for close to thirty years, eventually reaching the level of Vice President of Human Resources (e.g., hiring, firing, mediating), which was just a few steps below President and CEO. Especially in the last five years of her career, she noticed an exponential increase in employees of all ages coming to her office insisting that they should be promoted to top levels of leadership despite having been hired just a few months prior. The most common complaints came from employees under the age of 25. Perhaps they were overqualified or someone had taught them to be über-assertive in the corporate world. She did not know. Most often, she said, the easiest explanation was the correct one. They wanted a great salary and a nice office without the time and effort required to attain it. Some quit. Others had to be fired. Still others worked hard enough to advance; it was rarely by leaps and bounds; it was usually by taking small steps over time.

In the book of Proverbs, sluggards have a similar mindset to the employees that my mother-in-law supervised at her credit union. They believe that they are entitled to much and that they are talented. They are wiser than "seven people who answer discretely" (26:16). But they do not want to put in even a small amount of work. Throughout the book, those in the older generation warn those coming after them about the dangers of laziness. Of the thirteen times that the Hebrew word "sluggard" appears in the Old Testament, all thirteen occur in this book.[11]

Sometimes the writers use hyperbolic and sarcastic imagery to get their point across. According to Longman, "The sage is at his most sarcastically comedic when it comes to the lazy person."[12] Some of the statements almost sound like a punchline. How lazy is a lazy person? So lazy that he turns on his bed to oversleep as often as a door turns on its hinges. So lazy that he puts his hand in a food bowl for a snack, and he lacks the strength to bring his hand back to his mouth again (26:14–15; cf. 19:24).

Preach about the Danger of Laziness and the Value of Hard Work

When preaching from these texts, you have poetic license to use humor, hyperbole, and even a measured amount of sarcasm to emulate what the writers are doing with what they are saying. When preaching about the sluggard who "buries his hand in the dish," and is too lazy to bring it back (19:24; cf. 26:15), consider a visual aid. Why not show listeners a tub of popcorn, bury your hand in it, and refuse to bring it up again? If you want to mirror the rhetorical effect of this image, which is humor, pretend to get your hand stuck in the container, and do not remove it. Instead of trying to get it out, you can say that you have resigned yourself to being stuck there for the rest of your life.

Other times, the writers use antithesis. They talk about laziness in opposition to hard work to describe how one path is dangerous and the other beneficial. Antithesis proverbs on laziness and hard work show up at least nine times in the book.[13] For example, in Proverbs 10:4, we read: "Lazy hands make for poverty, but diligent

---

11 6:6, 9; 10:26; 13:4; 15:19; 19:24; 20:4; 21:25; 22:13; 24:30; 26:13, 14, 16.
12 Longman, *Proverbs*, 561.
13 10:4–5; 12:11, 24, 27; 13:4; 15:19; 21:25–26; 28:19.

hands bring wealth." Notice that one path leads to an undesirable outcome and the other leads to a different outcome that is desirable. Of course, most ancient readers understood (and most modern readers also understand) that there are many people who are poor but are not lazy, and many who are wealthy but not diligent. That is not the point of the proverb. The point is simple: most of the time, laziness leads to the outcomes that you do not want, and hard work leads to the outcomes that you do want.

When contrasting laziness and hard work, find a way to set the sermon up as a contrast. Each path has its own beginning. Each has a type of person on it who is characterized by particular virtues or vices. Each produces outcomes that are good or bad. Once again, the choice is ours to make.

Some proverbs warn the next generation that sluggards tend to lie and even create diversions so that they can avoid work. They cry out with falsehoods, "There's a lion in the road, a fierce lion roaming the streets!" not just because it will create a distraction, but more importantly, because it will keep them from having to go outside to work (26:13; cf. also 22:13). Other proverbs lift up the benefits that await the diligent who are not lazy:

> Do you see someone skilled in their work?
> > They will serve before kings;
> > they will not serve before officials of low rank. (22:29)

Other proverbs warn that sluggards irritate those who do business with them "like vinegar to the teeth and smoke to the eyes" (10:26). Still other proverbs warn against the poverty and even ruin that awaits the one who does not remain diligent.[14] Notice the description of extreme danger awaiting the sluggard:

> A little sleep, a little slumber,
> > a little folding of the hands to rest –
> And poverty will come on your like a thief
> > and scarcity like an armed man. (24:33–34, cf. also 6:10–11)

---

14 14:23; 18:9; 19:15; 20:4, 13; 21:25.

According to Waltke, the sluggard does not come to poverty because of mistreatment or trial, but through "moral degeneracy" that leads to loss of freedom, aimlessness, and loss of life.[15]

Especially in the present moment, preachers have a pastoral responsibility to bring Waltke's point to the attention of our listeners. In the book of Proverbs, those who are sluggards often become poor on account of their moral degeneracy. However, this does not mean that all those who are poor experience poverty because they are sluggards. Be sure to make a clear distinction. I will say more about wealth and poverty in my chapter on justice.

The Wife of Noble Character

Do Not Preach Cryptically about Proverbs 31 Women

Whenever I ask male seminarians or veteran male pastors about their experiences preaching from the book of Proverbs or listening to others preach it—how often it is preached, which texts, what themes, what occasions—I hear one answer more than any other: "Proverbs 31 on Mother's Day" regardless of differences in race, ethnicity, theology, or ecclesial tradition. Perhaps not coincidentally, female pastors and seminarians usually give the same answer, especially those who grew up in churches that were conservative or even fundamentalist. Some female pastors and seminarians heard great sermons. The majority did not. Their description of the sermons' impact on them usually catches most of the men by surprise. While there were certainly exceptions, the sermons almost never made their moms feel like better moms; they almost always implied that their chief end in life was to be a wife and a mother; and they usually made them feel terrible about themselves.

With that in mind, let me start with what to avoid. Watch out that you do not weigh people down with impossible expectations. Talk about how the character in the poem is an archetype rather than a standard of measurement. As Longman reminds us, "The description is an ideal and should not be used as a standard by

---

15 Waltke, *The Book of Proverbs*, 1:115.

which to measure and critique women."¹⁶ In modern terms, think *X Men* or *The Avengers*. Normal people do not have the extraordinary powers or abilities of superheroes, but they can be inspired by the ideals that the superheroes represent.

The character described in Proverbs 31:10–31 is a superhero, an "ideal," to use Longman's word. What human being could accomplish all that the wife of noble character is able to accomplish? She gets up "while it is still night" to provide food for her family with some leftovers for her servants (15). Yet, she still has enough energy left over so that "her lamp does not go out at night" (18). That is to say, she does not need the 6–8 hours that most other human beings need. She makes her own clothes as well as other amenities like bed linens whether these are for her home or for business purposes (13, 19, 22, 24). She makes clothing and linens with excellence, persistence, efficiency, and profitability. She "sets about her work vigorously" (17a) and "does not eat the bread of idleness" (27b). Moreover, she has no fear when trials come. She does not worry about herself or her family when a storm comes through town that could threaten their livelihood (21). Indeed, she can "laugh at the days to come" (25).

Anxiety-free. Check. Problem-free. Check. Levity-about-the-future. Check. Her husband has full confidence in her and praises her (11, 28b), for she knows how to bring him "good, not harm, all the days of her life" (12). Not some days or even most days. *All* days. If you think the husband thinks she is great, wait until you hear about the kids: "Her children arise and call her blessed" (28). The kids do not have time to tantrum or bicker, to engage in petty rivalries or act like little un-sanctified demon-children. They are so busy praising their mom that they have no time left to step out of line, act up in church, or have their mom include their middle name when she corrects them. Permit me to use my sanctified imagination a bit: her kids' hair is always cut, their nails are always clipped, their clothes are always ironed, their grammar is always correct, and their manners are always good. If having perfects kids is not enough, in her spare time, she teaches Bible Study with wisdom and loving-kindness (*chesed*) (26), considers a field

---

16 Longman, *Proverbs*, 540.

and plants a garden with the earnings (16), runs a successful business outside her home (18a, 24), and opens her arms to the poor and needy (20).

Just to keep track, this person knows how to win at home, win at marriage, win at business, win at lowering the costs of overhead, win at raising children, win at productivity, win at ministry, and win at being worry-free about herself, her family, and the future.

Are you feeling exhausted yet? Many female readers of Proverbs 31 feel that way, too, and many male readers do not understand why the passage could be heard that way. Male readers: imagine if all the feminine pronouns were replaced with masculine pronouns. In what world could a man "win" in all of these areas all the time? Who could meet these expectations? Why "honor," "praise," (31) and emulate someone who, at least at first glance, lives by an unreachable —and dare I say, impossible—standard? We have a word where I come from for a person who works 20 hours a day: workaholic.

Instead, Preach Poetically about Wise Living

So, now that we know what to avoid, what should we embrace, especially since it should be our desire to preach this text with skill and faithfulness? The book of Proverbs closes with this hymn of praise, which means the character's story was pretty important to those who completed the anthology. Before I offer a formal answer, let me draw your attention to two resources in the Appendices of this book. Appendix I is called, "Understanding and Preaching Proverbs 31:10–31." This poem is so rich, multi-layered, and intriguing that I recruited an OT scholar, Rebecca Poe Hays, to offer exegetical and homiletical insights designed to help us. In another section, Appendix II.3, you will find a sermon on Proverbs 31 in its entirety by another OT scholar, Ingrid Faro, who deals with many of the nuances and implications of the passage in sermon form. The insights that I offer here will supplement the great interpretive work that they provide as Bible scholars and preaching practitioners.

It will move us in the right direction if we consider the genre and sub-genre of the passage. The text comes to us in a larger chapter in a larger book that is about prioritizing wisdom and pursuing the fear of the Lord as our ground and our goal, the importance of which will emerge when we discuss the purpose of the text in its context.

Notice the sub-genre as well. The passage is as an acrostic poem. Each verse begins with a letter of the Hebrew alphabet in alphabetical order, 22 letters to make 22 verses. Then, like now, poets wrote acrostic poems for stylistic and pedagogical reasons. Stylistically, one must exert considerable effort to write a deep and compelling poem in which each new verse begins with a new Hebrew letter in alphabetical order. Pedagogically, an acrostic poem aids the learner in memorization since the person who hears and memorizes it will know that the next verse after this one is supposed to begin with the next letter in the alphabet.

As preachers, we might ask: "How can we aid the learner in memorization?" Of course, we can do this through easy-to-remember points or moves that people can write down and remember. You do not need to come up with an acrostic in order to emulate the emphasis on memorization, but you also do not need to discard the idea entirely either.

In a sermon that I preached on this text, I created an acrostic sentence that I repeated and restated as part of a larger message of good news to women from Proverbs 31:30. The acrostic used the first seven letters of the alphabet, which was the best I could do. Twenty-six English letters seemed like too much for everyone to remember in one sermon on one Sunday. Here is the acrostic I created: **A** Woman of **B**eautiful **C**haracter **D**evotes herself to **E**veryday **F**ellowship with **G**od. It was simple, true, and sticky enough for people to remember.

It also helps to consider the tone of the text. Adopt a celebratory tone when you preach from this passage. Albert M. Wolters points out this poem is actually a heroic hymn of praise modeled after hymns of celebration for soldiers that were victorious in battle.[17] The poem utilizes military language at various points such as, "he [the husband] lacks nothing of value" (11b) on account of her,

---

17 Al Wolters, *The Song of the Valiant Woman: Studies in the Interpretation of Proverbs 31:10–31* (Paternoster, 2001).

a phrase which in Hebrew reads as, "he does not lack plunder," that is, he does not lack the spoils of warfare.[18] Also, the word "noble" (*hayil*) in verse 10 as in "wife of *noble* character" usually refers to those who serve in military contexts, sometimes with great valiance and courage (Exod 18:25; 2 Sam 23:20; 2 Kgs 15:20).[19] Consider also that the book of Ruth follows Proverbs 31 in some orderings of the Hebrew canon, which is likely not by accident.[20] Boaz calls Ruth a "woman of noble character" (Ruth 3:11), the same phrase that is found here, but notice that he uses it to describe a woman who is a poor Moabite widow. Her profile and story overturns modern Victorian ideals for what women can and cannot do. Also, the writer of the book of Ruth refers to Boaz as a man of noble character or "standing" (Ruth 2:1), a reminder that the phrase is for both women and men.

So, how do we aim at being genre-conscious with this text? I have already mentioned the possibility of a simple acrostic, but there are other ways to be genre-conscious here. As when you preach about other characters, use characterization through a description of attributes or imaginative embodiment. Since the passage is hymnic, consider how you might take lyrics (composed or borrowed) and songs (composed or borrowed) and pair them with the sermon so that the sermon feels more hymnic. Since the passage challenges images of docility and passiveness, you can use stories, images, and personification that do the same thing. When I preached this sermon, I used the image of William Wallace in *Braveheart* to help my listeners do some category shifting. Since the passage is a hymn of *praise*, celebrate in the same way as the

---

18 Regarding the spoils imagery in verse 11, Longman writes: "The composer intends the reader to recognize warrior imagery here. In what follows, we see a woman who is engaged in the battle of life, dealing with people and winning and advantage for her family." Longman, *Proverbs*, 542.

19 The word "noble" (*hayil*) can also refer to a person with affluence (Prov 13:22; Ruth 2:1; Isa 30:6; Jer 15:13), one who is capable (Gen 47:6; Exod 18:21), one in a high position like a king (Judg 11:1), or a person with physical strength (1 Sam 2:4; Eccl 10:10).

20 Longman writes: "That this poem concludes the book helps explain why, in the Hebrew canon, Proverbs is followed by Ruth (who herself is called a 'noble woman' in Ruth 3:11), and then by the Song of Songs, a book in which the woman is the main speaker and initiates the relationship." Longman, *Proverbs*, 540.

passage celebrates. Yes, you can deconstruct the text to a certain extent so that people understand that it is an archetype rather than a standard. That way, they will not be crushed under the weight of it, but you should also use this opportunity to celebrate people who fear the Lord, whether they are men or women, married or single. Make sure to remind everyone listening that anybody who loves the Lord can fear the Lord. Anybody who fears the Lord is praiseworthy according to this text.

Let me offer some more concrete ways to help listeners, women in particular, experience the text as a hymn of praise. First, draw attention to what the poet omits. Notice that the poet does not highlight the woman's physical beauty, her sexual abilities, or private parts of her body, an important but oft-overlooked omission in a poem that has young males as its intended audience. The writer does mention the wife's hands with reference to physical work, such as making garments and linens (Prov 31:13, 19), and he also mentions her hands in a metaphorical sense, namely, opening her hands to the poor (20). But the poet has nothing else to say about her physical appearance. When he mentions "charm" he describes it as both superficial and deceptive, and also states that "beauty is fleeting" (30). In the sermon, we have an opportunity to illustrate the stark contrast between ideas of beauty in our sexualized society that impact body image, especially for women and girls, and the refreshing vision of beauty in a passage with a markedly different focus.

Second, ground Proverbs 31:10–31 in gospel hope. If charm is deceptive and beauty is fleeting, then what is left to aspire to in light of this idealized and hymnic celebration? The poet answers the question this way:

> Charm is deceptive, and beauty is fleeting
>   but a woman who fears the LORD is to be
>   praised. (31:30)

The most important attribute of a woman of noble character, one more important than any other, remains as it has always been: the fear of the Lord, the same ground and goal for the young men to whom Proverbs was written (1:7; 2:5). This is good news to modern listeners! We do not have to be charming or beautiful to fear the Lord. We do not have to be perfect spouses or have perfect children. We do not have to be superheroes or have superpowers. The fear of the Lord is what matters most. Alice Mathews makes this same point in a sermon on this chapter:

> Here's the bottom line: the wise person, the strong committed person, knows the difference between what passes and what lasts. And the wise person chooses to live for what is eternal. Verse 30 tells us that charm is deceitful and beauty is fleeting. Beauty is good, but it doesn't last. What lasts forever is our relationship to God.[21]

What does the biblical poet say we should do for someone who understands this profound truth? The final verse says: "Honor her" (31:31). Praise such a person! Why not praise someone who has the clarity of vision to focus on that which matters and lasts in life and eternity?

When we preach this text, we can preach in a hymnic, mnemonic, and redemptive mode. In so doing, we will mirror what the text itself is saying and doing as an acrostic poem of praise in the tradition of a military hymn. To do what the text does, celebrate women as *part* of what you do. Yes, you can preach this text on Mother's Day if you want to, as long as you do so in a manner that is celebrative and hope-filled, as opposed to limiting and stifling. The emphasis at the end on the fear of the Lord offers a gospel word that sets mothers (and daughters) free from unrealistic societal expectations, and it also reminds those around them why they are worthy of our esteem on a day that celebrates all that our mothers do for us.

Yet, the passage does more than this, which is why we can do more with it. The second-to-last verse reminds us all—men or women, young or old, single, married, divorced, or widowed—that

---

[21] Alice Mathews, "Responding the God We Know," Sermon delivered in 2010 for Christian Life Emphasis Week at Houghton College, Caneadea, New York. See also Mathews' recently published book: Alice Mathews, *Woman of Strength: Living the Best Life Possible for God in This Broken World* (Our Daily Bread, 2020).

those who fear the Lord are greatly to be praised. The ground of gospel hope is level regardless of our lot or station. With God's help and by God's grace, all of us can fear the Lord.

Conclusion

In this chapter, we considered how to use characterization as a genre-conscious strategy. We studied five characters: animals, Woman Wisdom, Woman Folly, the sluggard, and the wife of noble character. As was mentioned at the outset, I could have conducted character sketches on the fool or the neighbor, for example, but I refrained from an exhaustive treatment, especially since I will discuss these characters elsewhere in the book. I also mentioned that I love good movies, and these days I maintain a special interest in character development in films. To close, I will mention one example.

In *The Greatest Showman*, a movie musical based on the life of P. T. Barnum, the founder of the Barnum and Bailey Circus, the main character (Barnum), played by Hugh Jackman, dreams of a circus that will one day be the greatest show on earth. When the circus launches and the people come, he sings, "It's everything you ever want. It's everything you ever need. And it's right here in front of you. This is where you want to be." He is a huge success.

However, the music shifts as the film progresses. Barnum tries to build bigger and aim higher at great risk to himself and his family. The lyrics change to, "All the shine of a thousand spotlights; All the stars we steal from the night sky will never be enough, never be enough. Never enough. Never enough for me." Nothing he does, builds, or promotes will satisfy his deepest longings.

Near the end, the music shifts one last time when Barnum experiences a transformative change in his perspective. Yes, he still loves the circus, but he can also let it go in a way that he could not before. In the final scene, he and his wife sit in a concert hall watching his daughters perform ballet. He returns to the first song, but the words have new meaning: "It's everything you ever want. It's everything you ever need. And it's right here in front of you. This is where you want to be."

In a higher and holier way, the characters in the book of Proverbs call out to us with a similar message. The animals give God glory. Woman Wisdom invites you to her banquet. The diligent proclaim that work is worthy of your best efforts. A "beautiful" person fears God above all. All of this happens because God welcomes you into covenant relationship. If you pay close enough attention to the characters and what they teach you, you can almost hear them singing: "it's everything you ever want ... this is where you want to be."

For Further Study

- Newsom, Carol A. "Woman and the Discourse of Patriarchal Wisdom: A Study of Proverbs 1–9." Pages 142–61 in *Gender and Difference in Ancient Israel*. Edited by Peggy L. Day. Fortress, 1989.
- Ogden Bellis, Alice. *Proverbs*. Edited by Sarah Tanzer. Wisdom Commentary 23. Liturgical, 2018.
- Weeks, Stuart. *Instruction and Imagery in Proverbs 1–9*. Oxford University Press, 2009.
- Wolters, Al. *The Song of the Valiant Woman: Studies in the Interpretation of Proverbs 31:10–31*. Paternoster, 2001.
- Yoder, Christine Roy. *Wisdom as a Woman of Substance: A Socioeconomic Reading of Proverbs 1–9 and 31:10–31*. BZAW 304. de Gruyter, 2001.

Talk about It

How do the characters in Proverbs shape your interpretation of the text? How might they shape a sermon series on this book?

Dig Deeper

Read through Proverbs 8 and 9 paying special attention to Woman Wisdom and Woman Folly as characters. Write a story or script in which these two women are the central characters and are trying to persuade a young person to choose to answer their call.

Practice

After reading the resources in the Appendix from Rebecca Poe Hays and Ingrid Faro, write a sermon on Proverbs 31:10–31 in which you celebrate those who fear the Lord. Get input from both men and women on the rough draft before you revise it and preach it.

4

Themes

THE ICONIC TV SHOW *Jeopardy* reigns as one of the most popular general knowledge quiz shows in modern history. Alex Trebek's name immediately comes to mind for those who watch the show; he was the talented and hard-working Canadian who hosted the modern version of *Jeopardy* from its inception in 1984 and stayed with it until his death from pancreatic cancer on November 8, 2020.[1] Trebek seldom missed an episode even during cancer treatment. He logged thousands of hours of hosting as a result. We can surmise that he amassed a lot of general knowledge about a lot of different subjects over 26 years.

For those who do not know how *Jeopardy* works, three contestants compete to be the first to solve a clue. They choose from six different categories of general knowledge. If they know the "answer" which they must state in the form of question, then they ring the buzzer as fast as they can. They compete for two rounds total. The person who gives the correct answer first gets to control the board. A game board might have categories as diverse as Cities in Europe, Words that Begin with "Q," Household Pets, and Famous Presidents. Then, in "Final Jeopardy," they wager their winnings on one final category.

The contestants appear on the show because they have amassed a lot of knowledge about a lot of different topics. They have built up a veritable storehouse of knowledge spread out across different

---

1 An earlier version of *Jeopardy* aired from 1964–75 with Art Fleming as its host before the current iteration of the show launched in 1984.

areas, knowledge they can access in an instant, because they have honed their memories over time.

Without straining the analogy too much, let me propose that, in the book of Proverbs, the older sages expected their younger proteges to do something similar, that is, to build up their memories, to have a "storehouse" they could access in real-time.[2] Of course, accessing wisdom for how to love God and neighbor is a much higher and loftier goal than accessing data for knowledge retrieval in a game. While knowledge is involved in the pursuit of wisdom, knowledge alone does not make one wise.

In this chapter, I propose using a thematic approach to preaching proverbs as a way to construct a storehouse of wisdom for those who listen.

Strategy 4:
Use a Thematic Approach

In the ancient world, a young person internalized most proverbs in order to access categories of wisdom. In the modern world, only a select few of us could access all of these categories without needing considerable help. We will not be able to internalize most of the book as they did. According to Tremper Longman III, "The ancient sage apparently would know the book so well that circumstances would call to mind the relevant proverb for application. For us, however, it is helpful to take a theme or topic addressed in the book, isolate the relevant proverbs, then study them as a group."[3]

A thematic approach to preaching proverbs organizes wisdom into categories so that modern listeners can think and act wisely in particular areas of life. It helps them build up a wisdom storehouse, an access center for tools and resources to utilize when in real-life situations that require discernment. A genre-conscious thematic approach honors the larger groupings of themes that

---

[2] Saint Augustine used the metaphor of storehouse in his discussion of memory. See Arthurs' discussion of Augustine's use of this term in Jeffrey D. Arthurs, *Preaching as Reminding: Stirring Memory in an Age of Forgetfulness* (Intervarsity, 2017), 5. See also section 10.8.12 in Augustine, *Confessions* (Oxford University Press, 2008), 185.

[3] Longman, *How to Read Proverbs*, 117.

recur throughout the book, but that could otherwise get lost without sufficient attention.

Opportunities

For some preachers, a topical approach cuts against the way they were trained. They learned to preach verse-by-verse from a passage, a short pericope that usually had some logical or narrative flow: a beginning, middle, and end. It is good and right to preach verse-by-verse in some places in the book of Proverbs, especially in Chapters 1–9 and 30–31. That stated, most of the rest of the book does not offer readers the structure, order, and flow of these chapters.

Because of the instinct to go deep with a few verses rather than wide with verses spread across chapters and sections of Scripture, many preachers who attempt to preach from the book of Proverbs will resort to one of two strategies. They will only preach a recognizable pericope with a clear beginning, middle, and end, usually from Proverbs 1–9 or 30–31, or they will preach just a single verse because they conclude that the verses before and after have little to no connection to the verse they have chosen. "Better to preach one verse the right way and go deep with it than to jump around from verse to verse and chapter to chapter," they tell themselves. Even so, for many, the prospect of preaching one verse for 20–40 minutes makes them want to run the opposite direction which keeps them from preaching most of the chapters in the book.

If you are reluctant about a thematic approach, here are some possible ways to reduce your hesitation. First, remember how proverbs were used, their intended audience, and their formational purpose. Young people (young men in this case) heard them read aloud and memorized them so they could acquire wisdom for everyday life. They drew from the storehouse in their interactions with family, friends, and neighbors, and they tried to think and act wisely in their relationships with God, creation, money, the poor and oppressed, rulers, and others in society. They had themes or topics sorted into larger categories to make sense of these relationships and to do right by them.

Second, the chapters and verses that we study today came along thousands of years after biblical passages were heard, memorized, and applied by ancient sages. An English cleric Stephen Langton added the chapter numbers and breaks that we find in most Bibles today in the early 13th century C.E. while teaching at the University of Paris in France.[4] More than two hundred years later, around the middle of the 15th century, a French printer and scholar named Robert Estienne popularized the versification of chapters in the Bible.[5] As modern interpreters, we often forget how chapter and verse divisions impact the way that we read Scripture.

Finally, let scholars of various stripes provide you with reassurance. In his book on interpreting proverbs, biblical scholar Edward M. Curtis writes: "Because of the narrow focus of each proverb, it is often useful to put together a larger mosaic about what wisdom teaches about a topic.... This is why a topical approach to teaching from Proverbs is often beneficial."[6] Jeffrey D. Arthurs, a homiletician, also encourages a thematic approach as a viable approach for preachers:

> Although units often encompass more than one verse, a topical approach is also possible as a genre-sensitive way to preach from the catalog. The book of Proverbs tosses out observations on themes like old age, gossip, laziness, alcohol, and humility. You can gather all the proverbs on [a] theme and preach a message or series on the topic. In a sense, your "text" is the entire book from which you glean a number of short pericopes.[7]

Literary scholar Leland Ryken agrees when he writes: "It is relatively easy to arrange the Book of Proverbs into various topics.

---

4 Others tried to develop a chapter system before Langton but none of their proposals gained traction in the same way as his divisions. For more, see Joshua Benson and Mark Clark, eds., *Stephen Langton's Prologue to the Bible* (Oxford University Press, 2021).

5 Estienne took much of the work that Hebrew scribes had done centuries earlier with versification, and he systematized it through the whole Bible. For more, see Elizabeth Armstrong, *Robert Estienne: Royal Printer* (Cambridge University Press, 1954).

6 Curtis, *Interpreting the Wisdom Books*, 49–50.

7 Jeffrey D. Arthurs, *Preaching with Variety: How to Re-Create the Dynamics of Biblical Genres* (Kregel, 2007), 142.

Once we have put such proverbs into their topical 'family,' we can meditate on the complementary aspects of a single experience, much as we can turn a prism in the light to get various colors."[8]

I know this is a dated reference, but think of the themes in the book of Proverbs as if they were songs on a jukebox. You might find a whole section of Motown's Greatest Hits organized in order from Songs 21–40 on a jukebox. However, if the jukebox is alphabetized by last name, which it sometimes is, then the Motown songs will be scattered throughout the anthology. Only after you push a button labeled "Motown Music" will you discover where the songs are located (e.g., Song 18, 36, 51, 68, etc.). In a sense, a preacher who uses a thematic approach knows where to find the button on the jukebox, helping listeners discover a recurring theme.

Cautions

Although the book of Proverbs lends itself well to a thematic approach, bear in mind that there are better and worse ways to preach topical sermons. Let me offer some cautions for the sake of best practices. First, when preaching a topical sermon or series, *remember to talk about the bad and not just the good*. For instance, in the book of Proverbs, we learn about what good friendship looks like, but we also learn about what bad friendship looks like. We read about how good leaders act and how bad leaders act. Just as there are proverbs about good marriages and good parenting, there are proverbs about bad marriages and bad parenting. You might want to preach about wise speech in a sermon or a series, a major theme in the book, but as a way to honor the message of the *whole* book, talk about good speech versus bad speech and wise listening versus foolish listening.

Second, with a thematic approach, *watch out that you do not turn context-specific wisdom sayings into context-free unconditional promises*.[9] For instance, not every person who honors the Lord with his or her wealth will see barns filled with grain and vats filled

---

8 Leland Ryken, *How to Read the Bible as Literature* (Zondervan, 1984), 127–28.

9 See Bruce K. Waltke, "Does Proverbs Promise Too Much?," *Andrews University Seminary Studies* 34 (1996): 319–36.

with wine (3:9–10). Not every Christian parent who "starts off children in the way they should go," will see the second half of the verse realized in the way they might hope: "even when they are old they will not turn from it" (22:6). Ryken writes: "Those who utter proverbs do not worry about possible exceptions (neither do lyric poets); they trust people to use their common sense in recognizing that a proverb need not cover every possible situation."[10] Do not be afraid to name this discrepancy to help people apply proverbs as guidance, direction, and formation rather than as universal, unconditional promises.

Lastly, with a thematic approach, *watch out for tendencies to moralize or de-theologize*. If we fall into this trap, we sever the connection between the themes that we preach on and the God whom we preach. Our sermons sound flat, horizontal, and a-theological, even in our attempts to be textual. In *Setting Words on Fire,* Paul Scott Wilson mentions this tendency: "Perhaps I simply assumed that when the Bible was in the sermon, God was the subject. It slowly dawned on me that people were the main focus, and the reason many sermons had no power was that God was largely absent."[11] Although it is right to trace themes across the book and to conduct subject-studies, steer clear of sermons that lose sight of God as the main actor. A sermon that sounds textual does not always say much about God. A sermon in which God is talked about is not the same as a sermon in which God is the subject.

Alyce McKenzie offers a similar warning when she claims that sermons from the book of Proverbs will often sound too much like self-help or New Age wisdom. McKenzie observes:

> In self-help wisdom, we attain wisdom by following a list of rules about how we are to think and act. According to Proverbs, we attain wisdom by staying in touch with its source. Wisdom is more than following a set of rules, it is cultivating a lifelong human/divine relationship with a Person.[12]

---

10 Ryken, *How to Read the Bible as Literature,* 124.
11 Paul Scott Wilson, *Setting Words on Fire: Putting God at the Center of the Sermon* (Abingdon, 2008), xii.
12 Alyce M. McKenzie, *Preaching Biblical Wisdom in a Self-Help Society*

As pastors, we already know that Christianity does not elevate a set of rules over a Person. Without a strategic theological reading that shapes our thematic approach, we will end up preaching a message that draws people away from rather than toward God. To quote famed literary scholar and poet Mary Karr, our sermons have so "squeezed out any mention of God or Jesus, maybe to sound modern" that there is "no sense of history. The pastor asks for peace and gives thanks for plenty, but the homily might come from *Reader's Digest*."[13]

Yes, we can preach on themes, but not if our sermon sounds like it belongs in the self-help section of a bookstore. Ask and answer theological questions. Who does God call us to become and why? Talk about how horizontal relationships compare and contrast with the relationship that God initiates with us. What good news does God have for us concerning this theme? A sermon on a theme can also be an occasion to declare gospel reality. Do not just explain and describe. Announce and proclaim. Our listeners need sermons that are multi-dimensional, vertical, and God-saturated. Whether or not they know it, they long for a sermon that centers on God.

Preaching a Thematic Sermon or a Thematic Series

A preacher has many themes from which to choose when using a thematic approach. Some of the major themes in the book include:

1. Friendship – how to be a good friend or a bad friend especially during trials
2. Family Relationships – how parents relate to children, children to parents, spouses
3. Neighbor Love – what it looks like to be a good neighbor versus a bad neighbor
4. Leadership – how to be a leader with vision, how to relate to rulers, how to rule

---

(Abingdon, 2002), 98.
13 Mary Karr, *Lit: A Memoir* (Harper Memorial, 2009), 232.

5. Speech and Silence – knowing when to speak, how to speak, and when to listen
6. Wealth and Poverty – wealth as a blessing, wealth as fleeting, why poverty exists
7. Compassion and Justice – how to relate to those who are poor and marginalized

I have highlighted these seven themes knowing that other scholars on the book of Proverbs might offer a slightly different list of themes, perhaps a longer or shorter list.

In the next section, I will discuss the first four themes. I will examine the other three in subsequent chapters.

Friendship

A good friend offers loving encouragement, provides constructive counsel, and stands in solidarity with you during times of adversity. Loving encouragement looks like caring about someone at all times (Prov 17:17), offering pleasant counsel (27:9b), and having a purity of heart and graciousness of speech that can win even the king for a friend (22:11). A good friend tells the truth even if it hurts because he or she seeks the greater welfare of the friend who will be offended. Here are some ideas for how to preach this theme using a genre-conscious approach.

> *Say what friendship is not (as the book does) to help listeners know what it is.*

Based on the qualities of good friendship, one can infer that a bad friend does just the opposite. Bad friends discourage others; they offer poor counsel or no counsel at all; they run away during times of trial rather than stand with you. The book of Proverbs actually says more about what constitutes a bad friend than a good friend. A bad friend tries to create conflict in friendships simply for the sake of conflict on account of a "perverse" mindset. Also, he or she tries to "separate close friends" through resorting to gossip (16:28; cf. also 17:9). Just as a good friend knows how to wound you for your own good by speaking with unfiltered candor (27:6a), a bad friend plays the part of an "enemy" who "multiplies kisses" (27:5). Although bad friends talk and act like they are your friend or want to be your friend, you should beware of "kisses" that are fake and put on for show.

Use the narratives of the Bible to illustrate the themes.

Use biblical stories. We find powerful examples of deep and abiding kinship in David's relationship with Jonathan and in Ruth's bond with Naomi. For instance, when faced with a choice between abandonment and love in the midst of a crisis, Ruth declares to Naomi: "Where you go I will go, and where you stay I will stay. Your people will be my people and your God my God. Where you die I will die, and there I will be buried. May the Lord deal with me, be it ever so severely, if even death separates you and me" (Ruth 1:16b–17). We also find negative portrayals. In the New Testament, Peter declares his allegiance to Jesus right after Jesus washes his feet in the Upper Room (John 13). Within a span of hours, he denies Jesus three times (18:25–27). Likewise, Judas greets Jesus with a kiss in the Garden of Gethsemane, a cruel way to betray their bond (Matt 26:48–50).

Connect the theme to the purpose of the book.

Ask and answer questions congruent with the purpose of the book. What resonance does friendship at the horizontal level have with the vertical relationship between God and human beings? What does it mean to say that God is a friend to us and that we are friends to God? What are the similarities and differences? We might explain this friendship by referring to the way God spoke to Moses "as a man speaks to his friend" (Ex 33:11). Likewise, Abraham was called "God's friend" (Jas 2:23). God chooses to be a "friend" to us and invites us through Christ to be "friends of God." God also enters into friendships between humans (1 Sam 20:8, 23, 42; Job 6:14). Jesus uses the language of friendship in the Last Supper discourse as a way to talk about sacrificial obedience and status in relationships. "Greater love has no one than this: to lay down one's life for one's friends. You are my friends if you do what I command" (John 15:13–14). In the same passage, Jesus replaces the language of "servants" with the language of "friends." He says, "I no longer call you servants because a servant does not know his master's business. Instead, I have called you friends, for everything that I learned from the Father I made known to you" (15:15). Using cross references like these, we can adopt a more theological approach to the theme of friendship.

Bring the ancient theme into conversation with the theme in the modern world.

Consider modern resources that help listeners understand friendship better. Where do we see examples of good friendship and bad friendship in churches, schools, or communities, on social media or in popular culture? What does it look like to be a good friend today? What concrete steps would a person have to take in order to be a better friend? What proverbs do people use today to inscribe the values of friendship? If we listen carefully, we will hear people use them, proverbs such as:

- A friend in need is a friend indeed.
- A new friend will tell you what you want to hear; a best friend will tell you what you need to hear.
- A real friend walks in when the rest of the world walks out.
- A friend to all is a friend to none.
- A man (woman) is known by the company he (she) keeps

These and other sources of modern wisdom help us win a hearing with our listeners because we are appealing to modern sources that many of them already know.

Family Relationships

Key relationships in the family unit—parents to children, children to parents, spouse to spouse—require commitment, discipline, diligence, and, of course, wisdom to function as God intended them. Here are some ideas for how to preach about family relationships using a genre-conscious approach.

Show how the parent-child relationship frames the book's message and tone.

When it comes to family relationships, the parent-child bond receives the most attention, especially since the voice typically represented in the book is that of the father imparting wise instruction to his son through a series of lessons. The father makes his agenda clear in Proverbs 1:8: "Listen, my son, your father's instruction, and forsake not your mother's teaching." Readers will find the language of "my son" or "my sons" followed by some kind of exhortation 26 times, despite the fact that various sections were written at various times by various authors.[14]

According to Dominick S. Hernández, parent-child imagery has an important rhetorical function regardless of whether one's relationship to one's parents is positive or negative. Parent-child imagery "serves the purpose of creating a model of how wisdom and knowledge should be passed down in general—that is, those who walk in wisdom are open to instruction in knowledge and imitate those who have more experience traveling on the pathway."[15]

Good parents provide a godly example, train children in wisdom, and correct them to keep them on the path of righteousness. A godly example begets blessing for the next generation. Because these parents "lead blameless lives" characterized by righteousness, "blessed are their children after them" (20:7). The parents see it as their responsibility to train their children well. They correct their children when they have erred. They discipline them as a way to love and protect them.[16] For good reasons, the imagery of the rod as a form of discipline creates discomfort for many modern readers, since various forms of physical discipline have brought so

---

14 1:8, 10, 15; 2:1; 3:1, 11, 21; 4:10, 20; 5:1, 7, 20; 6:1, 3, 20; 7:1, 24; 8:32; 19:27; 23:15, 19, 26; 24:13, 21; 27:11; 31:2.

15 Dominick S. Hernández, *Proverbs: Pathways to Wisdom* (Abingdon, 2020), 85.

16 13:24; 19:18; 22:15; 23:13–14; 29:15, 17.

much harm to vulnerable children throughout history.[17] However, we miss the point if we use the metaphor to justify one particular method of discipline. As Kidner reminds us, "The rod is no panacea. The book tacitly condemns the martinet [harsh disciplinarian] by its own reasonable approach, its affectionate earnestness, and its assumption that the old find their natural crown, and the young their proper pride in each other."[18]

Talk about the bad and not just the good.

Good children bring joy to their parents (10:1; 15:20; 23:22–25; 29:3), they heed their instruction (28:7), and they bring peace and delight to them when they are willing to receive correction (29:17). By contrast, Proverbs has pointed and even harsh warnings for "bad" children who dishonor and disrespect good parents through their words and actions. The harshest warning comes in Proverbs 30:17:

> The eye that mocks a father,
>   that scorns an aged mother,
> will be pecked out by the ravens of the valley,
>   will be eaten by vultures.

A foolish son brings grief to his parents (10:1, cf. also 15:20) and brings about their ruin (19:13). Children who rob their parents or are gluttonous with companions bring disgrace upon them (19:26; 28:7, 24). Those who curse their parents will have their lamp snuffed out as a result (20:20, cf. also 30:11).

Draw attention to opportunities and dangers in a marriage.

The young receive instruction on what to look for in a spouse, and they also receive instruction on how to have a good marriage.

---

17 For instances of the rod as a form of discipline, see 13:24; 19:18; 22:15; 23:13–14; 29:15, 17.

18 Kidner, *Proverbs*, 47.

In today's world, both husbands and wives, sons and daughters should hear and heed these reminders, and in the case of negative examples, the warnings.[19]

Invest in your marriage relationship without inviting strangers into the intimacy that you share (5:15–20). Avoid sexual infidelity.[20] Do not be a quarrelsome person in your marriage as it will hinder and harm the person that you marry.[21] If you are married, enjoy your spouse and give thanks to God for your spouse's presence in your life.[22] If you are single, become the sort of person that you would want to marry.

Draw from stories and teachings in Scripture about families.

When preaching on family relationships, ask which resources are available in Scripture and which theological connections prevent us from preaching sermons that are too horizontal. On the negative side, examples abound in Scripture of dysfunctional families that distort and undermine the values of wise living. One does not need to look long in the Bible to find parents mistreating children, children mistreating parents, or spouses mistreating each other. On the positive side, remember the emphasis that is placed on parents passing on the story of God's faithfulness to their children and their children's children.[23]

---

19 For more on why the passages on healthy marriages and on finding a spouse speak also to modern female readers in addition to male readers, see Longman's "Excursus: A Word to Women Readers of Proverbs." To women readers, Longman writes: "Quite simply, I believe modern readers are invited to read Proverbs by flipping the text to the other side of the relational equation. For example, 'It's better to live alone in the corner of an attic than with a quarrelsome husband in a lovely home.'" (132) Longman does not argue that the passages now exclude men when they used to exclude women; rather, he wants *all* readers to see the importance of these lessons. See Longman, *How to Read Proverbs*, 132–33.

20 6:29, 32–33; 23:26–28.
21 19:13b; 21:9, 19; 25:24; 27:15.
22 12:4a; 18:22; 19:14b; 31:10.
23 Deut 6:1–9; Pss 71:18, 78:4–6; Joel 1:3.

Make theological connections and emphasize gospel motivations.

Let theology shape your sermon with a particular interest in a gospel focus. Consider what gospel motivations drive a person to be a godly parent, a godly child, or a godly spouse. Connect faithful discipleship to faithfulness in relationships. A disciple of Jesus extends discipleship into every relationship. Remember how much marriage language and imagery is used to describe God's relationship to humanity, whether that is faithfulness or infidelity in marriage on the part of the people, or covenant fidelity on God's part even when the people insist on infidelity. Also, emphasize the metaphorical language of family, especially "children of God," and talk about why it functions as such a salient and powerful metaphor in the New Testament to describe our relationship to God (e.g., John 1:12–13; Rom 8:14; Gal 3:26; 1 John 3:1–3).

Connect the dots between the theme and modern culture.

When preaching on family relationships, consider which contemporary resources will help listeners resonate with a sermon or series on the subject. Tell modern stories of good parenting and bad parenting. On the negative side of parenting, for example, the college admissions scandal which started in 2019 revealed that celebrity and corporate-world parents were using their influence to help their kids cheat on standardized tests and lie on their applications.[24] When we lived in Illinois, a nearby town had Silent Saturdays for the children's soccer league, a day in which parents could attend, but were not allowed to "coach" from the sidelines. Too many problems arose with parents complaining and screaming, so the league had to make a policy that prohibited all talking and shouting during the game.

What stories are already being told in books, movies, and songs

---

24 Kate Taylor, "College Admissions Scandal: Former Pimco CEO Gets 9 Months in Prison in College Admissions Case," *The New York Times*, October 8, 2021, https://www.nytimes.com/news-event/college-admissions-scandal.

about functional and dysfunctional family relationships? For instance, most kids love the movie *Toy Story 4* (2019) for its storyline, humor, and animation all of which are excellent. However, parents love it for a different reason that they cannot always fully articulate. For adults, the subliminal theme is how to let go of your kids and reclaim your personhood when they have reached adulthood. The movie mirrors the same tension that parents feel when they have to "let go" of their grown kids.

Pastor people in pain.

The vision presented in the book of Proverbs and the values that it commends quite often differ from what our society says we should value in a spouse, parents, or children. On the one hand, we have an opportunity to challenge the empty visions that are prevalent in our society, the values that are out of sorts with a life marked by wisdom. On the other hand, because we live in the real world—a broken world—we have a responsibility to pastor people who are suffering.[25] Many of their (and our) family relationships are marked by heartache, disappointment, and estrangement. Just as we have a responsibility to share wisdom with those who are young in marriage or with young parents, so also, we have a responsibility to provide hope and pastoral encouragement to those struggling in their marriage or in their parenting, wanting to be married, or recovering from a divorce. A person can strive to be wise, but he or she cannot control the choices of others.

Neighbor-Love

A good neighbor sets a godly example, avoids mistreatment of others in word and deed, and serves as a much-needed friend during times of trouble. The theme of neighbor-love overlaps with the theme of friendship, especially since one of the most common Hebrew words for friend (*reaʿ*) can also be translated as "neighbor."

---

25 For an excellent resource on preaching to people in pain, see Matthew D. Kim, *Preaching to People in Pain: How Suffering Can Shape Your Sermons and Connect with Your Congregation* (Baker Academic, 2021).

This overlap highlights why neighbor-love matters so much. The writers do not have a category for neighbor-as-adversary. They assume that a person pursuing godliness and wisdom will seek out friendship with his or her neighbors. Here are some ideas for how to preach about neighbor-love using a genre-conscious approach.

Celebrate the good neighbor (as the book does).

A righteous person serves as a "guide to his neighbor" (ESV) on how to live a godly life (12:26).[26] Through knowledge, he or she escapes the temptation of the godless to destroy neighbors rather than love them (11:9). A good neighbor refuses to make false pledges (3:28; 17:18; 24:28; 25:18; 26:19), plot evil (3:29), give out loans that complicate and ultimately destroy the relationship (6:1–6; 17:18), commit adultery (6:29), deride (11:12), despise (14:21), entice (16:29), or flatter (27:14; 29:5). When all is as it should be, the good neighbor to whom you have shown neighbor-love will also show neighbor-love to you.

Construct a biblical-theological framework for neighbor-love.

Consider again which scriptural and theological resources are available to you. A preacher has lots of great resources from which to draw that are connected to how to think, speak, and act in relation to the neighbor that is most proximate. Elsewhere in Scripture, however, we find scriptural statements and theological language for how to welcome neighbors that society might be tempted to disregard. For instance, in Deuteronomy 24:17–18, we read: "Do not deprive the foreigner or the fatherless of justice, or take the cloak of the widow as a pledge. Remember that you were slaves in Egypt and the Lord your God redeemed you from there. That is why I command you to do this." Notice the call to "remember." At one time, you too were in a similar predicament had it not been for the grace of God that delivered you. God calls you out to be a neighbor to those in need regardless of proximity, convenience, or status.

---

26 The NIV translates the word "neighbor" as "friend" here.

Tell the stories Jesus tells about neighbor-love.

Jesus talks about neighbor-love in Luke 10. A young expert in the law asks Jesus how he might inherit eternal life. Jesus asks him how he interprets the law, and the young man responds with an almost perfect answer. Jesus affirms that the law can be summarized as, "Love God and love neighbor," but the young expert in the law persists. He wants to "justify himself" by asking the question, "And who is my neighbor?" Jesus responds to his question by telling the Parable of the Good Samaritan. In the story, the neighbor that listeners least expect, the despised outsider, the Samaritan rather than the priest or the Levite, showed radical neighbor-love to the man who had fallen into the ditch. "Who of three was the true neighbor?" Jesus asks. The expert in the law replied, "'The one who had mercy on him.' Jesus told him, 'Go and do likewise'" (Luke 10:37).

Use the call to pursue neighbor-love to challenge listeners today.

Challenge listeners to imagine what neighbor-love looks like in the modern world in their relationships with proximate and non-proximate neighbors. Do we know our proximate neighbors' names? Do we pray for them? Do we communicate that we are willing and ready to help them in a time of need? Especially in a transient world, how can we be present to our neighbors rather than anonymous? Does our way of living guide our neighbor on how to find the path of wisdom? What virtues does God call us to pursue, and what vices does God call us to reject in our relationship to our neighbors? Moreover, how might we expand our horizon, develop our imagination, and move toward action in loving neighbors that are not proximate to us, those who might be lost, lonely, or left out of the wider society? A prayer of C. S. Lewis's comes to mind. In a *Grief Observed*, he prays: "Not my idea of God, but God ... not my idea of my neighbor, but my neighbor."[27]

---

27 C. S. Lewis, *A Grief Observed* (Harper One, 1967), 67.

Leadership

A wise leader works hard, chooses honesty and integrity, and avoids financial mismanagement such as giving bad loans or exacting usury on others. Here are some ideas for how to preach about leadership using a genre-conscious approach.

Provide a character sketch on good, godly leaders.

A leader exerts considerable effort in work, thus avoiding the highly dangerous path of laziness.[28] A leader also chooses the path of integrity. Take financial leadership as an example. God sees whether we have chosen to be honest and accurate in our estimates, accounting, and deal-making with others in work settings in particular. "The Lord detests dishonest scales, but accurate weights find favor with him" (11:1; cf. also 16:11; 20:10). Proverbs calls leaders to be shrewd. Watch out for the buyer who says, "Bad, bad, but he disappears and then brags" (20:14). At various points throughout the book, the older generation warns the young about the threat of financial mismanagement, such as loans with interest or promised loans that never materialize.[29] This does not imply that you should refrain from being generous and withhold from those in need. If anything, the expectation is that a person will give generously and give to those in need without expecting to be repaid (11:24–25). If you have it, give it and be set free as you do. If you do not have it or perhaps you have some of it and want to preserve your work relationships from unnecessary drama, then steer clear of situations that complicate and bring potential strain on your relationship with others.

Tell stories from Scripture about good leaders and bad leaders.

We see great leaders like Nehemiah helping the people rebuild the

---

28 For instance, see Prov 6:6–11; 10:4; 18:9; 19:15, 24; 20:4; 21:25–26; 26:13–16.

29 6:1–5; 11:15; 17:18; 20:16; 22:26–27; 27:13; 28:8.

wall, Esther acting with courage and conviction in the citadel of Susa, or Daniel remaining faithful in King Nebuchadnezzar's palace. We also see terrible leaders like Pharaoh oppressing the nation of Israel at the beginning of Exodus or most of the judges leading Israel and Judah astray in the book of Judges. Moreover, we see religious leaders who lose their moral compass like King Saul in 1 Samuel, Pashhur the priest in Jeremiah 20, and Amaziah the priest of Bethel in Amos 7.

Illustrate biblical proverbs using stories from today's context.

We do not need to search long or hard to find examples of leaders who bring out the best and leaders who bring out the worst in us regardless of who we vote for or follow on social media. We have plenty of negative examples. On the positive side, most of us can think of pastors and Christian leaders in our lives who have been mentors and models for us in ministry. Many of these influential leaders do not have a lot of letters after their names (i.e., degrees granted), and they have not read a book on leadership, yet they were the right person at the right time speaking into our lives in the right ways. Tell these inspiring stories so that those who hear your sermon get snapshots of leadership in action through regular people. Leaders do not need to be a CEO of a Fortune 500 company to be great leaders or to make a difference in the world. Some leaders follow that path. The rest of us seek to be faithful in our circles, no matter how big or small, in a way that honors God and blesses people.

Talk about Jesus as a leader to show how he fulfills proverbs on good leaders.

In Jesus, we see a radically different kind of leader who embodies and prescribes a set of kingdom values that are wholly out of step with the values of the dominant society. Service. Sacrifice. Generous love. Forgiveness. Truth-telling. Reconciliation. Hope. He invites would-be leaders into another way of seeing the world and acting in it. He calls his disciples into a Christ-honoring theology of power. In Mark 10:42–44, Jesus gathers his disciples and says, "You know that those who are regarded as rulers of the Gentiles lord it over them, and their officials exercise authority over them. Not so with you. Instead, whoever wants to become great among you must be your servant, and whoever wants to be first must be slave of all."

Connect leadership then to leadership now.

Ask people which leaders they look up to, which ones they model themselves after in leadership, and whether or not the values and commitments of the leaders they admire cohere with the values that Jesus names in Mark 10. Challenge people to care more about who they are becoming than the tasks they are accomplishing. Cast a vision for what it means to be a godly leader at school, at work, in our homes, and with our families. Invite people to take spiritual gifts inventories so that they can discern what their gifts are and decide how to use them, and call people to exercise their gifts in service to God and people.

Conclusion

A thematic approach helps listeners build a storehouse of wisdom to draw from in their relationships with friends, family, neighbors, and co-workers. A sermon or series that uses a thematic approach enables people to identify which virtues to pursue and which vices to avoid in common categories of living. It helps them think, speak, and act in their most important relationships. The decisions they make will depend largely on the specificity of the context and the people in it. The writers of the book of Proverbs knew this. They realized that most relationships require local, contingent, contextual decision-making. What they cared about most was this: who we are in our decisions, the path we choose to take, and the person we choose to become in all of the many areas of our lives. A wise person not only knows this to be true; he or she chooses to live out its implications daily in the context of concrete relationships.

For Further Study

- Clements, Ronald E. "The Good Neighbor in the Book of Proverbs." Pages 209–28 in *Of Prophets' Visions and the Wisdom of Sages: Essays in Honour of R. Norman Whybray on his Seventieth Birthday*. Edited by Heather A. McKay and David J. A. Clines. JSOTSup 162. JSOT, 1993.
- Curtis, Edward M. *Interpreting the Wisdom Books: An Exegetical Handbook*. Kregel, 2017.
- Hernández, Dominick S. *Proverbs: Pathways to Wisdom*. Abingdon, 2020.
- Kidner, Derek. *Proverbs*. Kidner Classic Commentaries. IVP Academic, 2008.
- Yoder, Christine Roy. *Proverbs*. AOTC. Abingdon, 2009.

Talk about It

- Discuss the opportunities and challenges of preaching the book of Proverbs thematically, especially if you are used to preaching a different way.
- Re-read the cautions section earlier in the chapter. Which of the three cautions named pose the biggest danger for you? Why?

Dig Deeper

- Choose one of the themes discussed in this chapter. What passages would need to be included for a sermon or series on that theme? What stories in Scripture would lead to a better and deeper understanding of that theme?
- Re-read the section on leadership. Engage in a biblical-theological study of leadership in the Bible. Generate ideas for both negative and positive examples. Spend time writing about what kind of leader Jesus was and what he taught his disciples about leadership through what he said and did. Spend time writing about what you aspire to be like as a leader.

Practice

- Plan and preach a 4-to-8-week series on one of the themes discussed in this chapter.
- Preach on the theme of neighbor-love. As a way to generate concrete application, commend at least five practical steps that people can take to practice neighbor-love toward their proximate neighbors and strangers and that the church as a whole can take in order to practice neighbor-love toward the surrounding community.

5

Timing

Sometimes we feel young in an older person's world. I started in church ministry as a youth pastor. One time, I surprised an eighth-grader in my youth group by having lunch with him at his public school. Imagine me as a 20-year-old wearing a hoodie, a baseball cap, and a backpack sitting down at an undersized rectangular cafeteria table. Suddenly, someone tapped me on the shoulder—a middle school teacher. In a stern voice, she exclaimed, "You know the rules, young man! Backpacks are supposed to be kept in lockers. You take this to your locker right now." My eighth-grade student tried to help me save face. "Uh, he's in college, Mrs. Jones." I thought the goatee, the clothing, and the fact that I was the tallest person in the room gave me away. "I just thought you looked old for your age," she said.

Other times we feel old in a younger person's world. If you are over 40 years old, talk with someone younger about actor Mark Wahlberg's hit singles and albums on Billboard before his blockbuster movie stardom, and you should expect some blank stares. A young professor like me feels old when a seminary student starts a sermon with, "When I was born in 1999 . . . ." An older professor feels this way when she tells a virtual classroom of students on Zoom or WebEx that the squares on the screen remind her of Hollywood Squares, an old game show. More blank stares. To them, Hollywood Squares sounds like a breakfast cereal.

In both situations, we must decide how we will say (or not say) the right thing in the right way. Possible responses include saying nothing, laughing it off, pretending like it did not happen, making light of the awkwardness, saying something that makes it more awkward, coming up with a witty retort, saying something rude or unfeeling, or perhaps even using the specific incident as a chance to reflect later. The situation requires of us an ability to make the right choice at the right time.

Herein lies the connection to the book of Proverbs along with the strategy that we will discuss in this chapter. A wise person associates timing with wisdom. That is to say, he or she develops and deploys practical know-how for what to say and what not to say, what to do and what not to do in concrete situations at just the right time.

Strategy 5: Associate Timing with Wisdom

Timing is everything. An understanding of timing in the book of Proverbs will not only help us understand its central role throughout the book, but it will also help us to give it an important role when we preach as a way to be more genre-conscious.

Knowing Roads and Seeing Signs

My mother grew up in Allentown, Pennsylvania. Whenever we would drive from the house where I grew up in New Jersey to visit my grandmother's house in eastern Pennsylvania, our family would drive part of the way through Amish country. My mother taught me how to tell which houses were Amish-owned. Many of the tell-tale signs had to do with technology. Look for the absence of cars or trucks in the driveway, a propane tank outside, or a clothesline for hand-washed clothes. She taught me to find particular objects and recurring patterns. As a result, I noticed that there were way more Amish-owned homes than I had realized on the same highways and roads that I thought I knew so well.

Although the analogy is imperfect, consider how it relates to timing in Proverbs. We know the highways and roads well, or at least we think we do. However, when we train our eyes to notice the recurrence of particular patterns and objects, we notice that there is far more here than we picked up at first glance.

The writers of the book of Proverbs wanted those coming after them to equate wise living with good timing. We could easily miss this. As a result, we could also miss opportunities to foreground timing in our sermons.

To associate timing with wisdom, I will set forth three ideas in particular: connect the appearance of contradictions with the importance of timing, help people make well-timed choices in concrete situations, and translate timing's importance for modern listeners.

Connect the Appearance of Contradictions with the Importance of Timing

One of the more obvious characteristics of the genre of proverb is brevity. Wherever you find brevity in the larger context of an anthology that spans centuries, you will also find contradictions. Let me mention one of the better-known examples. Later, I will connect the dots between apparent contradictions and the importance of good timing.

Proverbs 26:4 reads: "Do not answer a fool according to his folly; or you yourself will be just like him." Then, one verse later, we read: "Answer a fool according to his folly, or he will be wise in his own eyes" (26:5).[1] So which is it? Do we answer a fool according to his folly or do we refrain from answering a fool according to his folly? What do we do with contradictory statements like these, especially when they are paired in succession? The solution is to realize that these pithy statements are both true depending on the timing.

Many contemporary readers of Proverbs struggle to imagine a world in which contradictions are a sign of consistency rather than inconsistency, especially if our training teaches us to root it out and expose it as false. Interrogators in the Federal Bureau of Investigation (FBI) look for contradictions in the stories of those

---

[1] These are two examples of answer proverbs in that they answer questions that are not recorded in the text.

they apprehend in an attempt to find the truth. Prosecutors look for inconsistencies in an eyewitness's account to show that the details do not add up.

Now imagine that the contradictions that pop up at various points in the book of Proverbs were put there on purpose, that they might actually be intentional.[2] Although modern readers struggle to hold these contradictions together in their minds, ancient readers did not necessarily have the same struggle. Intentional inconsistency offers hearers a much-needed rhetorical effect. It forces us to ponder, to wrestle, or to talk to others and get advice. It takes wisdom to read wisdom.

Sometimes we find examples of contradictory statements in succession such as the one mentioned above: Proverbs 26:4–5. However, most often, the contradictions do not take place in succession; they are spread out across various chapters. Here are three non-successive examples among the many that we could highlight:

Lazy hands make for poverty,
    but diligent hands bring wealth. (10:4)
versus
The blessing of the Lord brings wealth,
    without painful toil for it. (10:22)

The greedy bring ruin to their households,
    but the one who hates bribes will live. (15:27)
versus
A gift given in secret soothes anger,
    and a bribe concealed in the cloak pacifies great wrath.
    (21:14)[3]

---

[2] For more on why and how proverbs are intentionally contradictory, see Peter T. H. Hatton, *Contradiction in the Book of Proverbs: The Deep Waters of Counsel* (Ashgate, 2008).

[3] In his commentary on Proverbs 18:16, a verse about bribes/gifts, Longman writes: "It is better to understand the circumstance of a gift to be the issue. If one gives a gift to circumvent justice, then it is wrong. But there are situations where a bribe can open doors to good ends. In other words, the purpose of the bribe is the issue here." See Longman, *Proverbs*, 552. For more on gifts and bribes in

> The house of the righteous contains great treasure,
>   but the income of the wicked brings ruin. (15:6)
>
> *versus*
>
> Better a little with the fear of the Lord
>   than great wealth with turmoil. (15:16)

Notice the tension. Again, our Enlightenment thinking resists apparently contradictory statements. The wealth that a righteous person produces usually comes about because of "diligent hands," but God can also bestow mercy and favor in such a way that one does not have to endure the same "painful toil" that others endure to acquire it. A God-fearing person who hates bribes will usually avoid the fate of those who are greedy, the latter bringing ruin to their households as a result of their avarice. However, even in many cultures today, a God-fearing person can initiate a bribe that is both blameless and right, especially in situations in which there is an offended party who has been shamed somehow. In some but not all situations, one can expect to find treasure in the house of the righteous, but if pressed to a decision, always choose a little with the fear of the Lord over a lot of treasure with turmoil.

Sometimes we find contradictions in Proverbs because the book itself is an anthology of wisdom sayings collected over time; it represents a cross-section of society. The book is like an eclectic anthology of music, the type of anthology that brings together diverse traditions and classes of people: folk, jazz, rock, classical, and opera. That is the reason why one proverb can sound like a folk-saying that is intended for the general masses in an agrarian society, whereas another proverb can sound like counsel to those in power such as kings, queens, and other rulers.

Often, contradictions appear in Proverbs because they serve an important pedagogical and rhetorical function. They teach us about the "situational nature of wisdom," to use Christine Roy Yoder's phrase.[4] In her commentary on Proverbs, Yoder observes that a wise person knows how to hold opposing perspectives, knowing

---

Proverbs, see also Hatton's chapter on the subject in Hatton, *Contradiction in the Book of Proverbs*, 137–48.

4 Yoder, *Proverbs*, xxiv.

which perspective to foreground in light of the situation. She writes: "Thoughtful people often hold views that are in conflict with one another and decide between them as circumstances warrant."[5] Ben Witherington makes a similar claim while taking aim at the particular pairing mentioned above. He writes:

> In various cases there are sayings paired together that seem almost flat contradictions of one another ("do not speak to a fool in his folly," followed by "speak to a fool in his folly" Prov 26:4–5). This raises the question of whether the author or editors saw this material as timeless truth, or whether such sayings placed in tandem were intended to have a dialogical rather than a didactic function. That is, rather than trying to offer Truth with a capital T, perhaps in some cases the function of a proverb was either to provide a general rule of thumb, not an exclusive rule, or the maxims were meant to aid the listener to discern the proper context in which to illuminate the human situation. Perhaps the function of Prov 26:4–5 is to show that either piece of advice might be appropriate in a given situation.[6]

So, do we answer a fool according to his folly or do we refrain from answering him? The answer depends on what the fool is saying. We must determine what is most fitting and appropriate in each particular situation. In other words, we associate good wisdom with good timing depending on the concrete situation.

In the case of Proverbs 26:4–5, the second half of each verse shapes what we do and do not do in specific situations. A wise person does not answer a fool according to his folly in specific situations that increase the odds that "you yourself will be just like him" as a result of what was said (26:4b). A wise person does answer a fool according to his folly in specific situations where the fool will end up "being wise in his own eyes" (26:5b).

Now, let me propose a few genre-conscious homiletical strategies that will highlight contradictions in a manner that is accessible.

---

5 Ibid.
6 Witherington, *Jesus the Sage*, 23.

Name the Tension So That People Feel the Tension

When preaching the contradictions, name the tension so that people *feel* the tension. Even if it makes our listeners uncomfortable, we have a responsibility to help them do what ancient listeners did on a regular basis: hold seemingly contradictory perspectives together in their minds at one and the same time. In so doing, we reproduce the rhetorical effect for modern listeners. Although there are many ways to raise tension in a sermon, let me commend two possibilities here. First, we can raise tension by asking rhetorical questions that challenge reductive binaries. For instance,

> Does the Bible tell us to do one thing, and then to do the opposite? How does that make sense? Are you supposed to answer a fool according to his folly or refrain from answering him? Which one is it anyway? It says at the beginning of Proverbs 10 that hard work from diligent hands brings wealth, but then it says in another place in the same chapter that God's blessing brings wealth and hard work may not be needed. So, does wealth come from hard work? From God? Both? What about those who work really hard who are poor? Why aren't they rich? What about those who are lazy who are rich? Did God bless them or did something else happen?

Second, we can raise tension by naming the emotions associated with it and helping people feel these emotions. Validate the discomfort, confusion, anger, and disappointment that our listeners feel when they encounter passages that say one thing and its opposite at the same time. Help listeners feel the emotional incongruity. Create space for the tension to be addressed, and in some ways, resolved in the sermon.

When our listeners see, hear, and feel that the contradictions are intentional, that they have something to teach them about how wisdom is situational and contextual, it helps them know whether to choose one option or its opposite, to be faithful in one way at one point in time and faithful in a different way at another point in time.

Present "Dueling Proverbs"

Alyce M. McKenzie argues that preachers should set up "dueling proverbs," as a way to highlight contradictions. McKenzie claims that it can be done with two or more biblical proverbs, or it can be done by putting conventional, idealized wisdom into dialogue with the radical and subversive wisdom found in Job and Ecclesiastes that calls it into question. When setting up dueling proverbs in the book of Proverbs, you can highlight a proverb that appears to prescribe one thing at one point and its opposite at another point.[7] For instance, here is a contradiction that occurs in successive verses:

> The poor are shunned even by their neighbors,
>   but the rich have many friends.
> It is a sin to despise one's neighbor,
>   but blessed is the one who is kind to the needy. (14:20–21)

Instead of preaching one verse or the other, preach both verses. These verses are "dueling verses" in the sense that they appear to compete with each other, but they are actually both true.

Help People Make Well-Timed Choices in Context-Specific Situations

Sometimes we have a clear idea concerning the right thing to do. If we crash our car into another car, we know that we should not flee the scene. If someone is about to walk into oncoming traffic, whether we know them or not, we will do what we can to stop them. If loved ones want to invest money in a Ponzi scheme that they believe is innocent, we will use research and stories to warn them. The way forward is clear in these scenarios. Sometimes the book of Proverbs presents us with clear-cut choices like these: the way of wisdom over the way of folly (Prov 9), the way of the righteous over the way of the wicked (15:29), the gifts of wisdom and insight over the seduction of silver and gold (16:16).

---

[7] Alyce M. McKenzie, *Preaching Proverbs* (Westminster John Knox, 1996), 127–28.

Although the writers present some clear right-versus-wrong choices, more often than not, they draw attention to different types of choices, what I am calling better-versus-worse choices. We can detect this tendency when we read the book in its entirety and notice the contrasts in it. Sometimes the writers call us to confront offenses, and other times they call us to overlook them. Sometimes they want us to act, and other times they want us to refrain from acting. Sometimes they expect us to speak, and other times they expect us to resist the urge to speak. When these contrasts appear, they show us the connection between timing and wisdom: there are indeed better and worse choices in the context of everyday situations.

A person with good timing asks: What is the wisest action to take in this situation for a person who fears the Lord? The answer varies depending on the situation. The wisest action might be to confront, to act, or to speak; or it might be to overlook, to refrain, or to remain silent. Context helps us choose. As Dave Bland writes, the proverb and the situation work together "in a dialectic manner to make sense out of the experience at hand. The situation provides a key element in the process of the proverb working to influence and change."[8] In addition to reading the situation, a wise person accesses memory and imagination in order to visualize possible outcomes and to determine which outcomes are best in the situation at hand.

Here are some homiletical ideas for how to help people make well-timed choices in concrete situations.

Use the Speech-Versus-Silence Contrast to Show Why Timing Is Important

Sometimes we need to speak and other times we need to refrain from speaking. The writers foreground thoughtful speaking and caring silence. Proverbs also gives us guidance on how often to speak, the manner in which to speak, and the value of choosing silence over speech:

---

8 Bland, *Proverbs and the Formation of Character*, 77.

- When we speak, our words should be words that bring healing rather than harm (12:18).
- When we speak, what comes out of our mouth should be characterized by gentleness (15:1a; 16:24; 25:15).
- Sometimes our words should sting those around us as a sign that we care about them too much to remain silent (27:5–6).
- Sometimes our words are the last thing that people need, especially when we speak them in haste (18:13).
- Silence over speaking can be a sign of wisdom and maturity (13:3, 17:28).
- Silence over speaking can be a sign of deception and falsehood (17:28).
- When we speak, we should avoid telling lies or resorting to flattery, especially since these harm other people in addition to harming us (26:28, cf. also 12:17, 19).
- When we speak, we should guard against self-promotion or branding ourselves wise (27:2).
- When we speak to our neighbor, we should guard against ill-timed remarks (27:14,[9] cf. 15:23; 25:11).
- We cannot and must not remain silent in the face of injustice, particularly when we find ourselves in positions of power and influence (31:8–9).

We do not have to walk people through all these passages to show them why timing matters in speech and in silence. In fact, it would be better just to highlight the tension between speech and silence in order to show why timing makes such a big difference.

A practical way to highlight the speech-silence contrast is to challenge listeners with questions and to give them time to write down answers. For instance, it could sound like this:

---

9 According to Proverbs 27:14, "If anyone loudly blesses their neighbor early in the morning, it will be taken as a curse." A loud blessing early in the morning does not sound much like a blessing, and it is likely intended to be heard by others rather than one's neighbor. Clements, however, argues that this proverb addresses motivation primarily: "It is not that the praise is spoken at the wrong time, but rather that it is spoken for others to hear." See Ronald E. Clements, "The Good Neighbor in the Book of Proverbs," in *Of Prophets' Visions and the Wisdom of Sages: Essays in Honour of R. Norman Whybray on his Seventieth Birthday*, ed. Heather A. McKay and David J.A. Clines, JSOTSup 162 (JSOT, 1993), 223.

In our speaking, would someone listening accuse us of being reckless or harsh with our words? What would it look like to choose the better way, to use words that are kind and gracious? In this situation, do we have a tendency to speak when it would be better to remain silent? In that situation, do we have a tendency to remain silent when what is called for is boldness to speak? What would it look like to choose the better way, to guard our lips more closely and to listen before answering in some situations, and to choose to speak without hesitation for those who cannot speak for themselves in other situations?

The speech-versus-silence theme functions as an invitation to make better choices about what you will say, how you will say it, when you will be quiet, and how well you will listen. A person needs good timing in order to make these choices.

Use a Dialectical Structure in the Sermon

The contradictory nature of proverbs suggests a homiletical strategy we might call "dialectical structure." I mean a structure that draws attention to both sides of an argument. The first section of the sermon would be "on the one hand," and the second part would be "on the other hand." In the third section, instead of resolving the tension with a one-size-fits-all solution, you would make it your aim to help listeners understand that situation A calls for an "on the one hand" decision whereas situation B calls for an "on the other hand" decision.

For instance, you could prepare a sermon on what to do when someone offends you. Do you confront an offense or overlook an offense? In the first section of the sermon, explain why we should confront an offense. Remember Proverbs 27:5? "Better is open rebuke than hidden love." Provide examples of why this path is good. In the second section, explain that the wise thing to do might be to let the offense go. "A person's wisdom yields patience; it is to one's glory to overlook an offense" (19:11). Provide examples of when this path is also good. Then, in the third section, associate timing with wisdom. Help people understand that sometimes they should confront an offense and other times they should overlook an offense. The answer depends on various factors in the concrete situation and on well-timed choices in the situation.

You could also use this structure to preach about saving versus giving. On the one hand, saving is both wise and virtuous (e.g., 6:7–8). Provide examples of why saving is wise. On the other hand, generosity has its virtues. It prevents us from becoming self-focused misers (e.g., 22:9). The one who "is kind [lit. "shows grace"] to the poor lends to the Lord, and he will reward [lit. "repay"] them for what they have done" (19:17, cf. 31:20). Think about that for a moment. We give a "loan" to God when we show grace to the poor.[10] Provide examples of why generosity is good and right. Sometimes, in a concrete situation, we need to double-down on saving as a form of diligence, and other times, in a concrete situation, we need to double-down on giving to cultivate generosity. Regardless of the situation, we need to grow in both. Explain why both-and rather than either-or is the wisest and most faithful way forward.

When we help listeners connect context-specificity to making better choices, they develop and deploy practical know-how for doing the right thing in the right way at the right time for the right reasons.

Translate Timing's Importance for Modern Listeners

Preachers do not need to look far to find modern proverbs that follow the same pattern of holding two opposing viewpoints in tension or making better-versus-worse choices. For this reason, use modern examples to help listeners translate timing's importance and relevance using scenarios from everyday life. Modern scenarios serve as yet another genre-conscious way to do what the text does, namely to produce the rhetorical effects of tension, contradiction, and context-specific decision making.

---

10 Waltke writes: "The one who gives generously to the destitute figuratively gives a loan to the Lord presumably because the Lord's honor is tied up with the poor, for he made them and they, too, are his image (14:31; 17:5; 22:2)." Bruce K. Waltke, *The Book of Proverbs: Chapters 15–31*, vol. 2, NICOT (Eerdmans, 2005), 111.

Let me offer some examples. In a situation in which people are trying to make a decision, they might hear, "Look before you leap." This proverb functions as a warning against rushing into decisions without deliberation. They might also hear, "He who hesitates is lost," or "Seize the day," proverbs that remind them that some windows of opportunity close if we wait too long or fail to act.

Every summer, high school seniors engaged in a serious romantic relationship get ready to go off to college. They wonder aloud together whether their new long-distance relationship will thrive or fracture when it is tested geographically over the course of the fall semester. For some couples, one modern proverb will apply: "Absence makes the heart grow fonder." For other couples, another modern proverb will apply: "Out of sight; out of mind."

In *How to Read Proverbs*, Tremper Longman provides readers with my favorite modern example of timing's relevance and importance. He writes:

> My grandmother was a veritable fountain of wisdom expressed in proverbs. As she prepared the turkey for Thanksgiving, she would say to my mother and my aunt, "Too many cooks spoil the broth." By this she meant "Leave me alone, the kitchen is too small, you will get in the way, I want to cook the turkey the right way, my way." However, after the meal, when we were all feeling sleepy and hardly able to move because of our full bellies, she would look at us and say, "Many hands make light work." The appropriate time had come for all of us to undertake clearing the table and washing, drying, and putting away the dishes, pots, and pans.[11]

A grandmother who wants to be left alone while preparing Thanksgiving dinner uses the first proverb, and the same grandmother who wants help after dinner because she is tired uses the second proverb. She knows which one to use at which time because she understands the connection between the concrete situation and practical know-how. These modern examples along with others help listeners associate good timing with wise choices.

---

11 Longman, *How to Read Proverbs*, 48.

Conclusion

Imagine that a major music anthology has been given to you on one condition: you have to curate it for others. (A curator is a fancy word for DJ, by the way.) Now, you have so much music that you could share, whether in a public venue or in a small gathering of friends and family! But, alas, there is a problem: the situation requires someone who not only knows the music well, but who also knows the people well. This person understands that there are better songs to play in this venue at this time, that the people in this space will expect a certain "something." With all of the music that is available, a good DJ knows how to do what the writers and hearers of Proverbs knew how to do: to play the right song in the right way at the right time for the right reasons for this particular audience. He or she knows that the old saying is true. Timing is everything.

For Further Study

- Clifford, Richard J. "Your Attention Please! Heeding the Proverbs." *JOST* 29.2 (December 2004): 155–63.
- Hatton, Peter T. H. *Contradiction in the Book of Proverbs: The Deep Waters of Counsel.* Ashgate, 2008.
- Holmgren, Fredrick. "Barking Dogs Never Bite Except Now and Then: Proverbs and Job." *The Anglican Theological Review* 61.3 (1979): 341–53.
- Longman, Tremper, III. *How to Read Proverbs.* Intervarsity, 2002.
- McKenzie, Alyce M. *Preaching Proverbs.* Westminster John Knox, 1996.
- McKenzie, Alyce M. *Wise Up! Four Biblical Virtues for Navigating Life.* Cascade, 2018.

Talk about It

- With a friend, discuss a time when you gave or received the right advice at the wrong time, or talk about a time when you gave

or received the right advice in the wrong circumstance. How do these experiences relate to the understanding of wisdom in Proverbs?
- Talk about a time in your life when wise action depended on the time or circumstance.
- Think about a time when you remained silent but wished you had spoken up, or when you spoke up but wished you had remained silent. How does speaking up and holding your tongue in everyday life help you understand the tension between these two things?

Dig Deeper

- In *Preaching Proverbs*, Alyce M. McKenzie claims that the ideal, conventional wisdom that we find in the book of Proverbs is different than the subversive, radical wisdom that we find in Job and Ecclesiastes. How is the wisdom in Proverbs ideal and conventional? How is the wisdom in Job and Ecclesiastes subversive and radical? How might you prepare a sermon in which these two visions of wisdom "duel" with each other?[12]

Practice

- Find a set of proverbs that seem to contradict each other. (If you struggle to find one, I have given three examples that you can choose from in the first section.) Spend time doing exegetical work on the two passages. Then, write down a contemporary situation in which each passage would be the wise action to take.
- Create a sermon file of modern proverbs that contain context-specific wisdom useful in some situations and not in others.
- Preach a sermon on ideas in the book that are in tension with one another. Use a dialectical sermon structure: "On the one hand ... On the other hand." Resolve the tension by helping your listeners appreciate when Option A or Option B is appropriate depending on the context.

---

12 McKenzie, *Preaching Proverbs*, 127–28.

6

Integrity

IN HER POPULAR NOVEL *Glittering Images,* Susan Howatch introduces readers to Rev. Charles Ashworth, a conflicted Anglican priest and canon trying to find his way in early twentieth-century England. John Darrow serves as Charles's mentor and spiritual director. John wants to break Charles free from the persona he has created for himself—the "glittering image." The dialogue between John and Charles in Howatch's novel reveals a common temptation that afflicts everyone: a human tendency to hide behind the persona that we create. In a memorable scene, Charles says he wants to remarry, but cannot bring himself to it. To complicate matters, the two women on his list for marriage are not interested in him. John asks Charles an incisive question: "Who's the one who wants to get married? After all," he continues, "we mustn't forget, must we, that there are two of you." The question confounds Charles. He mulls it over, and after a pause, responds: "It's the glittering image who wants to get married." It is the persona that desires remarriage as it will make him the ideal clergymen in an ideal situation.

"But what about your other self?" John asks. "Let's hear again what he thinks of remarriage?" His true self, Charles explains, is "so unfit and so unworthy that no woman could cope with him." John asks how long this person has been hiding. "Seven years," Charles responds. "Has he never been tempted to set down the burden by telling someone about it?" John asks. It would destroy the glittering image, Charles responds. "I'm becoming interested in this other self of yours, the self nobody meets. I'd like to help him come out from behind that glittering image and set down this appalling burden which has been tormenting him for so long," John says. Charles replies: "He can't come out. ... You wouldn't like him or approve of him."[1]

This scene reminds us that, as fallen creatures, we have an innate ability to hide from God, others, and ourselves. But it is curious, is it not, that the dialogue takes place between ministers? Although the temptation to put on a persona tempts all of us, ministers of the gospel remain especially vulnerable to the allure of the glittering image, the performance of a false self.

We know instinctively that God cares about our integrity and that we also should care about it. We know why God wants to reach beneath the surface, to find the person behind the glittering image that we have built for ourselves and for others, which is why we need to heed these reminders. Like everyone else, we need to be reminded of why integrity is important. As ministers, we have a responsibility to help listeners understand why it is important as well. In so doing, we honor both the message and the form of the book of Proverbs. With that in mind, we will consider our next homiletical strategy.

Strategy 6:
Tie Wisdom to Integrity

The book of Proverbs provides us with helpful guidance on how to tie wisdom to integrity. It foregrounds two indispensable prerequisites for living wisely in the world: internal integrity, what I am calling guarding one's heart, and external integrity, or practicing uprightness before others. It reminds us that the way to pursue wise living is through virtuous living (much like the book of James in the NT), with the understanding that virtue is both internal and external. Where you find a person of integrity, there you find someone pursuing godly wisdom in the manner that the book commends.

In this chapter, I will discuss why tying wisdom to integrity, through guarding one's heart and practicing uprightness before others, can be a strategic way to engage in genre-conscious

---

1 Susan Howatch, *Glittering Images: A Novel* (Fawcett Columbine, 1994), 223.

preaching. The writers point out the need for both a rich inner life and a rich outer life. As preachers, we have an opportunity to mirror this dual focus. When we pursue care of our own souls and uprightness before others, and when we call others to do the same, we say what the text says and do what the text does.

The Purpose of Proverbs

Before we turn our attention to what this could look like in our sermons, we will take a closer look at the book's purpose statement and its emphasis on character formation.

The Call to a Rich Inner Life and Outer Life

To get at why integrity is such an important theme, permit me to return to the book's purpose statement. The book of Proverbs exists because the older generation wanted those coming up behind them to be people of character and to be trained up in wisdom. They believed that the inculcation of wise thinking would beget wise decision making and produce wise behavior in the real world. Just a partial reading (the first three verses) of the larger purpose statement of the book (Proverbs 1:1–7) reveals as much:

> The proverbs of Solomon son of David, king of Israel;
> for gaining wisdom and instruction;
>   for understanding words of insight;
> for receiving instruction in prudent behavior,
>   doing what is just and right and fair. (1:1–3)

The expectation is clear. Hear and apply proverbs to your life, and you will gain more than "wisdom," "instruction," and "words of insight"—all of which will help you make good decisions. Wisdom, instruction, and insight will result in "prudent behavior." A wise person uses that which has been gained in order to behave in a manner that is upright, virtuous, and just.

On the one hand, these verses encourage us to focus on soul care, the inner life, protecting our heart and renewing our mind.

God cares about who we are on the inside (1 Sam 16:7). Yes, we need preaching that lives, but we also need lives that preach. Jesus warns us that all could be lost if we lose sight of our priorities when he asks: "What good is it for someone to gain the whole world, yet forfeit their soul?" (Mark 8:36).

On the other hand, these verses remind us that integrity reveals itself in uprightness before others, an outer life that engages human need. A focus on interiority must not become a need for insularity. We learn to love God better and to love ourselves better because we know that we are loved by God, but we cannot do either of these apart from loving others better. As the popular American philosopher and public intellectual Cornel West reminds us, "Justice is what love looks like in public."[2]

People with rich inner lives ask hard questions and take bold actions in their outer lives. Do I practice virtuous living with the people with whom I am in close relationship? Are the ethical judgments I make in line with God's will and God's ways? Do I care about those who are vulnerable, including strangers and outcasts? Do I care about creation? While no one can do what is "just and right and fair" perfectly overnight—we need God's help and mercy—no one can opt out either. The book of Proverbs does not leave that option open to us.

Proverbs as Character Formation

According to Dave Bland, the writers cared deeply about character formation for the next generation, especially since it feeds the sort of life transformation that everyday disciples desire for their lives. Bland writes:

> Wisdom is not content to leave us as we are but insists that we allow ourselves to be transformed by the power of God. Character, that cluster of virtues that forms into habits, is a product of one's relationship with God and with other fellow humans. In as much as this character is the natural outgrowth

---

[2] Cornel West with David Ritz, *Brother West: Living and Loving Out Loud, A Memoir* (Smiley, 2009), 232.

of wisdom, it is important to realize that wisdom, as expressed in Proverbs, is relational. In coming into relationship with God and becoming involved in the lives of others, character takes shape. Character, being shaped by these relationships, in turn rejuvenates them, continually refreshing our love for God and for others. Wisdom engenders character that is both shaped by and shapes community.[3]

Of course, a process like the one described by Bland requires considerable time, effort, and discipline. It would be naïve to suggest that pursuing it is easy or problem-free.

Renewed character may refresh and rejuvenate love for God and others, but not without cost and most certainly not without sacrifice. In a fallen world, considerable growth rarely occurs apart from considerable pain. We navigate our way through difficult relationships, broken systems and structures, the harm that we bring to others, and the harm that others bring to us. Add to that the disappointment and shame that we feel when we let ourselves and others down, and perhaps we feel that becoming a person of integrity is overwhelming and even impossible.

Yet, the book of Proverbs teaches us that such a path is not only possible with God's help, but also desirable to anyone who wants to become a more devoted disciple. The process of character formation should matter enough to us that we reorient our priorities around it. As leaders, it should also be our priority and burden to invite others to join us on the path of integrity. Consider the imagery that the apostle Paul used in his letter to the churches in Galatia. He wrote that he was like a mother "in the pains of childbirth until Christ is formed in you" (Gal 4:19).

So, how do we promote a rich interior life and exterior life when we preach from this book? No one would deny that ministers preach integrity best through believing it and living it. Ministers also have opportunities to communicate the value of both internal and external integrity through curriculum, programs, Bible studies, and in other ways. Assuming that we are well-balanced and wise in our emphasis outside of the pulpit, how might we also lift

---

3 Bland, *Proverbs and the Formation of Character*, 3.

up integrity in the pulpit? We do not want to sound overly moralistic or legalistic, but we also do not want to pretend that a theme so prominent in the book does not matter.

In the sections that follow, I propose the following: exhort people to protect the inner life that others do not see, call people to pursue uprightness before others, and remind people to live with "the dash'" in mind. I will explain later what I mean by "the dash."

Protecting the Inner Life that Others Do Not See

Who is the person behind the glittering image? The answer to the question posed at the beginning of this chapter remains both timeless and timely. The writers of the book of Proverbs wanted subsequent generations to ask the same question of themselves. No one else can answer it for us. Spiritual mentors or counselors can help us excavate our inner lives, but they cannot think our thoughts or feel what we feel, nor do they have the power to will us to change. They can assist us in rescripting or reframing the life narratives that we have constructed, but they cannot enter into our ongoing dialogue with God, nor can they know about the absence of such dialogue unless we tell them. The book of Proverbs helps today's congregations remember why nurturing the part of us that only we can see (that others do not see) remains vital to our walk with God and our witness to others.

Remind Listeners to Guard Their Hearts

"Above all else, guard your heart; for everything you do flows from it" (Proverbs 4:23). One of my former students likes to call verses like this one "stitchwork verses" since they are the sort of verses that we find in a cross-stitched pattern in a frame on a wall in someone's house. The problem with stitchwork verses is that they lose their force and intensity if we take them out of their literary context.

The larger context of Proverbs 3–4 tells the story of a father pleading with his son to keep his commands in his heart (3:1), to write love and faithfulness on his heart (3:3), to trust in the Lord

Integrity

with all his heart (3:5), to heed the counsel that his father once gave him: "Take hold of my words with all your heart" (4:4), and to be careful that he does not let these commands out of his sight, but keeps them in his heart (4:21). In the verses that immediately surround 4:23, the father makes clear that every part of the body is required in the pursuit of wisdom: the ear for listening, the eyes to keep the commands within sight and to look straight ahead, the feet to journey on the path of righteousness and to avoid the path of wickedness (4:20–27). Even so, above all, the heart is to be protected, looked after, and guarded, especially since everything one does in life flows from it. Here are some homiletical ideas for how to remind people to guard their hearts.

Use a parent-to-child framework in a sermon or a series.

The parent-to-child framework shows up throughout Proverbs 1–9 and not just in Chapters 3–4.[4] Find a way to emulate this framework in a sermon or series. A few verses before the command to "guard your heart," we see the framework on display: "My son, pay attention to what I say" (4:20).

Use your creativity to emulate the framework. For instance, you can use the same language in the structure, points, and moves of the sermon: "my son," "my child," "my children," "pay attention," "listen," "take hold." With this framework in particular, make sure that you do not sound holier-than-thou or condescending.

If you want to stretch yourself, try writing a letter to your congregation and read it in the sermon, one that uses the same parent-to-child framework. You can write it as yourself or you can write it as a character trying to communicate the importance of guarding one's heart to a child today with the same amount of emphasis that the parents had when speaking to their child in the ancient world. Most listeners can understand the genre of a letter, and most parents can wrap their minds around a parent imparting wisdom to children. If you want recent examples of letters from a parent to a

---

4 See Daniel J. Estes, *Hear, My Son: Teaching and Learning in Proverbs 1–9*, New Studies in Biblical Theology (Eerdmans, 1997).

child, try Jasmine L. Holmes's *Mother to Son: Letters to a Black Boy on Identity and Hope*.[5] In this book, she writes letters to her young son about what to expect growing up as a Black male Christian in the South and what her hopes are for him in life.

You can also take practical steps in a sermon, such as interviewing parents, children, or both in real-time or on video. You can tell stories about what your parents said to you, what they taught you, or what they failed to teach you that you wished they had.

Use stories and teachings from Jesus' life to illustrate why the inner life matters.

Draw a straight line to Jesus' teaching on the same subject. For instance, when Jesus eats at the home of a Pharisee in Luke 11, and the Pharisee expresses surprise when he does not wash before eating the meal, Jesus responds this way: "Now then, you Pharisees clean the outside of the cup and dish, but inside you are full of greed and wickedness" (Luke 11:39, cf. Matt 23:25–26). One cannot profess to be clean on the outside of the cup without attending to what is unclean on the inside of the cup. Also, in the Gospel of Luke, Jesus claims that just as good fruit indicates the health of a tree and bad fruit indicates its lack of health, so also good words from the mouth indicate heart health and evil words indicate heart sickness. He declares: "A good man brings good things out of the good stored up in his heart, and an evil man brings evil things out of the evil stored up in his heart. For the mouth speaks what the heart is full of" (Luke 6:45; cf. Matt 12:34).

Expand the meaning of "the heart" so that listeners protect all of it.

Clearly, the call to guard one's heart (in Hebrew: *leb/lebab*) mattered to the writers of Proverbs, but what they meant by "heart" was more expansive than what we typically mean by it. The word occurs 46 times in Proverbs, 858 times in the Hebrew Scriptures,

---

5 Jasmine L. Holmes, *Mother to Son: Letters to a Black Boy on Identity and Hope* (Intervarsity, 2020).

and the Greek equivalent (*kardia*) occurs 161 times in the New Testament. The English word "heart" usually falls short of all that is meant in the Scriptures. Tremper Longman III describes the heart as one's "innermost being," the "core personality" of a person that drives thinking, feeling, being, and doing.[6] Derek Kidner observes that the word translated as heart "most commonly stands for 'mind' (e.g., 3:3; 6:32a; 7:7b; etc.; cf. Hos 7:11), but it can go beyond to represent the emotions (Prov 15:15, 30), the will (11:20; 14:14), and the whole inner being (3:5)."[7] According to Bruce K. Waltke, in the Old Testament, the heart controls the "body's functions," the "psyche's functions," and the "spiritual functions."[8] He writes: "No other English word combines the complex interplay of intellect, sensibility, and will."[9]

Our hearts have the capacity to be wise and pure (14:33; 20:9) or to be perverse and wicked (17:20, 23–25). They can lead us on a path that brings life (14:30; 15:13) or a path that brings death (4:26–27; 12:20; 14:12; 17:22). It matters too much to life to neglect the core of our existence, to underestimate the power of the heart to lead us toward or away from God. In a sermon or series, remind people to invest, take care of, protect, and guard their hearts above all else. Although it is an imperfect and simple analogy, remind them of what would happen to a car if they never put gas in it, if they ignored the warning lights, if they never changed the oil, or if they attempted to do with a car what is not possible to do with a car.

Expand the definition of the heart. In Proverbs, the heart as the core of the person—emotions, mind, soul, will—needs to be protected above all else. You can do this through what you say. You can also create a simple visual like a drawing of a heart with words inside it such as "emotions, mind, motives, and worldview" and words outside it such as "will, behaviors, actions, and ethics." Finally, you can use examples from the English language that expand the definition. When a sports commentator says, "She left

---

6 Longman, *Proverbs*, 154.
7 Kidner, *Proverbs*, 65.
8 Waltke, *Proverbs* 1:90–91.
9 Ibid., 1:91.

her heart out there on the basketball court today," it means that the player gave everything she had, expended all effort and energy, and refused to quit in the face of adversity. In this example, the heart means emotions, mind, soul, and will. Help people expand their idea of what they need to protect.

Challenge People While Holding Out Hope That Growth Is Possible

Challenge people to pursue a rich inner life, but undergird the call to guard their hearts with reminders that the gospel empowers them to go places they cannot go in their own strength. The gas of the gospel drives the car of obedience.[10] If we over-challenge and under-promise, then we make the same mistake as the religious people whom Jesus confronted: we "load people down with burdens they can hardly carry" (Luke 11:46). Here are some strategies for how to hold out hope at the same time that you challenge people.

Balance challenge with promise.

God makes promises that we could miss at first glance. In the immediate context of Proverbs 4:20–27, the father reminds the son that God's instructions lead to "life for those who find them and health to one's whole body." In the wider context of Proverbs 3–4, God has stated that the "wise will inherit honor, but fools get only shame" (3:35). Moreover, God has promised to watch over the way of those who walk along the path of wisdom without the same promises being extended to those who pursue folly.[11]

---

10 I make this statement in classes on a regular basis, and I also discuss why a statement like this one is needed in my introduction to preaching textbook. "This idea comes from a conviction that preachers should not ask listeners to go where they want them to go without first giving them fuel to help them get there. It also arises from a belief that we preach the text in order to preach the gospel." Jared E. Alcántara, *The Practices of Christian Preaching: Essentials for Effective Proclamation* (Baker Academic, 2019), 22.

11 4:6; 6:22; 22:12.

For good reasons, our listeners will experience some fear and trembling when they consider that God weighs and tests their hearts both now and in eternity.[12] However, encourage them to look at the same situation differently. Remind them that their hearts are in the hands of a "forgiving God, gracious and compassionate, slow to anger, and abounding in love" (Neh 9:17), a phrase that is repeated at least eight times in the Hebrew Scriptures.[13] It changes a person in a court of law to know that the judge has a reputation for being generous and compassionate. It changes a person to know that his or her parent has consistently been loving and kind and has always been out for his or her growth and good.

Use answer proverbs to exhort listeners to realize that character matters.

The book of Proverbs warns its listeners not to trust those who sound wise when their character reveals that they are fools. Our interior character authorizes or invalidates our wisdom. The writers use vivid and even graphic imagery and simile to convey this same point:

> Like the useless legs of one who is lame
>   is a proverb in the mouth of a fool.[14] (26:7)
> Like a thornbush in a drunkard's hand
>   is a proverb in the mouth of a fool. (26:9)

Scholars would call these two verses answer proverbs in that they invite us to ask how Verset B answers the riddle posed in Verset A.[15] Here and in other places, the word "fool" has a connotation of wickedness and godlessness.[16] These proverbs about fools state

---

12 17:3; 21:2; 24:12.

13 Exod 34:6; Num 14:18; Neh 9:17; Pss 86:15; 103:8; 145:8; Joel 2:13; Jon 4:2.

14 With this particular parable, exercise pastoral sensitivity, especially since differently-abled members of your congregation might think this verse's imagery is insensitive.

15 Alter, *The Art of Biblical Poetry*, 212.

16 10:18, 21, 23; 13:19; 15:7; 17:7, 21; 19:1; 20:3; 26:11; 29:11; 30:22, 32.

a truth in the negative that can also be stated in the positive: the character of the person who speaks the proverb does matter after all.

To communicate the same truth, you can adapt the form of an answer proverb while using modern examples, for instance, "Like wings on a bird in a cage..." or "Like matches in the hand of an arsonist...." You can also provide short narrative vignettes, fictional or non-fictional, that illustrate that the character of the one speaking matters in the end.

Pursuing Uprightness Before Others

According to Thomáš Frydrych, "The whole of Proverbs is essentially about ethics, the distinction between good and evil is truly all pervasive."[17] A person of integrity knows how to cultivate a rich interior life, yes, but not to the neglect of uprightness before other people. A "good" person cultivates internal character while also building an outer life characterized by good values, habits, and actions (i.e., skills) for walking justly in the world.

In *Mere Christianity*, C. S. Lewis uses the metaphor of a fleet of ships to illustrate the connection between internal integrity and external integrity. A fleet of ships will achieve success "in the first place, if the ships do not collide and get in one another's way; and, secondly, if each ship is seaworthy and has her engines in good order."[18] Ships with poor internal gears, systems, and engines will not be able to function long "if their steering gears are out of order." This is why internal integrity matters so much. Where there is poor internal functioning, the ship will be incapacitated. So also, ships that fail to recognize their dependence on and operation within a larger fleet will either drift apart in ways that are damaging to the fleet, or they will "keep on having collisions." Either way, the ships

---

17 Thomáš Frydrych, *Living Under the Sun: Examination of Proverbs and Qoheleth*, VTSup 90 (Brill, 2002), 176. See also Clifford who argues: "Wisdom in Proverbs has a threefold dimension: sapiential (a way of knowing reality), ethical (a way of conducting oneself), and religious (a way of relating to the divinely designed order or to God)." Richard J. Clifford, *Proverbs: A Commentary* (Westminster John Knox, 1999), 19–20.

18 C. S. Lewis, *Mere Christianity* (Harper One, 2001), 71.

Integrity

"will not remain seaworthy for very long."[19] This is why external integrity is important. A person who drifts from people or crashes into them all the time does not understand how the parts relate to the whole. Lewis also argues for a third prerequisite to a successful voyage, one that is related to the destination, but we will save that for the next section.

So, what does the book of Proverbs tell us about the pursuit of *external* integrity, and how can we as preachers communicate that to listeners? For the sake of brevity, let me highlight some themes related to relational integrity, ideas that will communicate to listeners why it is so important to pursue uprightness before others.

Remind Listeners to Tell the Truth

A person of relational integrity pursues truth-telling in relationships and thus steers clear of deception and misrepresentation. For instance, in a courtroom setting:

> An honest witness tells the truth,
>   but a false witness tells lies. (12:17)

> An honest witness does not deceive,
>   but a false witness pours out lies. (14:5)

According to another antithesis proverb, truth-telling brings God pleasure:

> The Lord detests dishonest scales,
>   but accurate weights find favor with him. (11:1, cf. 12:22)

The writers use antithesis proverbs of description to contrast truth-tellers with liars and to show through description which path is good and right.[20] To be genre-conscious in preaching, you would

---

19 Ibid.
20 See also Proverbs 6:19 for lying in court as one of the "seven deadly sins," 14:25 and 21:28 for antithesis description proverbs on truth-telling versus lying in court, and 19:5 and 19:9 for elaboration proverbs on the consequences of lying

bring out the contrast between truth-telling and telling lies in both the proverb and the book.

Some proverbs warn against the consequences for habitually deceiving others: "A false witness will not go unpunished, and whoever pours out lies will not go free" (19:5), an elaboration proverb. Still other texts point to the blessings that come to others when we tell the truth: "An honest answer is like a kiss on the lips" (24:26). Wise rulers take notice of truth-telling and respond well to it: "Kings take pleasure in honest lips; they value the one who speaks what is right" (16:13). These last two proverbs can be considered answer proverbs. To be genre-conscious in preaching, you would warn listeners about the dangers of deceit in the way the text warns them (19:5), and you would encourage listeners with the blessings offered to truth-tellers in the way the text does (16:13; 24:26).

Challenge Listeners to Love their Spouse

A person of relational integrity chooses to share romantic love with one person. To paraphrase a Spanish proverb, "The one who loves many loves no one, but the one who loves one person loves everyone." In other words, we honor humanity when we fulfil the promises that we have made to the one we love. The writers of the book of Proverbs frame their instructions to an audience of young men. So, at first hearing, the proverbs that deal with romantic fidelity to one person might sound like they apply only to the single male young adult. However, as Dave Bland reminds us, "The teachers use the young adult male as an example for how they engage in the process of character formation, but the instructions of Proverbs apply to all ages and both genders."[21] One could argue further that the charge to love one person as an ideal extends beyond the marital relationship to any exclusive romantic relationship in which promises have been made and are meant to be kept.

Given that the book is written to everyone regardless of marital status, age, or gender, find a way to highlight this in the sermon. Use diverse illustrations about love: how God defines it, and how

---

in court.

21 Bland, *Proverbs and the Formation of Character*, 163.

a world that is passing away usually defines it. Interview married, single, or widowed people as part of the sermon. You can also use a "feed-forward" group[22] to get perspectives from people of different marital statuses, genders, and ages, and incorporate their stories with permission.

Sometimes the writers warn us that we reap what we sow when we are sexually unfaithful or indiscriminate in our choice of a spouse. To anyone who believes that he or she can love many rather than one without receiving or causing harm, the writers of Proverbs ask:

> Can a man [or woman] scoop fire into his [or her] lap
>   without his [or her] clothes being burned?
> Can a man [or woman] walk on hot coals
>   without his [or her] feet being scorched? (6:27–28)

The implied answer to the rhetorical questions is, "Of course not!"

The writers also warn the young that those contemplating marriage should steer clear of someone who is quarrelsome. Using answer proverbs of description, they compare the unwise decision to marry someone who is quarrelsome to the constant drip of a leaky roof (19:13; 27:15). They use better-than parallelism to argue that it would be better to live on the corner of a roof than to live with such a person (21:9, 25:24). Consider using the same strategies: rhetorical questions, evocative imagery, hyperbole, comparison, and answer proverb structures.

Finally, the writers extol the beauty, preciousness, and blessing that comes to those who find a marriage partner in life. Those who do this find "what is good," and they find "favor with God" (18:22; cf. 5:18). Waltke refers to Proverbs 18:22 as an "educational proverb," in that it both describes and instructs the learner about what is wise.[23] To be genre-conscious in preaching, you would use the language of blessing, promise, and favor as a way to frame the gift of a good marriage.

---

22 By this I mean a group that gives input to the sermon like a feedback group, but before the sermon is preached, instead of after.
23 Waltke, *The Book of Proverbs*, 2:94.

Exhort Listeners to Do the Right Thing

A person of relational integrity does the right thing. By "the right thing," I mean doing what is right and just within our circles of influence and beyond them. God honors and values this more highly than any offerings we might make in the context of formal worship: "To do what is right and just is more acceptable to the Lord than sacrifice" (21:3). This proverb functions like a better-than proverb in that it compares two relative values to make clear which is best. Notice the focus is on both righteousness and justice here. Sometimes, we pursue one and neglect the other. When preaching on this verse or others like it, call people to pursue both what is right and what is just, and remind them to expand their definition of justice beyond their circles of influence and identity.

The book warns us that there are dire consequences for the one who ignores the plight of those outside his or her circle of immediate relationships:

> The Lord tears down the house of the proud,
>   but he sets the widow's boundary stones in place. (15:25)

> Do not exploit the poor because they are poor
>   and do not crush the needy in court,
> for the Lord will take up their case
>   and will exact life for life. (22:22–23)

A wise person believes that God honors and defends those who are dishonored in society. The wise work to see this theological reality take place in the real world. Such work honors God. The person who brings honor to the "least of these" brings honor to God (14:31). The Lord has promised to bless our efforts.

Strike a balance between a tone of warning and a tone of hope when you preach. On the one hand, point to the serious consequences for those who ignore people in need. On the other hand, celebrate the promises God has made to those who do the right thing. I will elaborate further on the concern for justice in the final chapter.

Living with "the Dash" in Mind

On most tombstones, you find a date of birth and date of death with a dash between them. Although sobering, life happens in the dash. If death is the most inevitable event in human existence, then we must ask, "What will we do with the dash, our one and only life?"

A wise person pursues integrity in both the inner life and the outer life, giving time and energy to both, but always with a humble recognition that life itself is on loan as a gift from God. In the end, we remain stewards rather than owners.

The writers of the book of Proverbs understood that life was both frail and feeble, not in a fatalistic sense—who cares?—but in a teleological sense: what makes a life on loan worth living? They weighed in on the end and purpose of existence. The word "teleological" is a formal way in theology or philosophy of talking about the purpose and aim of human existence.

C. S. Lewis referred to the teleological aspect of morality as the third prerequisite to a successful voyage for a fleet of ships. The ships must have a clear understanding of the destination and a clear determination to get there. The voyage does not succeed if the destination is not reached. Lewis writes: "However well the fleet sailed, it would be a failure if it were meant to reach New York and actually arrived at Calcutta."[24]

Here is a short list of suggestions for preaching about the dash.

Use Examples from Scripture and Examples from Life to Illustrate Life's Brevity

As preachers, we have more than enough illustrations to remind our listeners that life is ephemeral. One strategy is to use the Scriptures as cross-references to show that this is true. The psalmist declares that life is but a "mere handbreadth ... everyone is a but a breath" (Ps 39:5). In the NT, James reminds us of life's brevity:

> Now, listen, you who say, "Tomorrow, we will go into this or that city, spend a year there, carry on business or make money."

---
24 Lewis, *Mere Christianity*, 72.

Why, you do not even know what will happen tomorrow. What is your life? You are a mist that appears for a little while and then vanishes. (Jas 4:13–14)

If life really is a mist, here "for a little while and then vanishes," then all we have as a guarantee is today. This stark truth can make us fatalistic and cynical, or it can drive us to change what we will do in the present. Will we give thanks for the moment? Will we live differently right now? To state that life is lived in the dash is to make the same point that James did. Life is so short and unpredictable that it forces us to ask what we will do with it.

Besides making appeals to Scripture, we can also use more recent examples of people whose lives ended abruptly to show that this is true: Whitney Houston, Kobe Bryant, and Chadwick Boseman, to name just a few. These are celebrities that millions of people know. We also have access to stories that resonate with our listeners from the congregation and community: the car accident that left behind a spouse and children, the terminal diagnosis, the suicide of a young person, or the sudden loss of a loved one due to COVID-19 (I am writing in the year 2022).

Talk about Teleology through Asking Big Questions

Ask people big-picture questions about life in general and the purpose of their lives in particular. What are we living for, and for whom are we living? What is our purpose? What does life mean? What is our destiny? How would our lives change if we remembered that we are human beings called to abundant life in the present (John 10:10b), yet we are also eternal beings who will one day stand before God (e.g., Heb 9:27)? When asking big-picture questions, we have freedom to talk about the answers that people give that are found wanting, answers like sex, power, money, celebrity, and luxury. Much like Qohelet in the book of Ecclesiastes, we try to find meaning in these things, only to discover that they are meaningless (Eccl 2:10–11).

Tell People to Watch Out for Being Tricked

In the book of Proverbs, unwise people trick themselves into believing that they are on the right path. However, in the end, it will be revealed that they were on a path to destruction the whole time. Warn people of the dangers of deception. If they invest their lives in things that do not matter or last, this will turn out terribly wrong in the end. Two times we read antithesis proverbs concerning the dangers of being on the wrong path:

> There is a way that appears to be right,
>   but in the end it leads to death. (14:12, 16:25)

Unwise people also mistakenly believe that their wealth will give them security and deliverance at the end when, in fact, neither is promised: "Riches do not endure forever, and a crown is not secure for all generations" (27:24). When compared to righteousness, wealth is useless as a deliverer: "Wealth is worthless in the day of wrath but righteousness delivers from death" (11:4). According to Proverbs 16:4, one day the Lord will set things right both for the wicked and for the righteous: "The Lord works out everything to its proper end—even the wicked for a day of disaster," yet another elaboration proverb.

Help People Connect the Purpose of the Book of Proverbs to Their Purpose in Life

Bring people back to the purpose of living wisely: state the purpose. What do wise people do with the dash? How do they come to terms with the goal of human existence in light of eternity? According to the book of Proverbs, they should use the dash to "fear of the Lord," which the writers identify as a purpose in living that can guide right thinking, right speaking, and right action. Fear of the Lord serves as a rubric for evaluating our relationship to God and others.

Someone who has reverential awe for humans alone, especially humans in power, makes a terrible mistake; it is an awful misread of the way things are in light of eternity. By contrast, the person who fears the Lord understands who has the power to create, redeem, and sustain all things. Perhaps you know people who live like the latter rather than the former. Tell their stories so that your listeners remember what matters most and focus on what endures forever.

Conclusion

The following story has a life of its own in oral preaching traditions. I have told it myself. A young pastor works late into the evening on a Saturday night in the study at the church trying to finish his sermon for Sunday morning. The pastor labors over every line especially since there are some Scripture texts that feel bigger than others. This week's text is Psalm 23 with its iconic opening verse: "The Lord is my shepherd; I shall not want." How can a preacher explain and proclaim all that is said in a verse like this one, let alone the whole psalm?

Someone else is working late at the church. The janitor has been mopping floors, vacuuming carpets, scrubbing toilets, and cleaning classrooms since early in the day. He is much older than the pastor. He has cleaned the church for decades. He loves his sixth pastor, whom he prays for daily.

During his nightly rounds, the janitor decides to pay the pastor a visit. He notices that the sermon preparation is not going well this week for some reason. "Reverend, would you like any help preparing your sermon on Psalm 23?" The pastor politely declines. After all, how much can a janitor help with all of the exegetical and homiletical hurdles that need to be overcome? Thirty minutes pass. The janitor returns and offers again. The pastor politely declines again. Another half hour passes. The janitor returns with the same offer, this time more insistent. "Reverend, if it's alright with you, I would like to help you with your sermon." At his wit's end, the pastor replies: "Ok, I guess. Now, why is it that you want to help me? Is there something I don't know?" The janitor responds: "Actually, yes. You see, Pastor, you know the psalm, but I know the shepherd."

A simple story like this one reminds us of what matters most. Every person can benefit from the realization that being smart is not the same as being wise. Sadly, you can know the Bible well without having a real relationship with God. Of course, a pastor can know Christ well and also love the Scriptures. Nevertheless, watch out for the preacher who knows Scripture well but has lost touch with the One to whom Scripture points.

God knows that we are human, sinful, and thus prone to wander. It does not surprise God when we try to perform a false self, when we are weak-willed, when our desires get misplaced. Even so, the same God who knows that we are human calls us to be holy, people who pursue a rich inner life and uprightness before others, not because it will make God love us more, but because it will help us love God more.

Everyone needs to hear this message, but perhaps preachers need to hear it most of all. Long after we preach our final sermon, teach our final class, perform our final baptism, or write our final liturgy, what will remain is the person beneath the tasks, the self behind the glittering image, the actions that supported or negated what we preached. Who is *that* person, the one beneath the work? Who is that person becoming behind the scenes and beyond the walls? In the final analysis, the great Scottish preacher Alexander Maclaren is right. It is "not what we possess but what we are" that matters to God.[25]

For Further Study

- Bland, Dave. *Proverbs and the Formation of Character.* Cascade, 2015.
- Brown, William P., ed. *Character and Scripture: Moral Formation, Community, and Biblical Interpretation.* Eerdmans, 2002.
- Crenshaw, James L. "A Proverb in the Mouth of a Fool." Pages 105–16 in *Seeking Out the Wisdom of the Ancients: Essays Offered to Honor Michael V. Fox on the Occasion of His Sixty-Fifth*

---

[25] Alexander Maclaren, *Expositions of Holy Scripture* (Eerdmans, 1952), 6:339–40.

Birthday. Edited by Ronald L. Troxel, Kelvin G. Friebel, and Dennis R. Magary. Eisenbrauns, 2005.
- Estes, Daniel J. *Hear, My Son: Teaching and Learning in Proverbs 1–9*. New Studies in Biblical Theology. Eerdmans, 1997.
- Northcutt, Kay L. *Kindling Desire for God: Preaching as Spiritual Direction*. Fortress, 2009.
- Shigematsu, Ken. *Survival Guide for the Soul: How to Flourish Spiritually in a World That Pressures Us to Achieve*. Zondervan, 2018.

Talk about It

- Have a conversation with someone you trust and who knows you well. Ask them if they notice any areas of your life where the real you hides behind a persona you project. Ask, "Are there any areas of my life where I regularly do not tell the truth, show love, or do the right and just thing?"
- Talk about an element of this chapter that led you to think more carefully about your own integrity.

Dig Deeper

- For the next week, take time every day to read through the obituaries in your local newspaper. As you do, reflect on the "the dash" of your own life and the lives of the people in your context.
- Read Dave Bland's *Proverbs and the Formation of Character*. Spend time writing about how the book of Proverbs relates to internal and external integrity.

Practice

- Read through Proverbs for 31 days, one chapter each day for one month. Every day, ask for God's help to practice one of the themes of integrity that come up in that chapter.
- Plan a sermon (or series) on "the dash." Highlight the theme in the book of Proverbs concerning the brevity and frailty of human life and the ultimate purpose in life given to us by God.

7

Justice

IN THE 1970s, A GROUP of Latin American Christian leaders rebuked a group of North American Christian leaders for what they said was an anemic vision of Christianity, a way of living that was detached from Jesus' call to radical discipleship. The two sides had been talking past each other for some time. The tensions boiled over when they convened for the Lausanne Congress for World Evangelization in 1974, an event that brought together leaders from every continent. The North Americans led by Billy Graham, Carl F. H. Henry, and John Stott (a British pastor and author who was a close ally) wanted to double down on proclamation and evangelism, while saying little to nothing about Christian social responsibility. They feared that the same social gospel movement that Walter Rauschenbusch had led in the early part of the century would reappear, a movement that they believed gave birth to modern liberal theology and watered-down evangelistic witness.[1] They also wanted to make a strong counter-statement to the Uppsala Assembly of the World Council of Churches of 1968, an event that, in their judgment, resulted in low Christology, an over-emphasis on political statements, and diminished evangelistic fervor.

Three Latin Americans in particular—C. René Padilla from Ecuador, Samuel Escobar from Peru, and Orlando E. Costas from Puerto Rico—refused to let the North Americans off the hook.[2]

---

1 Walter Rauschenbusch, *A Theology for the Social Gospel* (MacMillan, 1917).

2 C. René Padilla, "Evangelism and the World," in *Let the Earth Hear His Voice*, ed. J. D. Douglas (Worldwide, 1975), 116–33; Samuel E. Escobar, *Changing Tides: Latin America and World Mission Today* (Orbis, 2002); Orlando E. Costas,

By the way, none of them was appealing to Rauschenbusch's social gospel movement in the United States. When it was their turn to speak, they did not mince words. They challenged the church-growth and soul-counting movements in North America. They argued that many North Americans failed to disentangle themselves from cultural Christianity, setting the bar too low for discipleship, taking the sting away from the offense of the cross, and propagating a gospel in which accepting Christ cost people almost nothing. These trends, Padilla claimed, made the gospel into a "type of merchandise the acquisition of which guarantees the consumer the highest values—success in life and personal happiness now and forever."[3]

Padilla, Escobar, and Costas adopted a prophetic tone to speak into the impasse. As a result, John Stott chose to stand with them, and other leaders followed including Billy Graham. When the Congress produced the confessional document that came to be known as the Lausanne Covenant, the statement included a section on Christian social responsibility, a section that would not have been included had these leaders remained silent. The statement cast a vision of gospel witness as *misión integrál,* or integral mission, a term that many credit Padilla with coining.[4] Integral mission understands that repentance is not just individual work; it is also structural and systemic work. It pursues both vertical reconciliation with God and horizontal reconciliation among people. It pairs high Christology with strong social consciousness, calling for individual transformation along with the transformation of all

---

The Church and Its Mission: A Shattering Critique from the Third World (Tyndale House, 1974).

3 Padilla, "Evangelism and the World," 126. See also J. Daniel Salinas, *Taking Up the Mantle: Latin American Evangelical Theology in the 20th Century* (Langham Partnership, 2017), 97–117.

4 For more on integral mission, see C. René Padilla, *Misión Integrál: Ensayos Sobre El Reino y La Iglesia* (Nueva Creación / Eerdmans, 1986); C. René Padilla, "Hacia Una Definición de La Misión Integral [Toward a Definition of Integral Mission]," in *El Proyecto de Dios y Las Necesidades Humanas: Más Modelos de Ministerio Integral En América Latina,* ed. C. René Padilla and Tetsunao Yamamori (Kairos, 2000), 19–34; Ruth Padilla DeBorst, "An Integral Transformation Approach," in *The Mission of the Church: Five Views in Conversation,* ed. Craig Ott (Baker Academic, 2016), 41–67.

of life and creation according to the plans and purposes of the triune God.

So, what does integral mission have to do with the book of Proverbs? More than you might think. Assuming that you preach about biblical justice, where do you usually go in the Scriptures when you preach about it? What are your "go-to" texts? Many make a beeline to the Prophets. Others turn to Jesus' inaugural sermon in Luke 4, what has been described by some as a Great Compassion text, to complement the Great Commission text in Matthew 28. Still others find their footing in the book of James or perhaps go to narrative texts that challenge the status quo. No one would deny that these instincts are good and right. Keep going to these cisterns. You will find plenty of water. But, consider this possibility as well: the book of Proverbs also has plenty of water.

In this chapter, I will show why we can adopt a prophetic tone concerning God's vision for justice. This is the seventh and final recommended strategy.

Strategy 7: Adopt a Prophetic Tone

I use the word "tone" with intentionality here to show that adopting a prophetic tone is also a genre-conscious way to preach. Literary critics often talk about the tone of a text.[5] In various genres of literature authors adopt a tone such as sarcastic, dramatic, comedic, ironic, or nostalgic. The tone an author adopts produces a rhetorical effect for the reader, what some call the "mood" of the literary piece.[6]

---

5 In *The Princeton Encyclopedia of Poetics*, David Marno writes: "the mod[ern] literary use of tone usually refers precisely to those aspects of written lang[uage] that are neither lexical nor syntactical, but that appear, at least at first, somewhat intangibly, as a quality of the text as a whole, or of a significant part of it." David Marno, "Tone," in *The Princeton Encyclopedia of Poetry and Poetics*, ed. Roland Greene et al. (Princeton University Press, 2012), 1441. See also the entry on tone in Peter Auger, *The Anthem Dictionary of Literary Terms and Theory* (Anthem, 2010), 134.

6 See the entry on mood in Auger, *The Anthem Dictionary of Literary Terms and Theory*, 190.

When I claim that the book of Proverbs has a prophetic tone, I do not mean to imply that this is its only tone. The book also has a sapiential, pragmatic, and fairly optimistic tone. As a way to nuance my argument, let me propose that, because the book has a prophetic tone, which could easily be overlooked, we honor this undervalued rhetorical feature when we choose to preach with a prophetic tone. That is to say, by foregrounding the book's concern for justice, we do what the text does in a way that might not otherwise be noticed and appreciated. By preaching this way, the listeners in our contemporary context can hear a prophetic tone similar to the one that listeners would have heard in their ancient context.

Why (Some) Preachers Avoid Preaching about Justice from the Book of Proverbs

For various reasons, many preachers do not realize that justice is both a salient and recurring theme in the book of Proverbs, or at least they fail to leverage that theme to the benefit of others. As was already mentioned, we have our "go-to" texts that we think are best suited to a sermon on Christian social responsibility. We also have other reasons why we avoid this connection. First, perhaps we know where to find a proverb on God's call to care for the poor or release the oppressed, but we do not know how to build a sermon around that verse if the other verses around it deal with other subjects. Many of us learned to preach by preaching pericopes, texts that are typically four verses or longer, usually in the epistles or in narrative passages. I brought up this struggle in my chapter on preaching proverbs in a thematic rather than sequential way. The challenge bears repeating here, even in passing, as many of us do not know where to begin with a shorter passage of Scripture, especially if we preach in church traditions where the sermon takes longer than 20 minutes.

Second, many preachers struggle with preaching verses that promote justice when other passages seem to call into question or challenge that vision. Some (though not all) of the passages that come across as troubling to us might include:

> Honor the Lord with your wealth,
>> with the firstfruits of your crops;
>> then your barns will be filled to overflowing
>> and your vats will brim over with new wine. (3:9–10)
>
> The wealth of the rich is their fortified city,
>> but poverty is the ruin of the poor. (10:15)
>
> The righteous eat to their heart's content,
>> but the stomach of the wicked goes hungry. (13:25)
>
> The poor are shunned even by their neighbors,
>> but the rich have many friends. (14:20)
>
> Laziness brings on deep sleep,
>> and the shiftless go hungry. (19:15)

What do we make of passages like these? Perhaps they make us squirm, especially when we juxtapose them with Jesus' warnings against the love of money (Matt 6:24), his reminder: "Blessed are the poor" (Luke 6:20), the apostle Paul's call to remember those who are poor (Gal 2:10), or the apostle James's harsh words directed toward rich landowners (James 5:1–6).[7]

As I mentioned in my chapter on timing, be sure to place these verses into dialogue with the rest of the book of Proverbs, so that you can help listeners hold contradictory perspectives in tension with one another (as original hearers did in the ancient world). It will allow you to discern the larger message of the book to which the collection of verses points.

---

7 Walter J. Houston observes that the rich and powerful are warned against wealth that will lead to ruin in much the same way that the lazy are warned that laziness can beget poverty. He also challenges the misguided and destructive trope that often gets repeated by the upper-class that the poor are where they are because they are lazy. Houston writes: "There are various ways to get poor, but there are no condemnatory statements about poor people and how they have brought poverty on themselves." Walter J. Houston, "The Role of the Poor in Proverbs," in *Reading from Right to Left: Essays on the Hebrew Bible in Honour of David J. A. Clines*, ed. J. Cheryl Exum and H. G. M. Williamson, JSOTSup 373 (Sheffield Academic, 2003), 234.

According to Edward M. Curtis, a singular proverb represents one "tiny snippet of truth, which must then be integrated with other bits of truth to give us a more complete picture of God's order. God's people must then apply those principles to the various situations that confront them in life."[8] When we read verses like these, we always have more work to do so that we can move from the tiny snippet to the bigger picture. Remember that you can address the bigger picture in a sermon series and not just in a single message.

Third, many preachers struggle with reconciling the call to care for the oppressed and those who are poor with one of the book's primary audiences, young men with access to education, resources, and wealth.[9] With this audience in mind, what do we do with the many messages in the book about obeying rulers and pleasing kings?[10] We read in Proverbs 22:11, "One who loves a pure heart and who speaks with grace will have the king for a friend." On the one hand, preachers would be happy to have a king for a friend assuming that the king is a God-fearing, people-loving person who is not intrusive on religious matters. On the other hand, should a preacher want to have the king for a friend when there are so many examples from history of preachers being compromised by corrupt leaders? Amaziah the priest had the king for a friend (Amos 7:10–17), and Amos the prophet came from Judah to Bethel to confront him. Sometimes, a preacher must stand outside the circle of power in order to challenge the status quo. The prophet Nathan confronted King David for his assault on Bathsheba (2 Sam 12:1–14). The prophet Elijah called out King Ahab for his idolatry (1 Kgs 17:1–3). John the Baptist chided King Herod for his marriage to Herodias, his brother's wife, and for "all the other evil things he had done" (Luke 3:19).[11]

---

8 Curtis, *Interpreting the Wisdom Books*, 51.

9 Daniel J. Estes writes: "The particular focus of this book is the training of young men, for the reader is frequently addressed as 'my son.'" See Estes, *Handbook on the Wisdom Books and Psalms*, 218.

10 For instance, Prov 8:15; 14:35; 16:10, 13–15; 19:6; 20:2, 8, 26, 28; 22:11; 24:21; 25:2–6, 15; 28:2.

11 According to Walter J. Brueggemann, the prophet Jeremiah "*practices [a] radical criticism* against the royal consciousness," which constitutes a bold challenge to a vision of power and control that is in direct opposition to the worldview

When we read other passages in Proverbs about kings and rulers, we receive a more well-rounded picture. Yes, the writers promote a vision that prioritizes order and authority, but they also challenge educated elites to use their power and position in ways that honor God.[12] An underlying theology of power and how to use it persists throughout the book, especially since educated elites are the primary audience. In a passage on the writers of Proverbs and their goals, Walter J. Houston writes:

> They accept that society is divided into rich and poor: that appears to them to be a given.... But they are aware of the destructive effects that this division of society into power and powerless may have. And so they attempt to bring up the youth of the ruling classes to be aware of their responsibility towards those who will be in their power, and to treat them in a way that recognizes their common humanity. This would be part of the general responsibility, urged throughout the book, to act moderately and restrain their greed and other passions for the sake of peace in society.[13]

While some proverbs address what is appropriate in one's interaction with kings and rulers, other proverbs challenge those in power to fear the Lord, to shun evil, and to care for those in need. A leader with access to education and power should treat people "in a way that recognizes their common humanity." A follower of God understands that the call to "do what is right and just and fair" (1:3) applies in public with strangers as much as it does in private with family.

Proverbs in Three Dimensions

3D technology has come a long way since I was a kid. No more $0.99 plastic 3D glasses at the movie theater with one blue lens

---

of God. Walter Brueggemann, *The Prophetic Imagination* (Fortress, 2001), 115. Emphasis in original.

12 For instance, Prov 16:12; 17:2; 20:8, 26, 28; 25:5; 29:4; 31:1–9.

13 Houston, "The Role of the Poor in Proverbs," 237–38.

and one red lens. For today's moviegoers, if you are willing to pay extra money for your ticket, you get a pair of 3D glasses that look like a cross between expensive sunglasses and night vision goggles. You can also buy 3D televisions and use the glasses at home. If you have money to spend, you can buy a pair of VTR glasses (virtual reality). With these, you can play video games or be involved in real-time situations with avatars that are 3D rather than 2D. Of course, not every 3D experience is perfect. The technology has its flaws, but consider for a moment what is gained: a more accurate and textured portrayal of that which is in front of you.

In his commentary on the book of Proverbs, Richard J. Clifford argues that the best way to understand the book is through examining it in 3D. To use his language rather than mine, we need to see it in a "threefold dimension": "sapiential (a way of knowing reality), ethical (a way of conducting oneself), and religious (a way of relating to the divinely designed order or to God)."[14] The book's authors focus on all three: how we come to know what is wise in relating to the world around us (sapiential), how we interact with God and the divine ordering of creation (religious), and how we interact with people in ways that are just and equitable (ethical). Clifford points to Proverbs 10:1–3 as an example of all three dimensions in action in three consecutive verses:

> A wise son brings joy to his father
>   but a foolish son brings grief to his mother. (10:1, sapiential)
>
> Ill-gotten treasures have no lasting value,
>   but righteousness delivers from death. (10:2, ethical)
>
> The Lord does not let the righteous go hungry,
>   but he thwarts the cravings of the wicked. (10:3, religious)

Usually, the three dimensions that Clifford describes reveal themselves in a less sequential and tidy way than they do in those three consecutive verses. But the point remains the same. All three dimensions matter if one's goal is to understand what is going on

---

14 Clifford, *Proverbs: A Commentary*, 19–20.

Emphasize Three Dimensions Instead of Two

Proverbs is a three-dimensional book that requires three-dimensional preaching. We know that the book is about acquiring wisdom. It is one of the wisdom books, after all. Sapiential dimension? Check. We also know that the fear of the Lord anchors the whole book. Without fear of the Lord, one will join the ranks of the wicked: people who do not fear God or shun evil. Religious dimension? Check. However, what we often miss is the final dimension, what Clifford calls the ethical dimension: relating to others in ways that are right and just.

A person who seeks wisdom and fears God understands how all three dimensions are connected to one another and not just the first two. At least in theory, a person who is wise and who fears God already knows that "ill-gotten treasures have no lasting value" (10:2a). The pursuit and acquisition of ill-gotten treasures do not reflect a wise way of interacting with reality, a good way of interacting with God and the divine ordering of things, or a just way of interacting with people in ways that are right and equitable.

However, we know from experience that theory and practice do not always line up as they should. The wise need to be warned against their tendency to be foolish in real-world situations, "Do not be wise in your own eyes; fear the Lord and shun evil" (3:7).

Ask Probing Questions

To adopt a prophetic tone in preaching, first, ask probing questions that force people to wrestle with the "third dimension," that is, the ethical component of their faith. Here are some possible ideas for questions to ask:

- What would it look like for you to commit yourself to acting justly inside the church? What is one concrete action step you could take?

- What about outside of the church? What is one concrete action step you could take?
- What will you do with your "power to act" (3:27)?
- How might we as a congregation act justly both inside and outside of the church?
- How might we as a community participate in the building up rather than the tearing down of the common good in our society especially in such a polarized world?
- What would have to happen in the community around us so that people who are far from God would be able to say, "Now, there's a church that really loves people, loves its community, and seeks the welfare of everyone"?
- How do we move tangible aspects of love beyond concern only for those who look like us, and beyond the neighbors most proximate to us?

Many of these questions are abstract. It will take time for people to mull them over, so create space for people to answer them. You can assign homework. You can pause in the middle of the sermon so that people can write down their answers to the questions. You can have discussion groups ahead of the sermon or after the sermon in which people wrestle through their responses. You can make the main points of the sermon questions rather than statements. Try adapting these questions to interview people in your congregation who experience marginalization or who pursue ministries of justice for the marginalized. See if you can get permission from them to share their responses with the congregation.

Tell Stories about Injustice and Justice

Second, tell biblical and contemporary stories that lament injustice and promote justice. On the theme of injustice in the Bible, we have many stories to choose from, such as David having Uriah killed to cover up his assault on Uriah's wife Bathsheba (2 Sam 11), Solomon's pursuit of riches and women to the neglect of fearing God and loving people (1 Kgs 11:1–6; Eccl 12), or King Herod killing the innocents in Bethlehem (Matt 2:16–18). We have access to many contemporary stories as well, such as examples of genocide, apartheid, lynching as a form of racial terrorism, confiscation of land from indigenous people groups, the mistreatment of immigrants, and the abuse of innocent children.

On the theme of promoting justice, we have examples in Scripture as well, such as Elijah's confrontation of King Ahab (1 Kgs 18–19, 21) including the story of Naboth's vineyard (1 Kgs 21), Esther's advocacy for her people (Est 5–7), and Daniel's civil disobedience (Dan 6). Think also of all the Reformation and post-Reformation stories that we could tell about people who staked their lives on the pursuit of a more just society: Antonio Montesinos, John Wycliffe, John Knox, Harriet Livermore, Jarena Lee, William Wilberforce, Sojourner Truth, Harriet Tubman, Martin Luther King Jr., Gardner Taylor, Oscar Romero, Nelson Mandela. When we tell stories of people who honored the third dimension of living, it puts flesh on the bones of something that might be abstract for some listeners.

A Closer Reading of Proverbs' Purpose Statement

As preachers, we have a great opportunity to adopt a prophetic tone by returning to a key phrase in the book's purpose statement (1:1–7). Consider how these words frame the direction of the whole book, and how they instruct those seeking wisdom in the way they should go:

> The proverbs of Solomon son of David, king of Israel
> for gaining wisdom and instruction;
> for understanding words of insight;
> for receiving instruction in prudent behavior,
> doing what is right and just and fair;
> for giving prudence to those who are simple,
> knowledge and discretion to the young. (1:1–4)

So much could be written about these verses, especially since they (and the verses that follow them in 5–7) are the purpose statement for the book.

What are proverbs supposed to do in the lives of those who hear and heed them? According to verses 2–4, the proverbs are for gaining wisdom and instruction (1:2a), for understanding words of insight (1:2b), for receiving instruction in prudent behavior (1:3a), for giving prudence to those who are simple, knowledge and discretion to the young (1:4). Perhaps most of this language sounds familiar: wisdom and instruction, words of insight, instruction in prudent behavior, prudence for the simple, knowledge and discretion for the young.

Now, notice the phrase that I skipped. I left it out on purpose. Perhaps you read the passage quickly, which I tend to do when reading familiar biblical passages. As a result, you may not have noticed that I left out Proverbs 1:3b. Those who hear and heed proverbs are equipped in "doing what is right and just and fair." The ESV translates this phrase as "righteousness, justice, and equity." Let that sink in for a moment. Every person who hears and heeds the proverbs does so for the sake of pursuing righteousness, justice, and equity. They seek wisdom and fear God for other reasons as well, but it is this particular reason that could so easily be missed. The same three words also make an appearance in Proverbs 2:9. When you understand that the Lord and the Lord alone gives wisdom (2:6), that God guards the paths of justice and watches over the saints (2:8), *then* "you will understand what is right and just and fair—every good path" (2:9).

On a parenthetical but related note, in an older Spanish version of the Bible (La Reina Valera 1960), the words in Prov 1:3b appear as, "justicia, juicio, y equidad," which translates roughly as "justice, (good) judgment, and equity." Often, when we hear the word "righteousness" or the word "right" in English, our mind goes to moral uprightness, personal righteousness, blamelessness, or one's forensic status in Christ. Notice that the Hebrew word that we translate as "righteousness" is translated in Spanish as "justice."[15]

---

15 English translators often translate the Hebrew word *tsedek* and the Greek word *dikaiosune* with the English word, "righteousness," a word that has a moral connotation of uprightness and blamelessness. By contrast, Spanish translators often translate these same words with the Spanish word "justicia," which in English is translated as "justice." This translation adds layers of meaning and significance to verses in the New Testament such as Romans 3:21–26 or James 1:20, to name

One could draw attention to the first half of the verse—"for receiving instruction in prudent behavior"—in order to show how the first half relates to the second half: "for doing what is just and right and fair." The problem with the phrase "prudent behavior" is that it could inadvertently lead a western English-speaking interpreter toward a more privatized or individualistic way of thinking about discretionary behavior. The ESV and the NRSV get at the more public dimension of this phrase by translating prudent behavior as "wise dealing" (ESV). The NASB translates it as "wise behavior." The implications remain the same regardless of how one translates the phrase. Wise behavior looks like doing what is just and right and fair.

All three words share at least one thing in common when placed in dialogue with the larger argument of the book. Righteousness, justice, and equity are always outwardly facing and pursue the common good. That is to say, we seek them beyond the benefits they might provide to us as individuals or to our families. We act on them in public for the well-being of those around us regardless of who they are, and for the gifts they bring to the society, not the benefits we receive ourselves.

By pursuing and enacting these three virtues in public life, we demonstrate that we understand the difference between wise and foolish living, we attain more wisdom as a result, and we benefit the common good. We exhibit wisdom, get wisdom, and shape a society with wisdom to look more like the way things really are in Christ. Indeed, God's vision for the world is that it would be a place of righteousness, justice, and equity. A wise person knows this, believes it, and strives to make the vision a reality.

Preach the Purpose Statement

If you decide to build a sermon or a series around this key phrase in the purpose statement, here are some strategies for how to adopt a prophetic tone.

---

just two examples, layers that English readers might not account for when they read these passages. "But now apart from the law the *justice* of God has been made known, to which the Law and the Prophets testify. This *justice* is given through faith in Jesus Christ to all who believe" (Rom 3:21–22a), and "...human anger does not produce the *justice* that God desires" (James 1:20).

Distinguish between Compassion and Justice

First, distinguish between compassion and justice, comparing and contrasting them. Remind people that, although we can do what is "just and right and fair" through participating in and supporting ministries of compassion, it only takes us part of the way to the goal. Both of these virtues focus on people in need and both are outward-facing, but that does not mean that they are the same. Lisa Sharon Harper writes:

> We must not confuse compassion and justice. Both are needed, but they are different. Compassion is what happens when we are moved from the bowels to feel as God feels for the suffering of another. . . . It moves us to action to help someone up. It moves us to give ourselves to stop their suffering. Justice is what happens when we examine the suffering in our world, find the structural, policy, systemic, social, and personal causes, and work to make the world as it *should* be.[16]

We need ministries of compassion, and we also need ministries of justice. As a pastoral colleague of mine reminded me recently in a sermon, "As part of the job description, a pastor doesn't just have to feed the sheep. A pastor also has to fight off the wolves."

Emphasize God's Sovereignty over Human Affairs

Second, emphasize God's supernatural power to bring about justice in the world as a necessary contrast to earthly rulers and authorities. These stories set people free from a "sky is falling" way of engaging modern politics, government, and international conflicts. Of course, use discretion with topics that incite such passion and division.

---

16 Lisa Sharon Harper, "Will Evangelicalism Surrender?" in *Still Evangelical? Insiders Reconsider Political, Social, and Theological Meaning*, ed. Mark Labberton (Intervarsity, 2018), 28. Emphasis in original. See also Dominique DuBois Gilliard, *Subversive Witness: Scripture's Call to Leverage Privilege* (Zondervan, 2021).

Let me share a brief excerpt from a sermon on Proverbs by Ralph Douglas West on pride versus humility to offer an example of what I mean. In this sermon, West reminds his listeners to let God be in charge of human affairs and to reject pride:

> History is on our side to mock at the proud. All Napoleon Bonaparte had to do was listen to advice and make one turn toward England, and he would have rewritten western history. That's all he had to do. One turn, and we would be speaking of the Bonaparte in a different tone this morning. But instead of turning toward England, he turned toward Moscow. And he decided that he would take his French army into Russia and follow the soldiers, who knew that if he would follow them there, he would be defeated. And God took one little, delicate snowflake and destroyed the army of the Bonaparte. Froze in their very tracks, all because of pride.
>
> Let me tell you something: all of us have been touched with pride at some level or another.... And nobody's exempt from it. Presidents of countries are not exempt from pride. They start assuming that a seat of power gives them the authority to say and do whatever they want to do. Pride. But it's not just political. It could be a big military. We've seen that in history. Pride. We can see what unchecked academics can do. Pride.[17]

West shows us that leaders make a dangerous mistake when they believe that they are in charge. As a preacher, you can adopt a prophetic tone without necessarily adopting a partisan or sectarian tone that becomes distracting—or offensive—to people.

Tell stories of God humbling the proud and the powerful, overturning the status quo, and upending the plans of earthly rulers and authorities. In so doing, you remind people of God's power over unjust situations and God's will for a just world.

Now, we will turn our attention to God's promises toward those who practice justice.

---

17 Ralph Douglas West, "Pride versus Humility (Prov 29:23)," Sermon delivered October 25, 2020, the Church without Walls, Houston, TX.

God Makes Promises to Those Who Reach Out

To Do What the Text Does, First Do Not Miss the Message of the Text

Sometimes, I wonder if preachers pass too quickly over God's message to those who are poor, weak, and powerless because they already have a level of authority, position, and power that prevents them from noticing these passages. Preachers who come from minoritized preaching traditions have an advantage over majority-culture preachers—at least some advantage. Although minoritized preachers have authority, position, and power by virtue of holding the office of preacher, many preach to communities that know the pains of prejudice and dishonor. In the face of injustice, they proclaim a word of hope in a God who is unquestionably on the side of those who suffer, a God who hears their cries, who comes down to help them in their misery (Exod 2:24–25; 3:7–9).[18] If I might borrow a line from Howard Thurman's *Jesus and the Disinherited*, they preach about a God who hears and answers "people who stand with their backs against the wall."[19]

God knows how to honor and dignify those that the broader society renders as invisible or deems to be worthless. Proverbs says as much. The best-known example comes to us in Proverbs 3:34: "God mocks proud mockers but shows favor to the humble and the oppressed" (cf. 16:19). This verse provides necessary pushback against any tendencies toward a tiny-snippets approach to Proverbs that would associate God's favor with resources, wealth, and family.[20] Such things may be a sign of God's favor, but they do not have to be a sign of it. In fact, according to this passage, God's favor

---

18 For instance, LaRue writes: "A God who is unquestionably for them is what blacks see when they go to the Scriptures.... This is not to suggest that God is at work only for blacks, but it is to say with power and conviction that blacks have not been left out of the redemptive purposes of almighty God." Cleophus J. LaRue, *I Believe I'll Testify: The Art of African American Preaching* (Westminster John Knox, 2011), 60.

19 Howard Thurman, *Jesus and the Disinherited* (Beacon, 1976), 7.

20 Concerning the reversal shown in Prov 3:34, Waltke writes: "Climactically, the upright and the righteous poor are characterized as *the wise* (see p 94), and

comes to those who are weak and marginalized. This verse also appears in 1 Peter and James, two passages that are set in the context of Christians experiencing persecution (1 Pet 5:5), and the quarrels and infighting among those in danger of divisions (James 4:5). In both cases, the word of hope for believers who are weak and marginalized in their society remains the same: "God mocks proud mockers but shows favor to the humble and the oppressed."[21]

To Do What the Text Does, Use the Language of Divine Promise for Those Who Do Justly

In Proverbs 3:21–35 and in other texts like it, we see another theme in addition to the theme of God's favor toward the disinherited: God shows favor toward those who show favor toward the marginalized. God sees what the righteous do in the lives of those who are marginalized, whether in secret or public, and God honors what they do both now and in the future. For instance, those who are kind to the poor honor God (cf. 14:31), and God has promised in turn to honor them, not in some sort of transactional way, but as a sign of divine grace and loving kindness.

In a sermon or a series on justice in the book of Proverbs, one can draw attention to the promises of God and adopt a prophetic tone at the same time. Sometimes we make the mistake of believing that a preacher with a prophetic tone always has to sound angry, zealous, and impatient. This is misleading. A prophetic preacher can also have a hopeful, expectant, and even celebratory tone, in light of the fact that we are the beneficiaries of promises that have been made and kept by God through Jesus Christ.

For instance, in a sermon that I preached on Proverbs 3:21–35, which can be found in Appendix II.1, I told my listeners that the language of promise surrounds and permeates Proverbs 3:27–31. I used the language of promise in my main idea: "God will reach out to those who reach up and reach out." I followed an inductive form

---

the devious, wicked mockers are labeled as *fools*." See Waltke, *The Book of Proverbs*, 273. Emphasis in original.

21 In the NT version, the verse is translated from the Septuagint: "God opposes the proud but gives grace to the humble."

so that my listeners would hear the promise as good news after I had laid out two challenges in the first two moves of the sermon: "The power to reach out comes from a commitment to reach up," and "Those who reach up to God have to reach out to others." To show my listeners what they might otherwise have missed in the passage, I pointed back to all of the promises in the passage near the close of the sermon:

> We find our power when we reach up, and we release God's power when we reach out. But, you know, there's one more thing, something I have left out thus far. . . . I already mentioned how verses 19–20 frame verses 21–35, but there's more to it. Notice a theme emerge. Verse 26 says: *The Lord will be at your side.* Verse 32: *The Lord detests the perverse but takes the upright into his confidence.* Some translate that as counsel. Typically, the angels are the only ones who get to enjoy God's counsel (Ps 89:7). Verse 33: *The Lord's curse is on the house of the wicked, but he blesses the home of the righteous.* It's not just those who are righteous but those in the home of those who are righteous that God blesses. Verse 34: *The Lord mocks proud mockers but shows favor to the humble and the oppressed.* Curious, isn't it, that this specific verse makes it into 1 Peter 5:5 and James 4:5? Both of these texts are set in the context of Christians experiencing persecution. God has a way of humbling the proud and exalting the humble. God has a way of turning things around. Verse 35: *the wise inherit honor, but fools get only shame.* The apostle Peter said it well when he wrote that, through Jesus Christ, we have an inheritance "that can never perish, spoil, or fade," an inheritance that is "kept in heaven" for us.
>
> This text is tailored to teach us that *God will reach out to those who reach up and reach out.* It is not because God owes you or because this is transactional. One thing we know: we are debtors unto God. It's because God loves you that *God chooses to reach out to those who reach up and reach out.* It's not because God needs you. That would be presumptuous, wouldn't it? No, we need God. We fulfill our ultimate purpose

when we let God use us and work through us. God brings life to us. God reaches out to those who reach up and reach out.[22]

At least according to Proverbs 3:21–35, God has promised to do for the just what God has *not* promised to do for the wicked. Indeed, this is good news for those who take seriously the call to pursue justice.

We see the theme of divine promise elsewhere in Proverbs just as we also find warnings given to those who oppress and mistreat the marginalized.[23] Here are some of the divine promises in the book (two of which appear in my chapter on timing):

It is a sin to despise one's neighbor,
  but blessed is the one who is kind to the needy. (14:21)

Better to be lowly in spirit along with the oppressed
  than to share plunder with the proud. (16:19)

Whoever is kind to the poor lends to the Lord,
  and he will reward them for what they have done. (19:17)

The generous will themselves be blessed,
  for they share their food with the poor. (22:9)

Those who give to the poor will lack nothing,
  but those who close their eyes to them receive many curses. (28:27)

If a king judges the poor with fairness,
  his throne will be established forever. (29:14)

Pride brings a person low,
  but the lowly in spirit gain honor. (29:23)

---

22 Jared E. Alcántara, "Street Smarts (Proverbs 3:21–35)," a sermon preached on April 20, 2021, for the seminary community at the Paul W. Powell Chapel at Baylor University's George W. Truett Seminary in Waco, TX. See Appendix II.1.
23 For the warnings, see 17:5; 21:13; 22:16; 28:3, 8; 30:14.

Notice the verbs here. God blesses, rewards, provides for, establishes, and honors. God will be with, show favor toward, and work on behalf of those who honor the least and left out in society. When God's people see, honor, and dignify those whom God chooses to see, honor, and dignify, God promises to show up in concrete ways in their lives as a work of divine mercy and grace.

Conclusion

When we read the book of Proverbs, we discover that the third dimension, the ethical, strikes a tone that in ancient times would have been recognized right away. Preachers who seek to honor the genre of biblical proverbs have the freedom to use a prophetic tone. Ministries of justice matter to the cause of the gospel in addition to evangelistic witness. Those who pursue wisdom and seek understanding also choose to pursue what is "right and just and fair."

Especially in the North American context, we need more theologies that conceive of sin not only as an individual malady, but as a systemic and structural wound in desperate need of redress. Theologies like *misión integral* pursue the transformation of all aspects of human life and creation according to God's purposes while also grounding themselves in a high Christology. To paraphrase my friend Robert Smith, who teaches at Beeson Divinity School, if some North Americans are afraid to use the language of socializing the gospel, then perhaps we should use the language of gospelizing the social. Jesus seemed to care an awful lot about that, did he not?

In going to the book of Proverbs, we find a deep cistern filled with water for preaching about justice. Adopt a prophetic tone when you preach from this book. Not only will you be more faithful to the genre, but according to the book of Proverbs, God will bless you and honor you for it.

For Further Study

- Clifford, Richard J. *Proverbs: A Commentary*. Westminster John Knox, 1999.

- Gilbert, Kenyatta R. *Exodus Preaching: Crafting Sermons about Justice and Hope.* Abingdon, 2018.
- Houston, Walter J. "The Role of the Poor in Proverbs." Pages 229–40 in *Reading from Right to Left: Essays on the Hebrew Bible in Honour of David J. A. Clines.* Edited by J. Cheryl Exum and H. G. M. Williamson. JSOTSup 373. Sheffield Academic, 2003.
- Padilla DeBorst, Ruth. "An Integral Transformation Approach." Pages 41–67 in *The Mission of the Church: Five Views in Conversation.* Edited by Craig Ott. Baker Academic, 2016.
- Rah, Soong-Chan. *Prophetic Lament: A Call for Justice in Troubled Times.* Intervarsity, 2015.
- Sandoval, Timothy J. *The Discourse of Wealth and Poverty in the Book of Proverbs.* BibInt 77. Brill, 2006.

Talk about It

- Meet with another preacher from a different background than yours. If you come from a minoritized community, meet with a majority-culture preacher and vice versa. Discuss this chapter together, specifically this question: How does Proverbs contribute to diagnosing the systemic and structural aspects of sin?
- Why do you think that some Christian communities are quite open to talking about justice and others are afraid to talk about it? What risks are involved with talking about it too little or talking about it too much?

Dig Deeper

- Do a close reading of Proverbs 10. What does this chapter teach you about justice and injustice? What does it teach you about the righteous and wicked? What it does it teach you about God's heart for the marginalized and God's promises to those who serve them?
- Consider more deeply how the perspective of Christians from the Global South informs a richer understanding of the book of Proverbs. How might their perspectives challenge North Americans to think about individual *and* communal faith?

- Study the passages in the book that emphasize God's promises to those who care for the marginalized. What other passages of Scripture make a similar claim?

Practice

- Plan a sermon series from the book. As you plan your messages, include the three-fold dimensions of sapiential, ethical, and religious elements in your plan.
- Review a previous sermon that you preached from the book of Proverbs. Consider how much or little you drew attention to the ethical dimension of the text or texts. How will you emphasize it the next time that you preach from this book?

8

Conclusion

Two sisters fight like dogs almost every day. They have a bad case of sibling rivalry. Their mom has to remind them far too often: "Comparison is the thief of joy." The girls have to get up early to catch the bus for school. Like most kids, they would rather sleep. Their parents tell them: "The early bird catches the worm." They roll their eyes when they hear it, but they will remember it later when they start their first job after college. The mom heads off to work. As she walks by her administrative assistant, she flashes a grin at the cheeky placard on the desk even though she has seen it countless times before: "Your poor planning is not my emergency." The dad has an anger problem that he is struggling to overcome. When he feels the anger welling up, he reminds himself of what his counselor told him: "There is never an excuse for unkindness." This family lives by proverbs whether they realize it or not.

According to Alyce McKenzie, people around the world make sense of their lives with proverbs. Granted, not every proverb will be as wholesome and edifying as those mentioned above. Some proverbs will make them more selfish, entitled, or ethnocentric. The question, McKenzie argues, is not whether people will live by proverbs. They will. The question is whether their preachers will notice and do something about it. She writes:

> Preoccupied with pondering the sermon for the week, we most often pass by proverbs with unseeing eyes and upturned noses. We walk and drive by them on billboards, T-shirts, coffee

mugs, cartoons, magazine ads, bumper stickers, and posters. Busy reflecting on how we can put biblical wisdom in conversation with contemporary wisdom, we hear them with unlistening ears, as the refrains of songs, in media commercials, and in conversations. Proverbs! Constantly used by the people, consistently ignored by many preachers.[1]

Preachers live by proverbs, too, whether or not we realize it. Thomas G. Long is right when he claims that "people need the kind of portable and memorable wisdom of the nuts-and-bolts-variety that a proverb is designed to provide. The question is not will people live by proverbs, but what kinds of proverbs they will cherish?"[2]

In a sense, preachers face a similar challenge with wisdom to the one we face with narrative. In much the same way that our preaching helps people rescript the stories they tell themselves, so also, our preaching helps people reframe the proverbs they tell themselves—at least it should. Some proverbs we can affirm. "Comparison is the thief of joy" sure sounds a lot like, "A heart at peace gives life to the body, but envy rots the bones" (14:30). Other proverbs need to be exposed and challenged. "The one who dies with the most toys wins" does *not* win in the end.

How to Preach Proverbs has been written to help us meet this challenge. In this book, I commended seven integral aspects of the genre of biblical proverbs and I connected them to seven strategies:

Genre	Strategy 1: Do what the genre does.
Imagery	Strategy 2: Bring images to the center.
Characters	Strategy 3: Use characterization.
Themes	Strategy 4: Use a thematic approach.
Timing	Strategy 5: Associate timing with wisdom.
Integrity	Strategy 6: Tie wisdom to integrity.
Justice	Strategy 7: Adopt a prophetic tone.

---

1 McKenzie, *Preaching Proverbs*, xiii.
2 Long, *Preaching and the Literary Forms of the Bible*, 55.

Conclusion

With each of these strategies came concrete ideas for actualizing them in sermons. As I stated at the outset, you are the resident expert in your context. This means that you will know which ideas will work best in your community.

No doubt it will take some work to unstop our "unlistening ears" and to wipe clean our "unseeing eyes." We know by now that the solution is not to avoid preaching proverbs, as many of us have done in the past. I doubt that God has left that option available to us. The person who takes this easy path will never thicken the Letter P folder in their sermonic filing cabinet, and their preaching will be impoverished on account of it.

Neither is the solution to preach like we have preached before, to do things as we might have always done them, using general tools for a job that requires particular tools instead. It will take some work to preach differently, I think. To use genre-conscious strategies well, we will need to say and do in our context what the text says and does in its context better than we do now. Easier said than done! If we are doing it right, our sermons will probably sound like different sorts of sermons preached from a different sort of book.

The first few sermons may sound far from perfect. They may feel awkward. In the end, however, it will be worth the work that we put into it. To be sure, a genre-conscious strategy for reading and preaching proverbs is a form of neighbor-love, honoring the text that we preach and caring for the people to whom we preach. This sounds like a worthy pursuit to me, even if it takes time along the way.

Appendix 1

Understanding and Preaching Proverbs 31:10–31

Rebecca W. Poe Hays[1]

As a Christian woman who has spent decades attending worship services, Bible studies, and spiritual retreats, I have heard a significant amount of teaching and preaching on Proverbs 31 in my time. Some of this preaching has been, on the surface, fairly innocuous: the preacher spotlights the value of wives and their contributions and encourages the men-folk to express gratitude. Some of this preaching is much more problematic. Perhaps the preacher spotlights the value of wives but does so with the accompanying implication that singleness (or childlessness) is an inappropriate status for women or men. Perhaps the sermon becomes an instruction manual for how wives should be hard at work *in the home* so that they can bring honor to their husbands in the community. Perhaps the message of Scripture becomes twisted to support a misogynistic notion that women should be all things for their men: ever-happy, never-tiring, fertile, and beautiful. More often than not, the recurring charge for me and my fellow Christian women to be "a Proverbs 31 woman" has had these latter notions in mind. The unfortunate result is that many Christian women—and men!—secretly recoil from the idea of hearing a sermon on Proverbs 31.

When we understand a few contextual matters, both historical and literary, it will allow us to preach Proverbs 31:10–31 more responsibly and, hopefully, in ways that encourage people—women and men both—to embrace the true "Proverbs 31 woman" for

---

[1] Rebecca W. Poe Hays serves as Assistant Professor of Christian Scriptures at Baylor University's Truett Theological Seminary in Waco, TX.

themselves. I will draw your attention to three of these matters: the nuances of the passage in the original Hebrew, the use of personification in the ancient Near East, and the larger structure of the book of Proverbs. Space here is limited so I will direct you to consult good commentaries and reference sources as well as you prepare to preach on Proverbs 31.[2]

The Hebrew Text of Proverbs 31:10–31

As always, reading the biblical text itself carefully is an important part of understanding and preaching the text well. If you do not want to work with the Hebrew yourself or you do not know how to work with Hebrew, then a good exegetical-critical commentary should draw out the most important insights from the original language.

First, the title of the woman herself is significant. The Proverbs 31 woman is an *eshet hayil*. How English translations render this Hebrew phrase varies widely: a "capable" or "competent wife," a "virtuous woman," a "virtuous *and* capable wife," a "wife of noble character," a "good wife," an "excellent wife," a "worthy woman," and a "woman of valor" are just a sampling. Most often, however, the Hebrew term *hayil* actually connotes material wealth (e.g., Jer 15:13), physical strength (e.g., Josh 1:14), or military might (e.g., 2 Chr 26:13). The Septuagint, which is the Greek translation of the Old Testament that Peter, Paul, and Jesus seem to have used most often, actually translates *hayil* with the word *andreian*—which means "manly courage!" The image this description conjures is less that of a sweet, godly housewife and more that of a God-empowered warrior woman. A blending together of Joan of Arc and Wonder Woman.

Second, the text emphasizes the agency of this woman. The action verbs take feminine forms and have feminine pronouns

---

2 My top picks are the following: Ellen F. Davis, *Proverbs, Ecclesiastes, and the Song of Songs*, Westminster Bible Companion (Westminster John Knox, 2000); Roland E. Murphy, *The Tree of Life: An Exploration of Biblical Wisdom Literature* (Eerdmans, 2002); Karen L. H. Shaw, "Wisdom Incarnate: Preaching Proverbs 31," *Journal of the Evangelical Homiletics Society* 14 (2014): 44–53; Alice Ogden Bellis, *Proverbs*, ed. Sarah Tanzer, Wisdom Commentary 23 (Liturgical, 2018).

attached to them. While those of us used to hearing sermons on what a Proverbs 31 woman accomplishes might not immediately catch this nuance of the text, in the male-dominated culture of the ancient Near East with a masculine-dominated biblical text to match, the abundance of feminine forms is highly unusual and would have attracted attention. Even today, students in my Hebrew classes tell me that they are stumped when they come across these feminine forms because they are so rare! These repeated feminine verbs and pronouns pound into the heads of audiences that this is a woman who *possesses* things (the husband and sons are "hers") and who *does* things.

Furthermore, words that are related to power and strength dominate the poem. In addition to the opening and closing characterization of the woman as *hayil* (vv. 10, 29), the text describes her as mighty (*az*; vv. 17a, 25) and making strong (*amats*; v. 17b)—words generally used to describe men or God. The poem repeatedly talks about her hands (vv. 13, 16, 19, 20, 31), which are associated with physical strength. Moreover, Proverbs 31 is the only place in the Bible where the person "girding up their loins" is a woman (v. 17). All of this language amounts to an exceedingly *masculine* description—at least in stereotypical terms—of the poem's feminine subject.

Personification in the Ancient Near East

Personification is a literary device that gives flesh to abstract principles—like a human object lesson. We see remnants of this device today when we talk about someone like Adolf Hitler being "the personification of evil," or when we describe countries as "she" and citizens as "children" (e.g., "Mother Russia"). In the ancient Near East, personification was common. It features prominently in the book of Proverbs, especially as it relates to the nature of wisdom itself. What better way to explain wisdom and make it attractive to a bunch of young men—the original audience of Proverbs—than by personifying it as a beautiful woman! And thus, "Lady Wisdom" is born.[3]

---

3 Roland Murphy has a really nice chapter on "Lady Wisdom" as she appears

Proverbs introduces the character of Lady Wisdom early in the book. She makes her entrance right after the wicked and foolish offer their invitation to sin and death (Prov 1:11–14), and she begins calling out in the streets with an alternative invitation to righteousness and life (Prov 1:20–32). Subsequent chapters continue to flesh-out "Lady Wisdom," whom we should pursue, and the seductive "Dame Folly," whom we should resist, in semi-graphic detail.

For the purposes of understanding Proverbs 31:10–31, it is critical to recognize the similar descriptions of Lady Wisdom and the *eshet hayil* of Proverbs 31:

Characteristic	*eshet hayil*	Lady Wisdom
She is more precious than jewels	(31:10) An excellent wife, who can find? For her worth is far above jewels.	(3:15) [Wisdom] is more precious than jewels. (8:11) . . . wisdom is better than jewels.
Finding her results in material gains	(31:11–12) [Her husband] will have no lack of gain. She does him good and not evil all the days of her life.	(3:13–14) How blessed is the man who finds wisdom and the man who gains understanding. For her profit is better than the profit of silver and her gain better than fine gold. (8:17–19, 21) I [Wisdom] love those who love me; and those who diligently seek me will find me. Riches and honor are with me, enduring wealth and righteousness. My fruit is better than gold, even pure gold, and my yield *better* than choicest silver . . . . I endow those who love me with wealth, that I may fill their treasuries.

---

in the Old Testament broadly in Murphy, *The Tree of Life*, 133–49.

Characteristic	*eshet hayil*	Lady Wisdom
She provides food and sustenance	(31:14b–15) She brings her food from afar. She rises also while it is still night and gives food to her household and portions to her maidens.	(9:2–5) [Wisdom] has prepared her food, she has mixed her wine; she has also set her table; she has sent out her maidens, she calls from the tops of the heights of the city: "Whoever is naive, let him turn in here!" To him who lacks understanding she says, "Come, eat of my food and drink of the wine I have mixed."
She is located at and associated with the city gates	(31:23) Her husband is known in the gates, when he sits among the elders of the land. (31:31) . . . let her works praise her in the gates.	(1:20–21) Wisdom shouts in the street, she lifts her voice in the square; at the head of the noisy *streets* she cries out; at the entrance of the gates in the city she utters her sayings. (8:3) Beside the gates, at the opening to the city, at the entrance of the doors, [Wisdom] cries out.
She is characterized by fear of the Lord	(31:30) . . . a woman who fears the Lord, she shall be praised.	(1:7) The fear of the Lord is the beginning of knowledge; fools despise wisdom and instruction. (9:10) Fear of the Lord is the beginning of wisdom.

Of course, differences do exist between Lady Wisdom and the woman of Proverbs 31:10–31. Most obviously, Proverbs 31 begins by suggesting that finding an *eshet hayil* is a real challenge. Alternatively, Lady Wisdom shouts in the streets to make her presence and availability known to any and all who seek her (Prov 1:20–21; 8:1–3). But perhaps this difference between the two is as simple (or at least as ordinary) as the difference between *knowing* and *doing, hearing* and *obeying*. After making it all the way to the end of Proverbs, you recognize that living a life characterized by wisdom is indeed a challenge, though it is a challenge available to any who would take it on!

One more aspect of wisdom's personification is significant for understanding Proverbs 31:10–31: how it relates to the character of God. Ancient Near Eastern personification often toed the line between being a purely rhetorical device and reflecting belief in a pantheon of deities. For example, in polytheistic contexts, cities were often understood to have patron goddesses (e.g., the Sumerian Ningal is the goddess of Ur and the Greek Athena is the patron goddess of Athens). Even in the monotheistic Old Testament, cities often appear personified as women (e.g., Daughter Babylon in Isaiah 47 and Daughter Zion in Isaiah 49). In Egypt, the goddess Maat was the personification of harmony, order, justice, and truth—a constellation of ideas very similar to the Hebrew concept of *hokmah* or "wisdom" that dominates the book of Proverbs.

In line with this tradition, the personification of wisdom in Proverbs reflects aspects of divinity. Both Lady Wisdom (Prov 9:1, 3) and Dame Folly (Prov 9:14) build their houses at the highest points of the city, which is where temples—whether to the true God or to false ones—would be built. As is typical throughout the Old Testament, choosing wisdom here is thus equated with choosing right worship. Additionally, the description of Lady Wisdom's opening speech echoes the speeches of the prophets who came pouring out the "word of the Lord" to the people (Prov 1:20–33), and the hymn in Proverbs 8:22–31 places her there with God as the firstborn of creation. Theologians have long debated (and will continue, no doubt, to debate) how much Lady Wisdom should be associated with God. Is she a personification not only of wisdom generally but of God's wisdom specifically? Is she an Old Testament expression of the Holy Spirit or of Jesus, whom Colossians 1:15–20 describes with a hymn strongly reminiscent of Proverbs 8:22–31? Whatever the specifics, Proverbs makes clear that she originates with God, reflects God's attributes, and points us to God. Worth finding indeed!

The type of personification we see in Proverbs—and in the broader ancient Near East—is not concerned with nuance or creating complex characters. The proverbs allow for no gradation between wisdom and folly. Dame Folly is utterly foolish with no redeeming qualities. Lady Wisdom is *perfect*: everything one could ever want in a woman, and everything one could ever want in life. Similarly, Lady Wisdom as she appears in Proverbs 31:10–31 is perfect and does more than any real, live woman could ever hope to do on a regular basis (if ever). The purpose is not to give a realistic to-do list for what it means for each person to be wise but rather to characterize *memorably* the extremes of wisdom and folly so that each person can make his or her daily choices between those two paths—the paths of wisdom and folly, righteousness and wickedness—with eyes fully opened.

The Organizing Structure of Proverbs

When we pay attention to the way that Proverbs is organized, it helps us understand even more about the purpose of its concluding poem. The book begins with a royal father's advice to his son and his praise of a woman personifying the wisdom he should seek (Prov 1). Proverbs 1–9, which serves as an expanded introduction to the book, further builds out the character of Lady Wisdom before launching into the "proverbs of Solomon" proper in chapter 10. The book ends with a royal mother's advice to her son and her praise of a woman embodying—and also personifying?—the wisdom he should seek (Prov 31). Whoever did the final editing-together of Proverbs arranged the book in a way that emphasizes the gender-inclusivity of wisdom—whatever qualities make for a good woman make for a good man, too, and vice versa.

Significantly, some arrangements of the Hebrew Bible placed the book of Ruth right after Proverbs in the canon. This narrative about a pious, industrious, and courageous woman describes Ruth as an *eshet hayil* (Ruth 3:11), but it also describes Boaz as an *ish hayil*, or a *man* of valor (Ruth 2:1). Proverbs ends with a concrete example in poetic form about what a life characterized by wisdom looks like, and Ruth provides an even more concrete example (in prose form)—and does so for both women *and* men. This example is similar to what Psalm 1 does when it describes what a life characterized by righteousness looks like; the psalm only talks about a righteous man, but clearly the example serves women as well.

So How Should We Preach it?

Proverbs 18:22 affirms how wonderful it is for a man to find a wife, so in some ways understanding Proverbs 31:10–31 as a poem celebrating the actual finding of a good wife makes sense. The various tasks this Proverbs 31 woman performs are all fairly realistic for life in the land of Judah during the Persian period when the editing-together of the book of Proverbs was likely occurring. Women were indeed a valuable commodity, and the social norm was for them to work hard. The textile industry was booming at this time. Scholars have found depictions of women of all economic levels working with yarn and cloth. Women could even own property, so the reference to the wife buying and planting fields in Proverbs 31:16 would not have been shocking. In empowering, dignifying terms, the poem commends female industry and piety and acknowledges that society cannot thrive without the contributions of women.

This message can still preach—but we must preach it carefully and with sensitivity to how our twenty-first century Western context differs from the original audiences who heard Proverbs 31. For one thing, our entire economic system is different. The world of Proverbs 31:10–31 was one in which *everyone* worked in the home (though they might have different tasks and roles there), so this passage should not be used to make arguments for women's place being "in the home" today. Rigid patriarchy is no longer the preferred norm, and women are no longer considered the property of their husbands, fathers, or brothers. Women should still strive for industriousness, piety, and contribution to society, perhaps, but their ultimate purpose in life is not to serve the needs and whims of their menfolk—and their menfolk should be striving for industriousness, piety, and contribution to society as well! Furthermore, not all women will or should marry and have children, and their singleness or childlessness does not diminish their worth one jot. Preachers should therefore take extreme care not to make them *feel* diminished.

It is also more than possible to fall off the other side of the horse and elevate the woman of Proverbs so much that she *becomes* our God. From the earliest days of the church, we see the temptation to worship wisdom and to rely on secret knowledge. Some of the New Testament letters seek specifically to correct this kind of gnosticism (e.g., 1 Cor 1:18–31; Col 2:8; 1 Tim 6:20–21). At various points in history—including our own day—we have seen enthusiastic revivals in the worship of Sophia, the goddess of wisdom (and whose name is, in fact, the Greek word for "wisdom"). Proverbs' Lady Wisdom is not a goddess but, rather, a way to illustrate what the wisdom of God looks like on the ground.

As with every sermon, knowing one's audience and context is key for knowing what truths to emphasize and what stumbling blocks to avoid. We must attend to how our congregants are prone to receive, use, or abuse the biblical text. Within the context of the book of Proverbs and of Scripture as a whole, Proverbs 31 is about much more than finding a good spouse, and responsible preaching will reflect this larger message.

Appendix 2

Sermons

"Street Smarts"[1] – Proverbs 3:21–35

Jared E. Alcántara

If you know me personally or have had class with me, perhaps you know that I come from a strange and wonderful planet known as New Jersey. This planet is filled with alien beings like Buddy from Cake Boss, two members of the cast of the Jersey Shore, the Real Housewives of New Jersey, and three of our most famous aliens: Bon Jovi, Whitney Houston, and Bruce Springsteen. If you ever come into contact with us, always remember: *We come in peace ... so long as you don't cross us.* When you mash together my own alien sensibilities with my role as a father of kids that are soon to be 14, 12, and 8, the result is this: a guy who spends a lot of time thinking about what he was doing at their age in a time long ago in a land far away: a land with lead paint, no internet, no nutrition labels or content warnings, and no helicopter parents.

One of my favorite memories growing up would have to be when our family would take the train into Manhattan. Family members from Honduras would come to visit from time to time. They would want to see the sites, and we would take them. These memories are infused with both adventure and wonder. I would see something new, learn something new, discover something

---

[1] A sermon preached on April 20, 2021, for the seminary community at the Paul W. Powell Chapel at Baylor University's George W. Truett Seminary in Waco, TX.

new. What I didn't fully appreciate on all those train rides on NJ Transit is that my parents were also teaching me how to do this myself someday. They were teaching me to be street smart in a big city *with them* when I was young so that, someday, I could be street smart in a big city *without them* when I was older. A lot of these street smarts were caught rather than taught. Don't be a wise guy with the conductor on the train. He or she doesn't have the time or patience for it. Move your wallet from your back pocket to your front pocket. Disburse your cash in more than one place on your body so that you won't be unprepared if something bad happens. Watch out for strangers that are overly friendly with you because they might be trying to scam you. *Always* remember that not *all* of the characters dressed like Elmo in Times Square are friendly.

Streets smarts. These are not hard and fast principles that apply in all situations at all times—sometimes the conductor on NJ Transit will be in a *good* mood—but following these guidelines will help you know what to do and what not to do in real-life situations.

Now that I teach at a seminary, the importance of my parents' lesson is not lost on me. At every seminary we should ask ourselves if we're teaching you the right kinds of smarts in the right kinds of ways. At a seminary, if we're not careful, we could accidentally communicate to you that loving texts and loving people are the same. We could inadvertently elevate a vision of success in ministry when it appears that Jesus didn't say all that much about success in his own ministry. He said a lot more about faithfulness and fruitfulness. We could fail to remind you of what Scripture teaches you: a person could earn a PhD and still be called a fool.

Street smarts. We need them in life, and we need them in ministry. We need them as professors, and we need them as students. We need to learn about them when we're together so that we'll use them when we venture out on our own. They didn't know it at the time but, what my parents were doing with me on those train rides to New York was a secularized version of what Hebrew parents have been doing with their children for thousands of years. Maybe they were smarter than I thought. Survival skills. Life skills. Doing the right thing in the right way at the right time.

It turns out that the vision that I am describing is the vision that is cast in our text for this morning: Proverbs 3:21–35. *"My son, do not let wisdom and understanding out of your sight, preserve sound judgment and discretion; they will be life for you, an ornament to grace your neck."* In our text, we find parents in dialogue with their son in how to live and how to find life while you're living. You don't need to search very long or hard to find out this theme throughout the book of Proverbs, especially chapters 1–9. Look with me at 1:8: *Listen, my son, to your father's instruction and do not forsake your mother's teaching.* Skip ahead to Proverbs 2:1: *"My son, if you accept my words and store up my commands within you … (4) then you will understand the fear of the Lord."* Now, look at 3:1: *"My son, do not forget my teaching, but keep my command in your heart."* Again, 3:11: *"My son, do not despise the Lord's discipline, and do not resent his rebuke."* These are just some examples. Of course, if we zoom out to larger themes in Proverbs like the fear of the Lord, love of neighbor, and caring for the weak, we'll see that street smarts aren't just for sons. They're for daughters. They're not just for families in the privacy of their homes. They're for communities in the real world.

In our short time together, I want to suggest to you that the path to wisdom and understanding requires both a ground and a goal. I will introduce some imagery here as well since I tend to think a lot in images. In Proverbs 3:21–35, we have both an anchor to secure us to the one to whom we need to be secured, and we have a sail to guide us toward the places to which we're called to go. Let me start with the anchor.

The Anchor

The anchor is this: *the power to reach out comes from a commitment to reach up.* I will say more about what I mean in a moment. Verses 21–22 are rich in imagery. Do not let wisdom or understanding out of your sight. Now that I'm a parent, I appreciate this more because I remember how attuned I had to be when my kids were young. Eyes fixed. Alert. Aware. Attuned. Then you find this language of preservation. Preserve sound judgment and instruction. That word—preserve—is often used in connection to working on olive trees or vineyards or protecting a watchtower. If you're going to cultivate, prune, care for, protect, watch over something, let it be sound judgment and discretion. These will be life for you, an ornament to grace your neck. We already read about instruction and teaching as a chain around our necks in Proverbs 1:9. It shows up in Proverbs 3:3: bind love and faithfulness around your neck.

No doubt these phrases are powerful. The images are both rich and deep. That stated, we could so easily miss the connection between verses 21–22 and 19–20. It just so happens that the words "wisdom" and "understanding" are insertions in the English translation. They actually don't show up in the original. If we were being literal, we could roughly translate verse 21 this way: "Do not let these out of your sight." "Where do the 'these' come from," you ask? They come from the preceding verses. Look with me at verse 19. *"By wisdom the Lord laid the earth's foundations, by understanding he set the heavens in place; by his knowledge the watery depths were divided, and the clouds let drop the dew."*

That's why I put it this way: that the power to reach out comes from a commitment to reach up. God is the one who set the earth's foundations. God is the one who set the heavens in place. "The fear of the Lord is the beginning of wisdom," it says in Proverbs 1:7, the verse that frames the whole book. The "beginning" of wisdom, according to Derek Kidner, means "the first and controlling principle, not a stage that one leaves behind."[2] A God-anchored and God-centered way of living frames the book of Proverbs and it frames this chapter, chapter 3. Verse 7: *"Do not be wise in your own eyes; fear the Lord and shun evil."* Verse 9: *"Honor the Lord with your wealth."* Verse 11: *"Do not despise the Lord's discipline."* Wisdom and knowledge come from the Lord. Without remaining tethered to God, those who might seem wise and knowledgeable in the world's eyes could turn out to be fools. I will put it another way: a person with street smarts always remembers first who paved the streets, and who made the smarts.

---

2 Derek Kidner, *Proverbs*, Kidner Classic Commentaries (IVP Academic, 2008), 56.

The temptation is always there to leave God behind in our work and our witness, to turn into "pragmatic atheists," to use sociologist Robert Bellah's term.[3] Gospel ministers remain just as susceptible to rupturing the relationship between sacred worship and secular decision-making. Could it be that we invest so much time walking *for* God that we forget to walk *with* God? The life that is described in verse 22 is a life that comes from one source and one source only.

Then, in verses 23–25, we have these intriguing descriptions of what life could look like, what it should look like, in a world that is set and secure on these foundations. Look with me at verse 23: *"Then you will go your way in safety, and your foot will not stumble. When you lie down, you will not be afraid; when you lie down your sleep will be sweet. Have no fear of sudden disaster or of the ruin that overtakes the wicked. For the Lord will be at your side and will keep your foot from being snared."* It is important to understand that statements like these are not law-like guarantees or timeless promises that apply in all situations at all times. We'll do a great deal of harm to people if we apply modern reasoning to ancient proverbs. Instead, this is a vision of how the world could work when things work the way they're supposed to work. OT scholar Carol Newsom refers to this kind of language as "iconic narrative," that is, "a community's expression of how it understands the foundational structures of reality and the nature and tendencies of the world—in short, how the world 'works.'"[4]

Let me tell you why I know these are *not* timeless promises. Early last week, I did a deep dive into the exegesis for this text, and I was feeling pretty good about the work I had done. I went to bed sometime between 11:00 p.m. and midnight. Then, around 2:00 a.m., I had a terrible nightmare that jolted me awake, heart racing, sweating in bed, and I was up from 2:00 to 5:00 a.m. I slept from 5:00 to 6:00 a.m., and then I taught my 8:00 a.m. class. I assure you that my sleep was not sweet. I went home later that day and

---

3 Robert N. Bellah, et al., *Habits of the Heart: Individualism and Commitment in American Life* (University of California Press, 1996).

4 Carol A. Newsom, *The Book of Job: A Contest of Moral Imaginations* (Oxford University Press, 2003), 122–23.

tried to sleep a little bit, even just for 20 minutes, but I was a lost cause. I was stressing out and anxious about how this might have happened and why. But then I realized what happened that caused this whole series of unfortunate events. It wasn't my sin, but my kids' sin that caused this whole mess in the first place. Just kidding. Not really.

What matters most to these verses is the bookends around them. The Lord who laid the foundations of the earth is also the Lord who will "be at your side" according to verse 26. In the times when the world works as it should, and in the times when it most definitely does not, God will be your anchor. God will be the one who holds you fast. *The power to reach out comes from a commitment to reach up.*

But that's not all there is to this passage. In fact, there is much more in the second half that we have not touched on just yet. There is a ground, and there is a goal. There is an anchor that holds us, and there is a sail that sets us free to go where God wants us.

The Sail

The sail is this: *those who reach up to God will have to reach out to others.* Notice the immediate turn toward neighbor-love in verse 27: *"Do not withhold good from those to whom it is due."* The way this is phrased can be a bit misleading. Sometimes we interpret "those to whom it is due" as any person who we think deserves our love, which often means any person who looks like us, agrees with us, and sees things our way. The real call here is not to withhold good from any person who has a right to the good, that is, to any person. Michael V. Fox points out that this could even be our enemy. He points to a passage in Exodus 23:4–5. If your enemy's donkey wanders off, then you should return it. If your enemy's donkey falls into a ditch, you should find a way to help it out of the ditch.[5] What is most important in a situation like this one is not who is right and who is wrong in your quarrel. What is most important is what is right and what is wrong in this concrete situation.

---

5 Michael V. Fox, *Proverbs 1–9*, AB 18 (Yale University Press, 2000), 164–65.

Verse 28: Do not make promises that you do not intend to keep with your neighbor. The word "neighbor" here is broadly defined and not narrowly defined. It means any person in need of help. So, do not make promises that you do not intend to keep with any person who needs help. *Verse 29*: Do not plot harm or evil against your neighbor. *Verse 30*: Do not quarrel for no reason when your neighbor has done nothing evil; neither has he caused harm to you. Take special note of this that neither a critical spirit nor a sharp tongue have made it onto the spiritual gifts list. *Verse 31*: Do not envy a person of violence. Violence begets violence. According to Proverbs 14:30, envying others will rot your bones.

Now, here is where my parents' advice about taking the train into the city might break down a little bit. For them, street smarts look like this: "Look out for strangers." However, that's not the message here, is it? If anything, these verses tell us, "Look out for your neighbors." Our neighbor is any person in need of help including and especially our strangers and our enemies. I'm reminded of C. S. Lewis's prayer in his book, *A Grief Observed*: "Not my idea of God, but God. . . . Yes, and also not my idea of my neighbour, but my neighbour."[6]

The focus on neighbor-love leads us to ask some questions that I want you to consider as we reflect on the vital connection between reaching up and reaching out, between faith in God and love toward neighbor. These are questions that any and every minister must ask.

What will you do with your power to act? That is the phrase in verse 28. Each of us has some level of power to speak and, yes, power to act. Will you hoard your power or will you share it? Will you seek power or will you release it? Will you use your power in the ways that the Gentiles do, exercising it and lording it over others, or will you heed Jesus' call to his disciples in Mark 10:43: "Not so with you"?

How will you define your neighbor? Will you define your neighbor in a narrow way—those in close proximity, those who look like you, vote like you, speak your language, who do things your way, who always agree with you, and always want what you want? The

---

6 C. S. Lewis, *A Grief Observed* (Harper One, 1967), 67.

consequences of this kind of neglect are dire. I hear Jesus saying, "I was hungry and you fed me not. I was thirsty and you gave me nothing to drink. I was a stranger, and you didn't take me in. I was naked and you didn't clothe me. I was sick and in prison, and you didn't visit me. For whatever you did to the least of these, you did it unto me" (paraphrase of Matt 25:42–43, 45).

This leads me to one more question. *Will you choose to make the same vital connection that Proverbs 3 makes between reaching up to God and reaching out to others?* This is why Latin American theologians like Samuel Escobar from Peru and René Padilla from Ecuador forced the organizers of the Lausanne Congress to make a statement on Christian social responsibility.[7] To them, it was not a choice between *either* proclamation and evangelism *or* compassion and justice. It was *both* proclamation and evangelism *and* compassion and justice. The Lord Jesus does not leave room for first order and second order activities in the Greatest Commandment. When North Americans asked Escobar and Padilla why so many Latin Americans cared so much about socializing the gospel, they shined the mirror back on us by wondering why so many North Americans cared so little about gospelizing the social. Here is how Martin Luther King Jr. puts it in his sermon, "Why Jesus Called a Man a Fool."

> It's alright to talk about heaven. I talk about it because I believe firmly in immortality. But you've got to talk about the earth. It's alright to talk about long white robes over yonder, but I want a suit and shoes to wear down here. It's alright to talk about streets flowing with milk and honey in heaven, but I want some food to eat down here. It's even alright to talk about the new Jerusalem. But one day, we must begin to talk about the new Chicago, the new Atlanta, the new New York, the new America.[8]

---

[7] See C. René Padilla, "Evangelism and the World," in *Let the Earth Hear His Voice*, ed. J. D. Douglas (Worldwide, 1975), 116–33.

[8] Martin Luther King Jr, "Why Jesus Called a Man a Fool," in *A Knock at Midnight: Inspiration from the Great Sermons of Reverend Martin Luther King, Jr.*, ed. Clayborne Carson and Peter Holloran (Warner, 2000), 146–47.

Jesus does not force us to choose between up there and down here. Rather, he invites to pray and to act in such a way that what happens up there starts to happen down here.

So, there you have it, right? A ground and a goal, an anchor and a sail. We find our power when we reach up, and we release God's power when we reach out. But, you know, there's one more thing, something I have left out thus far. We could miss it if we make our focus too horizontal rather than vertical, too moralistic rather than redemptive, too humanistic rather than theological. Let me press it a little further and go a little deeper.

What do I mean? What am I getting at here? Here's how I would put it, if I could state it in a sentence: *God has promised to reach out for those who reach up and reach out.*

I already mentioned how verses 19–20 frame verses 21–35, but there's more to it. Notice a theme emerge. Verse 26 says: *The Lord will be at your side.* Verse 32: *The Lord detests the perverse but takes the upright into his confidence.* Some translate that as counsel. Typically, the angels are the only ones who get to enjoy God's counsel (Ps 89:7). Verse 33: *The Lord's curse is on the house of the wicked, but he blesses the home of the righteous.* It's not just those who are righteous but those in the home of those who are righteous that God blesses. Verse 34: *The Lord mocks proud mockers but shows favor to the humble and the oppressed.* Curious, isn't it, that this specific verse makes it into 1 Peter 5:5 and James 4:5? Both of these texts are set in the context of Christians experiencing persecution. God has a way of humbling the proud and exalting the humble. God has a way of turning things around. Verse 35: *the wise inherit honor, but fools get only shame.* The apostle Peter said it well when he wrote that, through Jesus Christ, we have an inheritance "that can never perish, spoil or fade," an inheritance that is "kept in heaven" for us.

This text is tailored to teach us that *God will reach out to those who reach up and reach out.* It is not because God owes you or because this is transactional. One thing we know: we are debtors unto God. It's because God loves you that *God chooses to reach out to those who reach up and reach out.* It's not because God needs you. That would be presumptuous, wouldn't it? No, we need God.

We fulfill our ultimate purpose when we let God use us and work through us. God brings life to us. God reaches out to those who reach up and reach out.

Yes, there is a ground in this text and there is a goal, but there is also something more important. There is a God who grounds the ground and who guides the goal. Yes, there is an anchor in this text, and there is a sail, but there is also something more important. There is a God who made the sea and everything in it, who made the boat and everyone in it. Some call him the captain of our salvation. He's the one who sets the course and controls the tide, who quiets the winds and calms the waves. If there's anyone who knows a thing or two about reversal, it would have to be God, wouldn't it? Who else could turn an instrument of torture into a symbol of hope? Who else could turn faith into sight, prayer into praise, a cross into a crown?

Conclusion

The last couple of weeks, I have been trying to chase down a story that I heard about George W. Truett, the namesake of Truett Seminary, shortly after arriving here three years ago now. Truett was not a perfect person. From what I know of him, he would have been the first to tell us. What we do know, based on reports, is that he was a man who loved God, who loved people, who loved Baylor, and who loved the church for which Christ died.

When he was pastoring his church in Dallas, Dr. Truett would gather with the members of his congregation every Wednesday night for Bible Study and for a congregational dinner. Many, many people would come from far and wide those Wednesday nights. Among them were three young children named Ann, Jim, and Jerry Vardaman. The three kids came from a single-parent home. Their dad was not around. They were poor. Every week, they would try to cobble their money together while their mom worked so that they could ride the bus over to the church for the Bible Study and the congregational supper. Some weeks, they had enough money for the bus fare and the supper. Other weeks, they only had enough money for the bus fare and not the supper. So, they would go hungry.

One night, Dr. Truett spotted them along the wall watching other people eat. He went over and discovered that they hadn't eaten any supper at all unlike like everyone else there. When he saw them sitting along the wall, he said: "You can sit at my table with me as my guests. You can even have dessert tonight if you like."

When I corresponded with the widow of the late Jim Vardaman, she told me that, if Jim were still alive, he would have made sure to tell me that on that particular night, they got to eat *cherry pie*. They had never had cherry pie before. When the kids grew up, they all went to Baylor. Jerry became a professor of Archaeology first at Southern Seminary and then at Mississippi College. Jim became a well-respected and much-loved professor of History here at Baylor. Ann, later Ann Vardaman Miller, became a brilliant teacher, a dynamic professor of English who blessed generations of students. She dedicated one of her poems to Truett.

All of this happened, of course, because God is rich in grace and mercy. Indeed, God can do extraordinary things through ordinary people who are simply willing to trust Him. But there is also something else going on in this story. I wonder if something supernatural happened in the Fellowship Hall that night. Could it be that God reached out through a person who chose to reach up and reach out? I wonder if God looked down and said, "Here is someone I can use, someone who knows how to reach up and reach out. Here is someone with some real street smarts."

"Wisdom for Times of Uncertainty"[9] – Proverbs 30:24–28

Ralph Douglas West

Well, we come to the end of a series of messages from this beautiful book called Proverbs, and I want to end it by giving you some wisdom to live by "for the living of these days."[10] In Proverbs, chapter 30, there's a series of images that Agur uses, but I want to look at verse 24 and following and hear what he has to say to us about wisdom that you and I can use, and of the peculiar place where we can find it. Agur reminds us, beginning at verse 24:

> Four things on earth are small,
>   yet they are extremely wise:
> Ants are creatures of little strength
>   yet they store up their food in the summer;
> Coneys are creatures of little power,
>   yet they make their home in the crags;
> Locusts have no king,
>   yet they advance together in ranks;
> A lizard can be caught with the hand,
>   yet it is found in kings' palaces. (30:24–28)

This is the Word of God. It's a wisdom that you and I can live by "for the living of these days." Agur was around about twenty-six hundred years ago. You meet him in First Kings, chapter 4. He's one of the companions to King Solomon. He's not a Jew, he's not a Christian, and yet he lands in the middle of sacred Scripture. Just mentioning his presence and his company with Solomon made me begin wondering.

King Solomon had been given the gift of wisdom. It was supposed that he was the wisest man on the planet. No one's wisdom has risen to the equality that he had. And yet, he surrounded himself by people of wisdom. I guess that's why he's wise. It's because wisdom knows how to hang out with the wise. In fact, if you meet

---

9 Sermon preached on November 8, 2020, as part of the Proverbs Series, "God's Viewpoint on Our Situation," at the Church without Walls in Houston, TX.
10 Harry Emerson Fosdick, "God of Grace, and God of Glory."

somebody who's wise, you might do good to sit down, pull your seat next to them, and listen to them and learn from them. Wise people have quite a bit to say.

And wisdom can come to us in multiple ways. I also noticed that since Agur had been in the company of the king, there's that unique possibility that wise people always look for someone who may have lived longer or at least have experienced what they are attempting to experience. They scale up. For instance, children look up to their parents. Students look up to their teachers. The sick depend upon their physicians. The unlearned look for someone who's unlearned. There's always this kind of scaling up, looking up, trying to learn from someone who has walked where you might be planning to walk.

But that's not always the case, is it? There are some times that it's not the upward look but the downward glance that gains our attention. That's what happened to Agur. In his chapter where he talks about numbers and animals, it actually sounds as if he's taking a tour through a zoo.

When I was a boy, they had a little box of cookies they called "animal crackers." And we could hardly wait to tear into that little package to eat those cookies and name the animals we were eating. That's exactly what it looks like when you read chapter 30. Agur is taking you on an excursion through a zoo and pointing out different animals and showing what you can learn when you spend time with these creatures.

There are four that I am concerned with today. Amidst the many, [we'll focus on] just these four that give us wisdom and teach us how you and I can live differently—maybe victoriously, certainly wisely—in times like these. And these are times when you need wisdom, to know how to make the right moral and ethical choice for life. That's the importance of wisdom. There's something about wisdom. When it's wedded to knowledge, it produces understanding. And I want to be a person who's wise.

The wise person is not always the smartest person in the room, by the way. Wisdom begins with the fear of God. It's the beginning of real wisdom and knowledge—a reverence of God, recognizing who God is. And when we do that, God sometimes pushes all of our toys off the play table.

What does Agur say to us, then, about wisdom from these little animals? I've read them to you, so look back with me, beginning at verse 24, as he gives us these brief descriptions of animals. And you notice immediately how small they are, and yet they are wiser than some of us that claim to have wisdom. What can you learn from them?

The Ant

Well, he begins with the ant. The ants teach us what time it is in life. The ant is small. It's weak. It's powerless in many ways. And yet, it can carry ten to fifty times its body weight. But these colonies of ants with their leaders that go out and explore the ground do more than that. They are really known according to verse 24, that they are extremely wise because they always have their eye on preparation.

In the summer of life, which could be an image where things are going well, it's not where they gobble up everything that they gather. But in the summer they actually gather so they are preparing for the winter. They're aware that winter is coming, that there is going to be a climate change when they live beneath the ground. And so, they prepare while the sun is shining. The flowers are in bloom. The fragrance of spring is sprayed. And at that very moment, they do their best work. So they begin at that moment gathering for a time of uncertainty.

There are people that live properly. The ants do. Ant-minded people, like the ant, live properly. That is, some people that you know live only in what they have done. Their whole life is spent in past tense. When you talk to them, they're the people who take big trips and take lots of pictures. They have pictures, but they don't experience anything. They're the ones who will take a trip to London and take pictures of Big Ben and go to Westminster, but they'll never experience touching the bricks, smelling the wharf off the Thames, tasting the delicatessens of the culinary delights. They're the people who never pause long enough to experience the music. They captured it on pictures, for sure. They sit down and always tell you where they've been, but they never experience anything.

It's like the cat that went to London, and all it saw was the seat it hid beneath in the palace. It had missed everything else. It had missed the monarchs. It had missed the pageantry and ceremony. Don't you live your life that way, that you're always in the past.

But then there are others who live for the moment. When you talk to them, it's as if all life began with them, that nothing came before them and there is nothing after them. They are the center of their whole world. They are narcissistic. The only image of life they see is the reflection of themselves. And the only satisfaction that they're interested in is their own massaging. Don't live just for the now. When you do that, you find yourself trying to anesthetize yourself to cope with the challenges of the now. There are some people that live like that.

And then there are others who only live for the future. The only thing they see is tomorrow, like Annie when she made her way to Washington, D.C., and she was inspired when she met President Roosevelt. And she began to sing, "Tomorrow, tomorrow." Because he had inspired optimism in her, she saw tomorrow, tomorrow.

There's a time when you don't live in the past. There's a time when you don't live in the present. There's a time when you don't always have your focus on the future. You learn to live, and you live by wisdom.

You remember the song Dorothy would sing, "Somewhere Over the Rainbow." She saw a better world in a lullaby that had been sung to her. That's not how Christians live. We live backwards *and* forwards. We know something about the God of our history, but we also know the God of our present and we know the God of our future. Like the ant, prepare your life in such a way because the time will come, won't it, when you'll need to be prepared.

How do you do that, then? What would Agur say to us? What are we to be collecting if we are collecting anything? Because ants ... I heard someone say it this way (I wish the idea were mine): He said, "Ants go to picnics too; they just don't enjoy it like you do." Because while you're eating, ants are collecting. I used to tell our church, and I say it to you, "Pay now and play later, or play now and pay later." That's what the ants teach.

Because what every student that's listening to me now is faced with. I just said this to my children. We were talking. I said, "You've heard people talking about how "I function better under the type. I'm a procrastinator.' That's nothing to boast about. You don't function better under procrastination. You've just got to get it done, so you're always against the gun."

What do you collect then, in life? One thing you can collect is to spend time in the Scriptures, reading them. I know what you're saying: "Oh, that's just religious jargon." No, it will shape the way you look at the world—to collect Scriptures by reflecting on them and memorizing and rehearsing them. It's no wonder that the Hebrew writers would say to their children, "Write down these Scriptures and put them on the wall and hang them on your wrists and put them on your foreheads; and read them over and over and over." It'll change the way you look at life.

This week, when you talk to people, raise any issue and watch the way they respond. They'll recite a scholar here and a scholar there. And they'll recite everybody other than God's Word, as if the Word of God and the Scriptures are just something you tag on in life. Collect the Scriptures. It will help you because there's a winter that's coming, and there's an uncertainty when you won't have time enough to collect.

And winter comes. You don't have to invite it; it just shows up. And winter can tear up some things. It can break your home, it can break your health, it can break your job and career. When winter comes along, the only way you can manage the uncertainty of winter is to have something that is certain and stable enough to keep you strong in those uncertain times.

The Coney

I wish I could stay with the ant longer because you could preach all of your twenty-eight minutes today just talking about the ant. The writer changes direction now in verse 24, and he raises up another little creature. He says, "The ant gives you wisdom for the living of life today." And then he uses this coney. He said, "The coneys give you the wisdom for the security of life." These little animals, these small creatures, look like little chipmunks. They're smaller than a rabbit, just maybe the size of a hamster. And they're weak and little and vulnerable. They make good eating for all of the creatures in the desert, these coneys. Probably in some of your NIVs they call them "hyraxes." They're little, small, timid things.

Another description calls them "rock badgers." They're about the color of the rock, and when their predators come to devour them, they're able to blend in with the rocks, and they search out immediately for a crack in the crags, a crevice that they can crawl in. And so, any predator, like an eagle coming along, would have to rip apart the whole mountain just to get that coney.

I know now you have to see the image that Agur is giving us about this. He's saying that our only security is really in the Rock. Our real security is inside the stability of the Rock, a metaphor that the Bible frequently uses to speak of the power of God and God's ability to keep us. He's our Rock. He's our stability, but He's also our security. In the Scriptures, that's what some psalmists would call Him: He's our Rock.

I grew up in the African American preaching tradition, and there was nothing like the close of a sermon when the pastor would begin to cite these tropes of who God is. He would say, "He's bread when you're hungry, water when you're thirsty, and a bridge over troubled water." But then he would get to this, "He's a rock in a weary land."

> ... a rock in a weary land,
> A shelter in the time of storm.[11]

Each one of these were reinforcements to remind us of the security of who God is and what God provides for us.

That's what the coney teaches us. The coney reminds us that God is our Rock and God is our security.

The apostle Paul comes along, and he gets in on this in his writings to the Ephesians when he speaks of God as being our strong power. And in a world of insecurities and uncertainties, you ought to live like the ant and prepare so that you can be like the coney, and you have the experience of the saints who sing,

---

11 African American spiritual, "Jesus Is a Rock in a Weary Land."

Rock of ages, cleft for me,
Let me hide myself in Thee.[12]

That's where security is—in God. And there will come a moment when you will need that security. Let people laugh and mock you about your faith and what you believe. I can assure you of this much: the time will come when you'll need that security.

In times like these you need an anchor;
Be very sure, be very sure
Your anchor holds and grips the Solid Rock![13]

The Locust

There's another image here that Agur gives as he was talking to me, and he raises it and says, "Don't stop at the coney." He says, "I want you to look at a very strange picture, and that is of the locust." He says, "Locusts tell us where our power lies, where real power exists." Did you notice the one line, what it says? "The locusts have no king, but it knows where its power comes from." He knows who his power is.

The locusts don't get a good report throughout the Scriptures, do they? Even when the spies went out to look at the Promised Land, they said, "We are like grasshoppers in our own eyes" (Num 13:33). They don't get a really glorious picture. In fact, a grasshopper alone poses no threat. A grasshopper? Pop 'em away. They're little and insignificant. You can step on them or swat them away. But when they band together, they become a force that's so powerful, they can destroy anything in their wake.

In 1915, in Palestine the sound was heard before the locusts were seen. The sun at mid-morning was blackened by the swarm of millions of locusts that dropped their excrement throughout the ground. And when they were gone, every leaf from every branch was gone, even the bark from the trees, and the little, beautiful brown Palestinian children that were left beneath the trees when

---

12 Augustus M. Toplady, "Rock of Ages."
13 Ruth C. Jones, "The Solid Rock."

the swarm came were all devoured.¹⁴ It left nothing. Life was gone. In fact, boys from sixteen years of age to men of sixty years of age were commanded to collect seven pounds of locust eggs every day and bring them to the officials. It gives you some sense of the enormity of what happens when locusts work together. They have no leaders, but they organize and they have a strange way, without a king, of really getting together.

Biblical writers understood something about this. They give us a lesson that we can learn. It speaks of the awkwardness of a speech that many of us have incorporated in our Christianity, where we have personalized our Christianity and individualized it. This is anti-Christian, by the way. I challenge you to do your study. I challenge you to take issue with me. You can have a personal faith, but you can't have an individual faith. That's not biblical Christianity. As long as you start hearing Christians that begin to become divisive and dismissive, they're acting out of another kind of religiosity but not out of biblical historical Christianity.

You know what you don't find in the Scriptures? You never find the word "saint." It's always in the plural—"saints." You can have your personal faith in God, but you don't have it with God alone. You do it in community with people. You don't even have to be a careful reader of the Scripture; you come across this.

You meet Jesus, and what is the first thing the King of Kings and Lord of Lords does? He incorporates: He calls people to follow Him and partner with Him in ministry. That's the first thing that you meet in Jesus and His act of ministry. It's not just His preaching and teaching and healing. You find in Him that He's already made up His mind that "after prayer, I'm going to call some men and women to come and follow Me." I'm not trying to be inclusive. That's what you find in the Scriptures, that He didn't just work on one side of the street; He worked on both sides of the street. He had men and women that were in His ministry, and they served Him and He served them.

Paul, who left his handprint upon the New Testament church, didn't do anything that he did without the help of somebody else.

---

14 Note: the Palestinian locust plague of 1915 lasted from March to October, and it killed tens of thousands of Jews and Palestinians.

His most significant letter in helping the church understand the teachings of who God is, Romans, he entrusted in the hands of Phoebe. And that sister took that letter to its destination. When he needed an offering collected, he called Epaphroditus. When he needed to straighten out a schism in the church, he had to talk to Onesimus. When he needed someone to be a companion for him, he had Tychicus. When he needed missionary people on the journey, he had two sons in the faith: Titus, who stayed in Crete, and Timothy, who stayed over in Ephesus. He didn't do it by himself. He knew that one planted, another watered, but it was God who gave the increase.

I mean, even Marvel Comics has the good sense to know that you can't do what you do alone. Batman had to have Robin. The Lone Ranger had Tonto. The Green Hornet had Kato. The Black Panther had them bad sisters fighting on the side, down in Wakanda. It's an image that it seems everybody gets but the Christian.

You see, all of us face a temptation in life, and you're able to overcome it when you can face it with somebody else. That's the significance of being in community with one another. It's that I don't have to face my hurt alone. There's somebody else in the fellowship who has experienced that pain. That's what you learn from the locusts.

I think I heard them singing it this morning. I don't know; I got in after it. A. J. Showalter taught music, and two of his former students almost within a matter of days of each other, both lost their wives who had succumbed to death. They were seeking consolation, and this is how he responded:

What a fellowship, what a joy divine,
Leaning on the everlasting arms;
What a blessedness, what a peace is mine,
Leaning on the everlasting arms.
Leaning, leaning, ...
Leaning on the everlasting arms.[15]

---

15 Anthony J. Showalter and Elisha A. Hoffman, "Leaning on the Everlasting Arms."

And I'll tell you, it's the hardest lesson to get Christians to comprehend. It's that you were not called to be a solo act. You're not that wise. And that's what our God says. You're not wise enough to negotiate yourself out of these kinds of circumstances. Like the locusts, when you're together, there's a power generated that elevates you out of your circumstances.

The Lizard

Let me sit down now. He holds up one more image for us. He says, "This ant comes along and tells us, 'This is how you are to live life—in preparation and provision.' You may be vulnerable like the coney, but God will give you the security that you need. Like a locust, there's a power outside of yourself that God would give to you, and a power that's generated when we come together."

He says, "But finally, there's a lizard here. I want you to pay attention to this lizard because this lizard provides for us a peculiarity." It's the best word that I can describe for this lizard, of the wisdom that it teaches us. Maybe this is a better way to say it: The lizard teaches us how God works in reverse.

They have a screw that they call the "reverse screw," and it works exactly by the way that it's named—in reverse. Many times you find it on cranks or the pedals of a bike. When you turn it clockwise rather than counterclockwise, it releases the tension, and then it's in reverse. What ought to be tightening up loosens, and what ought to be loosening tightens.

It sounds like God, doesn't it? Because in this, he says, "There's a lizard. It's small enough to be caught in your hand, and yet it's found in kings' palaces." I want you to use your imagination. Let the childishness of your faith come alive again. You see that picture. The lizard can be caught in hand, and yet it's found in kings' palaces.

Where I live, I seem to live in the land of lizards. When I sit out back of my house alone, I'm never quite alone because some lizard is always lurking around. They're just everywhere. One year in Milan, sitting overlooking the garden in our hotel room, Ree and I were sitting there, and I thought, "Who packed this lizard to take a trip to come go with me?" I mean, what was he doing in the Four Seasons? I said, "Well, he must have bought a ticket and took a flight. Or nobody told him that he wasn't supposed to be there. He just showed up on his own."

Lizards have a way of rising up in the strangest places. They're small enough to be grabbed in the palm of your hand, and yet it rises up to places where some of us would say it doesn't belong. It would be a peculiarity, a paradox, a particularity. But that's how God works—lizards in kings' palaces, in places that you don't belong. And it works out.

Now, I know who I'm preaching to. In a majority of my church, you believe that whatever you have—and has been given to you—was not really given to you; you deserved it and were entitled of it. But I can't say that. My life is more like that of a lizard in that I'm surprised when I end up in certain places. I want to know, "How in the world did I get here?" I don't really belong there. I know the images people have of me when they encounter me, but I know me better than people know me. And I know that the most surprised person in the king's palace is the lizard in me.

I can't even begin to explain how I got there, and yet I hear the gospel of the Scripture preaching to me. I hear what Jesus says about life in reverse. He says, "West, you want to live? You have to learn how to die. You want to gain? You have to learn how to give it away. You want to climb up the ladder? You'd better know how to come down that ladder. You want to wear a crown? You'd better be ready to bear your cross. You want to be mature in Christ? Learn how to suffer, for suffering becomes eternal life."

And so, like the lizard, I'm that way. And I meet people ... my whole life now and my adulthood has been around people. And I make mental notations of people when I meet them of how they don't say it, but they say it—that they believe they deserve to be—and then you want to know why they're so sour. It's because they live a life that doesn't know anything about amazing grace. Grace people truly know, in the private moments of their lives, that when they get on their knees, they are able to say, "Lord, I don't deserve it." And it's only then that you're really, really ready to be used by God. That's what it means. That's what the lizard teaches us.

C.S. Lewis, in his sermon, "The Weight of Glory," makes this comment. He says, "Just think of the most ordinary Christian that you can think about—someone that annoys you, somebody that gets on your nerves. Think about that Christian, and then think of that Christian once they're in the presence of God. And once they're in His presence, imagine if that Christian could return back to earth and you saw them. He would look so much like God that you would be tempted to bow down and worship him."

That's what it means. That's what God reminds us. It's that none of us, like the lizard, have paid our fare to be in the palace of the king, and yet God puts you there for some reason. Learn now in your home during this season. I hope you're not wasting moments. Today would be a good day after worship to ask each other or call someone and say, "What are you most thankful for, lizard? Where has God put you where you know you don't deserve?" I can go down the line. I really can. I marvel daily that God could use the limitations of somebody like me.

Conclusion

I have to sit down now. You get the picture, I believe. Agur raises all of these great questions. And in these questions in chapter 30, he begins to raise a series of fours. You'll notice how he plays on numbers. And he asks these questions: Who's gone up to heaven, and who's coming down? Who's able to wrap the waters up in his cloak? Who's established the ends of the earth? Whose name is it?

Well, by now you don't have to be a Rhodes scholar to know the answer to some of those questions. You may not know them in depth, but you know the answer of whose name it is. He's got a lot of names. You can call Him El-Shaddai, or you can call Him El-Elyon or Elohim, or you can call Him Yawheh, Jehovah God. You can call him a lot of things. You can call Him what we've already talked about, some metaphors. But you can call Him Wonderful Counselor and Mighty God and Everlasting Father.

Whoever His name is, and whatever it is, it answers one of the series of fours in chapter 30 that Agur raises about the subject of dissatisfaction. And I close on that. When you look at around verses 14 through 16 and following, he gives us another series of fours. He looks at nature and sees grace in nature. And in that, he looks at things like death. He says, "Death is never satisfied; it's always hoping for the next body. A barren womb is never satisfied; it's always empty." He says, "The earth is never satisfied; it's always thirsting for water. Fire is never satisfied; it's burning up everything and turning everything into fuel."

Yet God said, "In a world of dissatisfaction, I'll send somebody to bring My message." When Jesus stepped on the scene, John the Baptist was preaching from the outside in, but Jesus said, "I'm going to preach from the inside out." He saw John, and John was preaching on revolution, but Jesus said, "I'm going to preach on redemption." He saw John, and John was going over there talking about the way down, and Jesus said, "I'm going to show you what it means to live on the way up."

God has called us to live a life of wisdom, to learn that if you can take wisdom and marry it over to knowledge, God will give you a good understanding. And the understanding that all of us need to know is who the real way, and who the real truth, and who the real life really belongs to. And it reminds us of this: if we just trust in the Lord, if we put our confidence in Him, He will guide our path, and He will make our lives straight.

Today, I thank God. I do thank Him for the lesson of the ant. "Lord, thank You for teaching me how to live right now. I don't want to wait until I die to learn how to live. I want to live now. But in my moments of uncertainty, thank You that You are my security. And when I'm powerless, thank You that You are my power. But most of all, thank You for Your grace, for Your grace saw me where I was, and grace led me to where I need to be. Grace looked beyond my faults and saw my needs."

> Amazing grace, how sweet the sound
> That saved a wretch like me.
> I once was lost, but now I'm found,
> Blind, but now I see.[16]

---

16 John Newton, "Amazing Grace."

Have I got company here today? Grace, amazing grace, wonderful grace, saving grace. Of all of you today who are saying, "I need to know how to live," look at the ant, look at the coney, the locust, and the lizard. And in their timid, vulnerable lives, they're wiser than the most-wise. And they are teaching us on how we can live.

I want you to live. I want you to have life with meaning and purpose, a life where you are now preparing for the not-yet. And we do that by coming and giving ourselves to the Lord Jesus Christ. He's the difference. He makes the difference. He's the one who changes what the future destination is all about. He is our security and our safety.

You know, a lot of strange things have been said about God over the last several months in this highly contested season of politics, especially from preachers from their pulpits, making false prophecies and claims. I shouldn't say it, but I've enjoyed ... I sat up longer than what I should have. I was just searching, listening to what these prophets, whose prophecies were wrong, were saying. And that's not my issue. I just wondered about what God had told them and what God demanded and who God cursed and who He was going to curse. And so, I was interested as a theologian of the church to see how they were going to work their way out. And they began to start backtracking. And one lady started talking about her prophecy ten years ago. Now last week it was one thing; this week it's something else.

I'm going somewhere. Listen, all of that foolish religious mumbo-jumbo doesn't mean a thing if you don't have a bedrock relationship with the Lord Jesus Christ. And when you have Him ... When you have Him, I celebrate everything that always happens. But the reason why I lose no sleep is because my hope ain't never been in Washington, D.C. My hope has never been in Austin, Texas. My hope is not there. My hope is in no one but the Lord Jesus Christ. And I say that, and I want you to know that for your life. Vote, because it is right to do that. Express yourself; that's why we're Americans. But when you start letting that determine how you're going to worship and love God, you've got a problem.

This morning I want to say, number one: I need Jesus Christ as Lord of life, yes, you do. Secondly, some of you need to turn from where you've put your trust in—the wrong things—and put it back in Christ Jesus. Because I'm going to tell you something that I know: one day, heaven and earth will pass away, but the Word of our God will stand forever. This is not escapism, this is not a cop-out. This is a matter of saying that if you put your hope in anything and anyone other than Christ, you're going to be dissatisfied. You want satisfaction, guaranteed? Put your hope in Christ Jesus. That doesn't mean that winter won't come and storms will cease. But it does mean that you have now security for the storm, and you have certainty for the future.

"Proverbs 31"[17] – Proverbs 31:1-31

Ingrid Faro

Where can wisdom be found? Where will you look for her? How will you know her deeds when you see them? Will you recognize her voice when you hear it?

These are the questions we have addressed throughout the book of Proverbs. In the last session on Proverbs 30, Dr. Billy Pohl shared with us an overview of the book of Proverbs. Chapter 30 provides an excellent review of the themes in which the key is humility based upon the fear of the Lord. That is the foundation of wisdom. So today, I will proceed to the book of Proverbs chapter 31. There, we will look and see that wisdom, firmly rooted in the fear of the Lord will make you a person of excellence, nobility, and godly character. *Let's pray: Father, open up your word to us. Teach us your ways so that we may be wise, well equipped to do all of your good works. Amen.*

Some years ago, as my son was in the process of returning to the Lord after five years of turning his back on God, he asked me these questions.

"Mom, why is this so hard? Why doesn't God make this easier?"

And I said to him, "My son, God is a good Father. He wants to pour out all His blessings on you. He wants your life to be good and rich. He wants your way to be smooth before you. He's a good Father and what He wants even more, He wants you to be wise. He wants you to grow up to be a strong and godly man. He wants you to be a person who leads others in the way of the Lord. This, my son, requires the fear of the Lord. This, my son, is a process that you must learn. God wants you to be like Him."

This is the processes that all of us must enter who seek to live godly in Christ. Today, as we look at this final chapter, this capstone of the book of Proverbs, we learn what wisdom looks like lived out, what the deeds of wisdom look like. This chapter teaches

---

[17] Sermon preached on April 28, 2016, as part of a Proverbs series at Trinity Evangelical Divinity School Chapel in Deerfield, IL. See https://www.youtube.com/watch?v=cN9BckJvZYE&t=696s.

us in two ways. First, [in] verses 1–9, through the exhortation of a mother to her royal son. Second, verses 10–31 teach us through an acrostic royal poem describing a woman of valor.

Turn with me now to Proverbs 31. We are going to walk through the passage and see what wisdom looks like rooted in the fear of the Lord and what it looks like to be a person of excellence, nobility, and valor.

"The words of king Lemuel,[18] the words of his mother, which his mother taught him" (31:1).[19] And she says:

> What, Oh my son, what oh son of my womb, and what oh son of my vows. Do not give your strength to women or your ways to that which destroys kings. It is not for kings, O Lemuel, it is not for kings to drink wine, or rulers to drink strong drink, for they will drink and forget what is decreed and pervert the rights of the afflicted. Give strong drink to him who is perishing and wine to him whose life is bitter. Let him drink and forget his poverty and remember his trouble no more. But you, open your mouth for the mute (or the voiceless), for the rights of those who are passed over. Open your mouth and judge righteously and defend the rights of the afflicted and needy. (31:2–9)

Starting with verse 2, are the words that the mother taught her royal son. In listening to her words, "Son of my womb, son of my vows," you can almost hear Hannah's prayer. "Lord, give me a son, and if you will, I will raise him to serve you. I will give him to you. He will be your servant." These are the vows a godly mother makes before the Lord as she is crying out for the son or daughter that she has not had. Of course, all are precious before the Lord, but here she is crying out, "Child of my womb." It seems, she makes these vows before the child was born. Just like with Timothy—the mother and his grandmother—to obey the teaching of his mother, and grandmother was his heritage. As it says in Proverbs 1:8 and 6:20, "My son, listen to the exhortation (or commandments) of

---

18 Some versions say, "King Massa."
19 Unless otherwise noted, all translations are the author's own.

your father. And do not forsake the Torah of your mother." Listen to what your mother teaches you.

In this passage, we will see how even the way we understand the word "mother" can be expanded. For this is her exhortation to the king and *to all of us* who would be noble in the Lord and live a life of excellence.

"Do not give away your strength."

And here is an important Hebrew word. There are some words in Hebrew that just don't translate well into English. Like the word *hesed*. English has multiple ways of translating that word. This word [in verse three] is one of those important words that have expansive meaning. So, I will use the Hebrew word and I want you to say it with me: *ha'yil* (pronunciation: ha'eel). Okay, if you can say *chutzpah*, you can say *ha'yil*. Say it again, "*ha'yil*." Alright, there are different ways that word is translated depending on the context. This word, *ha'yil*, is one of the most common words used for the "men of valor," David's warriors. They are "mighty men of valor." *Ha'yil* is a word that was used to describe them. *Ha'yil* is also used for people of excellence, people of wealth. Boaz was called a man of *ha'yil*. He was a person of wealth, influence, and excellence. He blessed his people and looked after them. He took care of all [the people], even the strangers, the aliens, and the people of unknown origin who were in his field. Boaz was a man of valor.

"Do not give your *excellence* (*ha'yil*) to women, or your ways to that which destroys kings."

In other words, do not forfeit your excellence for power plays over women. Do not forfeit your excellence to try and squash those who may seem like your opposition or to put them down, whether in a debate or in a discussion. That is unbecoming for a person of valor. "Don't do that," says Lemuel's mother to her son and God's Word to all of us.

For it is not for kings, for those of us who are part of a royal priesthood, to dull our minds with various things. There are many ways to dull our minds. We have far more creative ways these days of dulling our minds than they did back in the times of King Lemuel. There they had different wines, strong liquors, and beer. Now we have many more options. We dull our minds in any variety of ways, we do things just as a distraction, just for entertainment. We can even play 60 hours of a video game. When we do those things, it simply dulls our minds. When we dull our minds, we forget what God has decreed. Then we will pervert the rights of the afflicted, take advantage of others, and forget who we are as children of God. Do not dull your minds. When you do, stop it. Your mother says, "Stop it!"

I have a dear friend who just called me again this week. She is working through some really difficult things. She grew up in a family where the language is foul. Her family is in a horrible situation. She is the only believer. When she called me after she had gotten into a heated fight with a family member who was incredibly foul and cruel. She said, "I started to use foul language and then I remembered: no. Ingrid wouldn't say that." That reminded me of Lemuel's mother. Sometimes it's good to have that voice of a mother speaking to our conscience. But it is also the Word of God speaking to us. As Paul says repeatedly, "Follow my example."[20]

We need this voice. We need to hear these words. Don't dull your minds. Don't do it! Because you will forget God's Words and you may take advantage of other people.

If Christians knew that they could compromise their integrity, their excellence, by walking into a certain situation, and they knew that the Lord was right there watching them, would they walk into it? Would you walk into it?

Keep your mind sober. You are the child of the most-high God. Never forget that He is with you at all times. He is looking at everything you do. Knowing this, is part of the fear of the Lord. When we face compromising situations, these are the times when we need the fear of the Lord. In those times the fear of the Lord is right and it is clean. When you are about to do or say something and suddenly you remember, "What would the Lord say? He is watching. He is right here with me."

I've heard some really funny stories (but they're too embarrassing to share) of people who have been in situations where all of a sudden, they heard the Lord speak. It happened to my son's father. He heard the Lord say, "Walter, what are you doing?" Then

---

[20] 1 Cor 4:16; 11:1; Phil 3:17; 4:9.

he remembered, "The Lord is right here with me." We need to remember and not dull our minds.

Now, we also need compassion for those who do dull their minds. In Lemuel's day they did not have pain medications. When people are in deep despair and they are behaving improperly, just love them. Have compassion on them. But you, maintain your nobility. Come around those who are in despair. Comfort them and try to help raise them up. Be the mothers and fathers to the afflicted.

Then Lemuel's mother concludes, "Open your mouth for the mute, for the rights of all the unfortunate."

This means, speak up! Speak up for the voiceless. Speak up for those who don't have authority, power, or influence. Speak up for those who are too afraid to speak.

How many times have I missed opportunities to do that? Even right here on campus and certainly in different places in our community. I have seen people being belittled. It could be the cashier in a store. It could be anybody. We must use our voice for those who are silenced.

I heard it said once, and I think this is so wise, "One of the ways you know if you are a servant is the way you respond when you're treated like one." Similarly, one of the ways that you know if you are a servant is how you treat those who are serving you. We are all accountable to God. The primary title for a leader in the entire Old and New Testament is, "Servant of the Lord." We must maintain the fear of the Lord, knowing that we are His servants. We are serving Him, nobody else. We are accountable to One. There is One to whom we will give an answer for every word and every deed. Let the fear of the Lord guide us into wisdom [so that] we shut our mouth when we need to and open our mouth when the time is right. We must speak up for the voiceless and for the rights of those who are passed over.

From the Hebrew, I use the word "passed over." There are a lot of different translations for that word, but the word talks about those who have been passed over. Many of us feel that way at different times and situations in our lives. We feel that we have been passed over, overlooked. When we do, we know we can go to the

Lord as our Father. But when we see others who have been passed over, with godly wisdom and the fear of the Lord we are to speak up for them. There are so many situations right now, within our own churches and communities that fall into this.

The next verse says, "Speak up. Judge righteously. Do what is right and defend the rights of the afflicted and the needy."

How many times have we seen in our own churches those who are being abused and mistreated and we say and do nothing? Rather than doing what is right and godly in the fear of the Lord, we shut up to protect the mighty, the influential, and, perhaps, our friends. We are answerable to the Lord. We have to remember in the fear of the Lord, that God takes personally how we respond. He wants us to be wise in the fear of the Lord because God wants us to be like Him. God is the one who has taught those who are noble, those who are excellent, those who have valor, to protect and speak up on behalf of those who cannot. That is who God is. Just as he told the people as they were coming out of Egypt to remember that they were slaves in that land. Therefore, always treat the alien and stranger among you with kindness, take care of them, and protect them. Because the Lord says, the way you treat them is the way you are treating Me.

These are the words of King Lemuel's mother; these are the words of the Lord for us today.

Then Proverbs 31 continues with the final acrostic poem. I have many women friends who don't like this part of Proverbs. They say, "This is impossible! A woman of valor, who can find? No one can, because no woman exists like this one." Some take offense when people bring up Proverbs 31. Look at this first verse.

"A woman of excellence, who can find? Her worth is far above jewels"[21] (31:10).

There is a precedent from the Word of God to interpret Proverbs 31 as a metaphor for wisdom. The question is, "Is this a metaphor for wisdom? Or, is this about a woman of valor?" The answer is: Yes. It is both. That is a little bit of comfort, perhaps, especially for women who say, "You're just picking on me saying that I should be better." Set all of that aside. Because Psalm 112 is also an

---

21 Jewels could be translated as rubies or corals.

acrostic but it is for men. "How blessed is the man who fears the Lord." That evens the score, if you like, that there's also a Proverb for men. Proverbs 20:6 asks, "A faithful," or "A trustworthy man, who can find?"

So the question is: Who can find this person of excellence? Can we find anyone? Hopefully, we can find a woman of valor and a trustworthy man.

"For her wealth is far above jewels."

Here you can see where understanding the correspondence between wisdom and the person comes in. The value of this woman is above jewels. In Proverbs 3:15 and 8:11 wisdom is said to be sought for more than jewels. Wisdom is to be treasured more than jewels. Wisdom is a tree of life and those who hold on to her and cling to her will be blessed.

We can equate this description in Proverbs 31 to a metaphor for wisdom. But do not miss the fact that the Word of God has chosen to embody wisdom as a woman, a woman of valor. Do not forget that. For men who feel intimidated by this description of a woman or for women who say, "I can't do all of those things," maybe you cannot do them all or be all of those, but you can be any of them. You can be more of them. Men and women do not forget this is the Word of the Lord which is profitable for teaching, reproof, correction, and training in righteousness.[22] Do not forget that and so interpret this text simply metaphorically. God is providing us with a message here that if we miss it, we are missing His voice.

The one great precedence for tree-hugging is considering wisdom as the tree of life. Hold on to her. Hold on to wisdom. That is biblical tree hugging. Hold on to the tree of life. Wisdom is the voice of God which we come to through the fear of the Lord. It produces fruits of righteousness and goodness. Then the text goes on.

Now for verses 11 through 18, that's *bet* through *tet*. Note that each line begins with a verb. Then verses 19 and 20 form the center, the turning point of the poem.

In the first half of this acrostic, we have verbs beginning every line and we have many uses of the word *kaph*, meaning hand or

---

22 2 Tim 3:16.

palm. There are a lot of strong military terms used in these first eight verses.

In the second half of this acrostic there is a change. We no longer have verbs beginning every line. Instead, we have references to clothing. The clothing of the household, the clothing of the tongue, and so forth. This second half turns more to the internal life, life within the home and community.

Some of the qualities here—through the verbs—reveal that wisdom takes action. The fruit of wisdom which is rooted in the fear of the Lord produces deeds. We see that, of course, in the book of James as well. Notice some of these actions.

She is trusted. This says she is trusted by the heart of her husband. So, some women and men will say, "Well this text doesn't apply to me, because it is just referring to a wife." Or they will ask, "Why does this only apply to married women?" That's because most translations read, "An excellent wife, who can find?" Right? It is true that in Proverbs there is a reference to an excellent wife as a crown to her husband. But there is one other place in the Old Testament where we find this phrase in verse 10 "*esheth ha'yil*," woman of excellence. It is in Ruth 3:11. When Ruth is gleaning in the barley fields, she is called an "*esheth ha'yil*," a woman of valor. She is a stranger, single, a widow with no children. She has no nobility, no wealth, no influence, no husband, and no children. But what she has is a godly character. Ruth is an "*esheth ha'yil*." She is a woman of valor. That means every woman is to be a woman of valor because it is who we are. Men, as we discussed, and women are to be people of valor. We saw that in King Lemuel. Before we have any influence, any family, any power, or any money, it is who you are in the Lord that will determine who you will become. Will you be a godly man or woman? Or will you be a person who has been conformed to this world, who is using their power wrongly, who is not producing godly fruit of righteousness?

Esheth ha'yil, a person of valor. It applies to Ruth, so it applies to all of us women. What a fabulous example in the genealogy of the Messiah, the ancestor of King David. She was an *esheth ha'yil*. The city recognized her as a woman of valor, but only because of her character and courage.

"The woman of valor is trusted by her husband and they have no lack of gain" (31:11).

That word translated "gain" in Hebrew is *shalal*. It is usually used in military terms. There are a tremendous number of military terms in this passage. This is reflected in the Septuagint as well describing a woman of valor. I might be contextually insensitive saying this, but the Greek word used in the Septuagint to translate *esheth ha'yil* is a manly woman, or a heroic or courageous woman.

In our context some of the images we get of godly women, women of wisdom, are not the image in this text. We sometimes think that a godly woman may say, "Oh, excuse me, do I have permission to speak now?" This is not what you see in Scripture. That is not an *esheth ha'yil*. "Oh, I'm sorry I opened my mouth. I'll go hide now." No! That is not a woman of valor. You single young men should be looking for a woman of valor. Be like Boaz. A wise man will cling to and seek a strong woman the same way he will seek wisdom because that is the kind of woman who speaks with wisdom. That woman will speak out and not be afraid. She will open her mouth.

"She deals out good and not evil" (31:12).

The text deals out another verb. She does not return evil, even if evil has been done to her. She deals out good. The word here is not just the word for doing good it is the word for dealing out. The word can mean recompense, payback. Even if evil is dealt to her, she will pay back good because her trust is in the Lord. She will do good all the days of her life.

She also seeks quality. Now in these days we do not generally seek wool or flax (31:13), so we have to contextualize those commodities. But she seeks quality in the things that she is looking for, in the things she buys for the household, and in the things she buys for herself. She also works with her hands and works with delight. This is not just, "Oh I gotta go do this today." She does her work with delight. She enjoys what she does, just as the Lord does. This is a word that is used for the Lord delighting in His creation. She delights in the things that she is creating. She searches for the best stuff and takes great delight in that. This is the description of wisdom.

Men, don't be turning off here. Because this is also a metaphor for wisdom. This is the kind of person that you look for, work with, be around, and to have around you. Gather around you people who exemplify these qualities. Gather them in your churches, your businesses, your families, and in your communities. Do not be afraid of women. There are some men that I see who are so afraid to even speak to a woman because she might be the woman of folly. Ugh, no! Come on. Do not do that.

Verse 14 continues: a woman of valor "is like a merchant ship."

She is abundant. All of us who love to go to Trader Joe's can relate to this woman. Understanding this metaphor is a little bit easier. She brings her food from afar. There is a delight, enjoyment, abundance, and fullness.

"She considers a field and buys it from her earnings. She plants a vineyard" (31:16).

It is perfectly fine according to the Bible for a woman to work outside of the home. We have to realize that is contextualizing this passage because in those days it was before the Industrial Revolution. The Industrial Revolution is something we tend to read into the text. But that was millennia after this text was written. It was an agricultural community. Yes, there were cities, but the household and even the household codes reflect that setting. The household was a business. As Dean Graham Cole has pointed out in some of his classes, the woman was frequently, basically, the master over the household. It was her responsibility to take care and make sure that the household was being run well.

"She girds herself with strength. She makes her arms strong" (31:17).

Again, military terms. The words of strength, strong. She continues to work.

The core of this is verse 20. "She spreads out her palm to the poor and she extends her hand to the needy, and she is not afraid for her household" (31:20–21a).

This is the same kind of exhortation that was given to King Lemuel. "Defend the rights of the afflicted and needy" (31:9).

Now in the following verses, 21–28, we see her clothing her household so that they are warm and not afraid. She laughs at days to come because she has planned ahead. She is taking care of things. Wisdom trusts in the Lord and wisdom plans. She, herself, is dressed royally. Her husband is known at the gates when he sits among the elders. Strength and dignity are her clothing. She is clothed well but her main clothing is her strength and her dignity. She strategically looks after the household. She is not idle. And, her children rise up and bless her.

Children can be also the children within the church or children in the community. I have many, many children. We have to see beyond the mentality that says "Us four, no more." That is not the biblical context, community is. We are a community and we have responsibility one for another.

Her husband also praises her and says, "Many have done nobly, (excellently, with valor, *ha'yil*), but you excel them all. Charm is deceitful, and beauty is vain. But the woman who fears the Lord she shall be praised" (31:29–30). There we see that word again, *ha'yil*. It forms an inclusio with verse 10.

Give her the fruit of her hands. And let her hands praise her in the gates. The woman who is being productive and godly and using her gifts fully for the Lord, who is speaking out and helping and doing it with the joyful strength, nobility, and character, she is to be praised among those who have governing authority within the community. So, let us not forget that this is the Word of the Lord. This is what the Lord wants us to know. Wisdom, firmly rooted in the fear of the Lord, will make you a person of excellence, nobility, and valor. Wisdom that is rooted in the fear of the Lord will help you to recognize those who have that spirit of excellence within them. If you silence or shut down the women, you're silencing the voice and acts of God.

Here I asked, "Lord, Lord, why did you choose women so much in Proverbs? Why did you choose the voice of a woman for the voice of wisdom?" And I'm out of time to go into it much more deeply but let me give you just a few hints that you can trace.

One of the funny ones is in Job 38 when God is talking about His creation, and He refers to the ostrich whom he deprived of wisdom. The ostrich lays her egg and flaps away joyfully not realizing that someone can come behind her and trample it. That is a mother deprived of wisdom. But a woman who has wisdom, a person of leadership, that mother will care for her young. They will not just flap away joyfully. Those within the church, the poor, the needy, the alien, they will care for them because that is the quality of God. That is reflecting the image of God, being His representative.

The imagery of mothers is used elsewhere in Job 38:3 and 29. The imagery of God as a mother is used in Isaiah 40–45 and 66. I was just reading parts of someone's dissertation on that because God says, "I brought you forth from the womb. Even though a mother may forget her suckling child I will not forget even into your old age. I will be there for you."[23]

There is a mother quality of God. He is our Father, but He also portrays Himself as a mother who protects and nourishes. And boy, you haven't seen anybody as fierce as a mother who is mad about somebody who is trying to mess with her child. I never knew anger like the time someone came after my son. But not only him, but also for those whose stories I have been entrusted with. Don't mess with my kids, because I will come after you!

That is the heart of God for each of us. That is the heart that we need to have for one another. Let's pray: *Heavenly Father, we thank you so much for your great love. Lord, teach us wisdom. We desire to learn wisdom. We desire to know your voice. We desire to know your ways. Lord, continue to work your ways, your will, your wisdom in each of our hearts so that we can continue to grow to become people of valor, people of excellence, and people of nobility. So that everywhere we go, we are representing you. That everywhere we go people will look at us and say, "There is God!" For Lord, we remember that what we do to the least we have done to you. So, Lord, give us your grace. You have given us your spirit. Enlighten our minds and our eyes so that we will be more and more like you. We give you praise in Jesus's name. Amen.*

---

23 Isa 49:14–15.

Bibliography

Alcántara, Jared E. *The Practices of Christian Preaching: Essentials for Effective Proclamation.* Baker Academic, 2019.

Alter, Robert. *The Art of Biblical Poetry.* Basic, 2011.

Armstrong, Elizabeth. *Robert Estienne: Royal Printer.* Cambridge University Press, 1954.

Arthurs, Jeffrey D. *Preaching as Reminding: Stirring Memory in an Age of Forgetfulness.* Intervarsity, 2017.

Arthurs, Jeffrey D. *Preaching with Variety: How to Re-Create the Dynamics of Biblical Genres.* Kregel, 2007.

Auger, Peter. *The Anthem Dictionary of Literary Terms and Theory.* Anthem, 2010.

Augustine. *Confessions.* Oxford University Press, 2008.

Barton, John. *Reading the Old Testament: Method in Biblical Study.* Westminster John Knox, 1984.

Bellah, Robert N., Richard Madsen, William N. Sullivan, Ann Swidler, and Steven M. Tipton. *Habits of the Heart: Individualism and Commitment in American Life.* University of California Press, 1996.

Benson, Joshua, and Mark Clark, eds. *Stephen Langton's Prologue to the Bible.* Oxford University Press, 2021.

Bland, Dave. *Proverbs and the Formation of Character.* Cascade, 2015.

Blocher, Henri. "The Fear of the Lord as the 'Principle' of Wisdom." *TynBul* 28 (1977): 3–28.

Brown, William P., ed. *Character and Scripture: Moral Formation, Community, and Biblical Interpretation.* Eerdmans, 2002.

Brown, William P. "The Didactic Power of Metaphor in the Aphoristic Sayings of Proverbs." *JSOT* 29.2 (December 2004): 133–54.

Brueggemann, Walter. *The Prophetic Imagination.* Fortress, 2001.

Buttrick, David G. *Homiletic: Moves and Structures.* Fortress, 1987.

Camp, Claudia V., and Carole Fontaine. "The Words of the Wise and Their Riddles." Pages 127–59 in *Text and Tradition: The Hebrew Bible and Folklore.* Edited by Susan Niditch. Semeia Studies. Scholars, 1990.

Clements, Ronald E. "The Good Neighbor in the Book of Proverbs." Pages 209–28 in *Of Prophets' Visions and the Wisdom of Sages: Essays in Honour of R. Norman Whybray on his Seventieth Birthday.* Edited by Heather A. McKay and David J. A. Clines. JSOTSup 162. JSOT, 1993.

Clifford, Richard J. *Proverbs: A Commentary.* Westminster John Knox, 1999.

Clifford, Richard J. "Your Attention Please! Heeding the Proverbs." *JSOT* 29.2 (December 2004): 155–63.

Costas, Orlando E. *The Church and Its Mission: A Shattering Critique from the Third World.* Tyndale House, 1974.

Crenshaw, James L. "A Proverb in the Mouth of a Fool." Pages 105–16 in *Seeking Out the Wisdom of the Ancients: Essays Offered to Honor Michael V. Fox on the Occasion of His Sixty-Fifth Birthday.* Edited by Ronald L. Troxel, Kelvin G. Friebel, and Dennis R. Magary. Eisenbrauns, 2005.

Curtis, Edward M. *Interpreting the Wisdom Books: An Exegetical Handbook.* Kregel, 2017.

Davis, Ellen F. *Proverbs, Ecclesiastes, and the Song of Songs.* Westminster Bible Companion. Westminster John Knox, 2000.

Dixon, W. Macneile. *The Human Situation.* Edward Arnold, 1954.

Escobar, Samuel E. *Changing Tides: Latin America and World Mission Today.* Orbis, 2002.

Estes, Daniel J. *Handbook on the Wisdom Books and Psalms.* Baker Academic, 2005.

Estes, Daniel J. *Hear, My Son: Teaching and Learning in Proverbs 1–9.* New Studies in Biblical Theology. Eerdmans, 1997.

Fox, Michael V. *Proverbs 1–9.* AB 18. Yale University Press, 2000.

Frydrych, Tomáš. *Living Under the Sun: Examination of Proverbs and Qoheleth.* VTSup 90. Brill, 2002.

Gibson, Scott M., and Matthew D. Kim, eds. *Homiletics and Hermeneutics: Four Views on Preaching Today.* Baker Academic, 2018.

Gilbert, Kenyatta R. *Exodus Preaching: Crafting Sermons about Justice and Hope.* Abingdon, 2018.

Gilliard, Dominique DuBois. *Subversive Witness: Scripture's Call to Leverage Privilege.* Zondervan, 2021.

Harper, Lisa Sharon. "Will Evangelicalism Surrender?" Pages 19–30 in *Still Evangelical? Insiders Reconsider Political, Social, and Theological Meaning.* Edited by Mark Labberton. Intervarsity, 2018.

Hatton, Peter T. H. *Contradiction in the Book of Proverbs: The Deep Waters of Counsel.* Ashgate, 2008.

Heath, Chip, and Dan Heath. *Made to Stick: Why Some Ideas Survive and Others Die.* Random House, 2007.

Hernández, Dominick S. *Proverbs: Pathways to Wisdom.* Abingdon, 2020.

Holmes, Jasmine L. *Mother to Son: Letters to a Black Boy on Identity and Hope.* Intervarsity, 2020.

Holmgren, Fredrick. "Barking Dogs Never Bite Except Now and Then: Proverbs and Job." *The AThR* 61.3 (1979): 341–53.

Houston, Walter J. "The Role of the Poor in Proverbs." Pages 229–40 in *Reading from Right to Left: Essays on the Hebrew Bible in Honour of David J. A. Clines.* Edited by J. Cheryl Exum and H. G. M. Williamson. JSOTSup 373. Sheffield Academic, 2003.

Howatch, Susan. *Glittering Images: A Novel*. Fawcett Columbine, 1994.
Hubbard, David. *Mastering the Old Testament: Proverbs*. WBC 15a. Word, 1989.
Jonker, Peter. *Preaching in Pictures: Using Images for Sermons That Connect*. Abingdon, 2015.
Karr, Mary. *Lit: A Memoir*. Harper Memorial, 2009.
Kidner, Derek. *Proverbs*. Kidner Classic Commentaries. IVP Academic, 2008.
Kim, Matthew D. *Preaching to People in Pain: How Suffering Can Shape Your Sermons and Connect with Your Congregation*. Baker Academic, 2021.
King, Martin Luther, Jr. "Why Jesus Called a Man a Fool." Pages 141–64 in *A Knock at Midnight: Inspiration from the Great Sermons of Reverend Martin Luther King, Jr.* Edited by Clayborne Carson and Peter Holloran. Warner, 2000.
Kugel, James. *The Idea of Biblical Poetry: Parallelism and Its History*. Yale University Press, 1981.
LaRue, Cleophus J. *I Believe I'll Testify: The Art of African American Preaching*. Westminster John Knox, 2011.
Lewis, C. S. *A Grief Observed*. Harper One, 1967.
Lewis, C. S. *Mere Christianity*. Harper One, 2001.
Long, Thomas G. *Preaching and the Literary Forms of the Bible*. Fortress, 1989.
Longman, Tremper, III. *How to Read Proverbs*. Intervarsity, 2002.
Longman, Tremper, III. *Proverbs*. BCOTWP. Baker Academic, 2015.
Lucas, Ernest C. *Proverbs*. Eerdmans, 2015.
Maclaren, Alexander. *Expositions of Holy Scripture*. Vol. 6. Eerdmans, 1952.
Marno, David. "Tone." Pages 1441–42 in *The Princeton Encyclopedia of Poetry and Poetics*. Edited by Roland Greene, Stephen Cushman, Clare Cavanagh, Jahan Ramazani, Paul Rouzer, Harris Feinsod, David Marno, and Alexandra Slessarev. Princeton University Press, 2012.
Maslow, Abraham Harold. *The Psychology of Science: A Reconnaissance*. Harper & Row, 1966.
Mathews, Alice. *Woman of Strength: Living the Best Life Possible for God in This Broken World*. Our Daily Bread, 2020.
McKenzie, Alyce M. *Preaching Biblical Wisdom in a Self-Help Society*. Abingdon, 2002.
McKenzie, Alyce M. *Preaching Proverbs*. Westminster John Knox, 1996.
McKenzie, Alyce M. *Wise Up! Four Biblical Virtues for Navigating Life*. Cascade, 2018.
Murphy, Roland E. *The Tree of Life: An Exploration of Biblical Wisdom Literature*. Eerdmans, 2002.

Newsom, Carol A. *The Book of Job: A Contest of Moral Imaginations.* Oxford University Press, 2003.

Newsom, Carol A. "Woman and the Discourse of Patriarchal Wisdom: A Study of Proverbs 1–9." Pages 142–61 in *Gender and Difference in Ancient Israel.* Edited by Peggy L. Day. Fortress, 1989.

Northcutt, Kay L. *Kindling Desire for God: Preaching as Spiritual Direction.* Fortress, 2009.

Ogden Bellis, Alice. *Proverbs.* Edited by Sarah Tanzer. Wisdom Commentary 23. Liturgical, 2018.

Padilla, C. René. "Evangelism and the World." Pages 116–33 in *Let the Earth Hear His Voice.* Edited by J. D. Douglas. Worldwide, 1975.

Padilla, C. René. "Hacia Una Definición de La Misión Integral [Toward a Definition of Integral Mission]." Pages 19–34 in *El Proyecto de Dios y Las Necesidades Humanas: Más Modelos de Ministerio Integral En América Latina.* Edited by C. René Padilla and Tetsunao Yamamori. Kairos, 2000.

Padilla, C. René. *Misión Integrál: Ensayos Sobre El Reino y La Iglesia.* Nueva Creación / Eerdmans, 1986.

Padilla DeBorst, Ruth. "An Integral Transformation Approach." Pages 41–67 in *The Mission of the Church: Five Views in Conversation.* Edited by Craig Ott. Baker Academic, 2016.

Perdue, Leo G. *Proverbs.* IBC. Westminster John Knox, 2000.

Perdue, Leo G. *The Sword and the Stylus: An Introduction to Wisdom in the Age of Empires.* Eerdmans, 2008.

Rah, Soong-Chan. *Prophetic Lament: A Call for Justice in Troubled Times.* Intervarsity, 2015.

Rauschenbusch, Walter. *A Theology for the Social Gospel.* MacMillan, 1917.

Ryken, Leland. *How to Read the Bible as Literature.* Zondervan, 1984.

Ryken, Leland. *Words of Delight: A Literary Introduction to the Bible.* Baker Academic, 1993.

Salinas, J. Daniel. *Taking Up the Mantle: Latin American Evangelical Theology in the 20th Century.* Langham Partnership, 2017.

Saayman, Willem, ed. *Embracing the Baobab Tree: The African Proverb in the 21st Century.* University of South Africa, 1997.

Sandoval, Timothy J. *The Discourse of Wealth and Poverty in the Book of Proverbs.* BibInt 77. Brill, 2006.

Shaw, Karen L. H. "Wisdom Incarnate: Preaching Proverbs 31." *Journal of the Evangelical Homiletics Society* 14 (2014): 44–53.

Shigematsu, Ken. *Survival Guide for the Soul: How to Flourish Spiritually in a World That Pressures Us to Achieve.* Zondervan, 2018.

Spolin, Viola. *Theater Games for Rehearsal: A Director's Handbook.* Northwestern University Press, 1985.

Sunukjian, Donald R. *Invitation to Biblical Preaching*. Kregel, 2007.
Taylor, Kate. "College Admissions Scandal: Former Pimco CEO Gets 9 Months in Prison in College Admissions Case." *The New York Times*, October 8, 2021. https://www.nytimes.com/news-event/college-admissions-scandal.
Thurman, Howard. *Jesus and the Disinherited*. Beacon, 1976.
Troeger, Thomas H. *Creating Fresh Images for Preaching*. Judson, 1982.
Troeger, Thomas H. *Imagining a Sermon*. Abingdon, 1990.
Waltke, Bruce K. "Does Proverbs Promise Too Much?" *AUSS* 34 (1996): 319–36.
Waltke, Bruce K. *The Book of Proverbs: Chapters 1–15*. Vol. 1. NICOT. Eerdmans, 2004.
Waltke, Bruce K. *The Book of Proverbs: Chapters 15–31*. Vol. 2. NICOT. Eerdmans, 2005.
Waltke, Bruce K., and Ivan D. V. De Silva. *Proverbs: A Shorter Commentary*. Eerdmans, 2021.
Weeks, Stuart. *Instruction and Imagery in Proverbs 1–9*. Oxford University Press, 2009.
West, Cornel, with David Ritz. *Brother West: Living and Loving Out Loud, A Memoir*. Smiley, 2009.
Wilson, Paul Scott. *Preaching as Poetry: Beauty, Goodness, and Truth in Every Sermon*. Abingdon, 2014.
Wilson, Paul Scott. *Setting Words on Fire: Putting God at the Center of the Sermon*. Abingdon, 2008.
Witherington, Benjamin, III. *Jesus the Sage: The Pilgrimage of Wisdom*. Fortress, 2000.
Wolters, Al. *The Song of the Valiant Woman: Studies in the Interpretation of Proverbs 31:10–31* Paternoster, 2001.
Yoder, Christine Roy. *Proverbs*. AOTC. Abingdon, 2009.
Yoder, Christine Roy. *Wisdom as a Woman of Substance: A Socioeconomic Reading of Proverbs 1–9 and 31:10–31*. BZAW 304. de Gruyter, 2001.

Scripture Index

Genesis
  47:6   62

Exodus
  2:24–25   144
  3:7–9   144
  18:21   62
  18:25   62
  23:4–5   170
  33:11   77
  34:6   117

Numbers
  13:33   182
  14:18   117

Deuteronomy
  6:1–9   81
  24:17–18   84

Joshua
  1:14   156
  6:20   34

Judges
  11:1   62

Ruth
  1:16–17   77
  2:1   62, 161
  3:11   62, 161, 198

1 Samuel
  2:4   62
  16:7   110
  20:8   77
  20:23   77
  20:42   77

2 Samuel
  11   138
  12:1–14   134

  23:20   62

1 Kings
  4:29–32   5
  11:1–6   138
  17:1–3   134
  18–19   139
  21   139

2 Kings
  15:20   62

2 Chronicles
  26:13   156

Nehemiah
  1:4   34
  9:17   117

Esther
  5–7   139

Job
  6:14   77
  38   201–02
  38:3   202
  38:29   202

Psalms
  18:2   26
  23   26, 126
  23:1   26
  27:1   27
  39:5   123
  71:18   81
  78:4–6   81
  86:15   117
  89:7   146, 173
  100:3   42
  103:8   117
  112   196

145:8	117	3:3	32, 112, 115, 168
		3:4	18
Proverbs		3:5	18, 113, 115
1:1	4	3:7	20, 137
1:1–3	109	3:9	18
1:1–4	139	3:9–10	19, 74, 133
1:1–7	4, 109, 139	3:11	79, 167
1:1–9:18	6	3:11–12	18
1:2	140	3:12	30
1:3	135, 140	3:13–14	158
1:4	5, 140	3:14–15	32
1:6	4	3:15	51, 158, 197
1:7	20–21, 63, 159, 168	3:18	31
		3:19–20	18
1:8	79, 167, 192	3:21	79, 168
1:8–8:36	50	3:21–22	167–68
1:9	15, 32, 168	3:21–35	145–47, 165–76
1:10	79	3:22	32, 169
1:10–19	53	3:23–25	169
1:11–14	158	3:26	18, 170, 173
1:15	31, 79	3:27	138, 170
1:17	29, 32	3:27–31	145
1:19	31	3:28	84, 171
1:20–21	9, 50, 159	3:29	84, 171
1:20–32	158	3:30	171
1:20–33	160	3:31	171
1–9	xix, 19, 32, 50, 54, 71, 113, 161, 167	3:32	18, 173
		3:33	18, 173
		3:34	144, 173
2:1	79, 167	3:35	11, 116, 173
2:5	18, 20–21, 63	4:4	113
2:6	140	4:6	116
2:7	31	4:9	15, 32, 194
2:8	140	4:10	79
2:9	140	4:14–19	53
2:12–15	53	4:19	52
2:17	18	4:20	79, 113
3	172	4:20–27	113, 116
3:1	79, 112, 167	4:21	113
3:1–6	13	4:23	112–13
3:1–20	42	4:26–27	115

5:1	79	8:1–2	54
5:1–22	53	8:1–3	9, 50, 159
5:6	52	8:1–36	50
5:7	79	8:3	159
5:15–20	81	8:4	51
5:18	121	8:5	51–52
5:19	31, 47	8:9	9
5:20	79	8:10–11	51
5:21	18	8:11	32, 51, 158, 197
6:1	79	8:13	20
6:1–5	86	8:15	134
6:1–6	84	8:17	51
6:3	79	8:17–19	158
6:5	32, 47	8:18–21	51
6:6	56	8:19	32, 51
6:6–8	47	8:21	158
6:6–11	86	8:22	51
6:7–8	102	8:22–31	18, 160
6:9	56	8:23	51
6:10–11	30, 57	8:24	51
6:12–15	53	8:25	51
6:16–19	18	8:26	51
6:19	119	8:30	51
6:20	79, 192	8:32	79
6:20–29	53	8:32–34	51
6:21	32	8:35–36	51
6:22	116	8–9	50, 52
6:23	8, 31	9	98
6:27–28	121	9:1	160
6:29	81, 84	9:1–3	54
6:32	115	9:1–12	50, 54
6:32–33	81	9:2–5	159
7:1	79	9:3	54
7:1–27	53	9:4	54
7:3	32	9:6	52, 54
7:7	52, 115	9:10	20, 159
7:11	52	9:13	52, 54
7:22–23	30	9:13–18	50, 54
7:23	52	9:14	54, 160
7:24	79	9:15	54
7–9	29	9:16	54

9:17	54	12:20	115
9:18	54	12:22	18, 119
10:1	4, 36, 80, 136	12:24	56
10:1–3	136	12:26	84
10:1–21:31	6	12:27	56
10:2	136–37	13:3	100
10:3	19, 136	13:4	56
10:4	56, 86, 94	13:14	32–33, 43
10:4–5	56	13:19	117
10:9	29	13:22	62
10:11	32	13:24	79–80
10:15	133	13:25	133
10:18	117	14:4	47
10:21	117	14:5	119
10:22	19, 94	14:12	20, 115, 125
10:23	117	14:14	115
10:26	56–57	14:20	133
10:27	19	14:20–21	98
10:29	18	14:21	84, 147
10–15	36	14:23	57
11:1	18, 86, 119	14:25	119
11:1–4	36	14:27	32
11:2	28, 29	14:30	115, 152, 171
11:4	125	14:31	18, 102, 122, 145
11:6	32	14:33	115
11:9	84	14:35	134
11:12	84	15:1	100
11:15	86	15:3	18
11:20	18, 115	15:6	95
11:22	30	15:7	117
11:24–25	86	15:8	18
12:1	8	15:8–9	18
12:2	18	15:9	18
12:4	81	15:11	18
12:9	7	15:13	115
12:10	48	15:15	78, 115
12:11	56	15:16	7, 95
12:13	32	15:16–17	7
12:17	100, 119	15:17	40
12:18	29, 37–38, 100	15:19	56
12:19	100, 119	15:20	80

15:23	100	17:20	115
15:25	18, 122	17:21	117
15:26	18	17:22	115
15:27	94	17:23–25	115
15:29	18, 98	17:28	100
15:30	115	18:4	32
15:32	28	18:7	32
16:1–6	18	18:9	57, 86
16:3	28	18:10	18
16:4	125	18:13	100
16:5	18	18:16	94
16:7	19	18:22	19, 81, 121, 162
16:8	7	19:1	7, 117
16:9	18	19:5	119–20
16:10	134	19:6	134
16:11	86	19:9	119
16:12	135	19:11	101
16:13	120	19:12	29, 48
16:13–15	134	19:13	80–81, 121
16:16	7, 32, 98	19:14	19, 81
16:19	7, 144, 147	19:15	57, 86, 133
16:20	18	19:17	18, 102, 147
16:22	32	19:18	79–80
16:24	100	19:21	18
16:25	125	19:22	7
16:28	76	19:24	14, 56, 86
16:29	84	19:26	80
16:31	29	19:27	79
16:32	7	20:2	48, 134
16:33	18	20:3	117
17:1	7	20·4	56–57, 86
17:2	135	20:6	197
17:3	18, 117	20:7	79
17:5	18, 102, 147	20:8	134
17:7	117	20:9	115
17:9	76	20:10	18, 86
17:12	7, 48	20:12	18
17:14	39	20:13	57
17:15	18	20:14	86
17:17	8, 76	20:15	32
17:18	84, 86	20:16	86

20:16–19	28	24:12	117
20:20	80	24:13	79
20:23	18	24:21	20, 79, 134
20:24	18	24:23	4
20:26	134–35	24:26	30, 120
20:28	134–35	24:28	84
20:29	29	24:30	56
21:1–2	18	24:33–34	57
21:2	117	25:1	4
21:3	18, 122	25:1–29:27	6
21:6	32	25:2	18
21:9	7, 31, 81, 121	25:2–6	134
21:13	147	25:5	135
21:14	94	25:9	31
21:19	7, 31, 81	25:11	30, 100
21:25	56–57	25:12–14	30
21:25–26	56, 86	25:15	31, 100, 134
21:28	119	25:18	14, 84
21:30	18	25:19	8
22:2	18, 102	25:24	7, 81, 121
22:5	32	25:26	14
22:6	74	25:28	34
22:9	102, 147	26:1–2	48
22:11	76, 134	26:4	93, 96
22:12	116	26:4–5	94, 96
22:13	56–57	26:5	93, 96
22:15	79–80	26:7	4, 117
22:16	147	26:9	4, 117
22:17	4	26:11	117
22:17–24:34	6	26:11–12	48
22:19	18	26:13	56–57
22:22–23	18, 122	26:13–16	86
22:29	57	26:14	30, 56
22:26–27	86	26:14–15	56
23:13–14	79–80	26:15	14, 56
23:15	79	26:16	56
23:19	79	26:19	84
23:22–25	80	26:28	100
23:26	79	27:2	100
23:26–28	81	27:5	7, 77, 101
23:27	29	27:5–6	100

27:6	12, 77	30:22	117
27:8	13	30:24	47
27:9	12, 76	30:24–28	47, 176–190
27:11	79	30:29–31	47
27:13	86	30:32	117
27:14	84, 100	31	58–65, 155–63, 191–202
27:15	81, 121		
27:23–27	48	31:1	4, 192
27:24	9, 29, 125	31:1–9	6, 135
28–29	18	31:1–31	191–202
28:2	134	31:2	79
28:3	147	31:2–9	192
28:4	18	31:6	29
28:6	7	31:8–9	100
28:7	80	31:9	200
28:8	86, 147	31:10	32, 81, 157–58, 196, 201
28:10	32		
28:15	48	31:10–31	4, 6, 59–65, 196–202
28:19	56		
28:24	80	31:11	59, 199
28:25	18	31:11–12	158
28:27	147	31:12	59, 199
29:3	80	31:13	59, 63, 157, 199
29:4	135	31:14	200
29:5	84	31:14–15	159
29:6	32	31:15	59
29:11	117	31:16	157, 200
29:13	18	31:17	59, 157, 200
29:14	147	31:18	59
29:15	19, 79–80	31:19	59, 63, 157
29:17	79–80	31:20	63, 157, 200
29:23	143, 147	31:20–21	200
29:25	15–16, 18	31:21	59
29:26	18	31:21–28	200–01
30:1	4, 18	31:22	59
30:1–33	6	31:23	159
30:5	13, 18–19	31:24	59
30:9	18	31:25	59, 157
30:11	80	31:26	59
30:14	147	31:27	59
30:17	80	31:28	59

31:29–30	201	23:25–26	114
31:30	63–64, 159	25:42–43, 45	172
31:31	157, 159	26:48–50	77

Ecclesiastes
2:10–11	124
10:10	62
12	138

Mark
8:36	110
10:42–44	88
10:43	171

Isaiah
30:6	62
66	202
40–45	202
49:14–15	202

Luke
3:19	134
4:23	xix
6:20	133
6:45	114
10:37	85
11:39	114
11:46	116

Jeremiah
15:13	62, 156

Ezekiel
12:22	xix

John
1:12–13	82
1:29	27
6:35	27
10:7–9	27
10:10	124
13	77
15:13–14	78
15:15	78
18:25–27	77

Daniel
6	139

Hosea
7:11	115

Amos
7:10–17	134

Romans
3:21–22	141
3:21–26	140
8:14	82

Joel
1:3	81
2:13	117

1 Corinthians
1:18–31	163
4:16	194
5:7–8	26
11:1	194

Jonah
4:2	117

Matthew
2:16–18	138
6:24	133
12:34	114

Galatians
2:10	133

3:26	82
4:19	111

Philippians
3:17	194
4:9	194

Colossians
1:15–20	160
2:8	163
3:1–3	26

1 Timothy
6:20–21	163

2 Timothy
3:16	197

Hebrews
9:27	124

James
1:20	140–41
2:23	77
4:5	145–46, 173
4:13–14	123–24
5:1–6	133

1 Peter
5:5	145–46, 173

2 Peter
2:20–22	48

1 John
3:1–3	82

Revelation
5:5–6	27

Subject Index

a fortiori argument 12–13
acrostic, *see poetics*
Agur, sayings of 4, 47, 176–179, 181–182, 187
Alcántara, Jared E. 116 n. 10, 147 n. 22, 165
Alter, Robert 7 n. 18, 117 n. 15
animals 25, 46–50, 65, 66, 177–178, 180
   ant 47, 49, 178–180, 188–189
   caring for 48
   dog 25, 48–49
   flocks 48
   pig 28, 30–31, 33–34
   wild 49
   see also
      Waltke, Bruce
      West, Ralph Douglas
answer proverb 3, 3 n. 4, 7, 7 n. 18, 8, 12, 13, 47, 56, 63, 93, 93 n. 1, 96, 97, 99, 101–102, 112, 117–118, 120–121, 138
anthology xix, 4, 5, 60, 73, 93, 95, 104
antithetical parallelism, *see poetics*
Arthurs, Jeffrey D. xv, xviii, 22, 70 n. 2, 72, 72 n. 7
Bellis, Alice Ogden 6 n. 13, 53, 53 n. 8, 54 n. 9, 66, 156 n. 2
Bland, Dave 8 n. 21, 9, 99, 110–111, 120
brevity 5–8, 8 n. 20, 10–12, 14, 15, 28, 93, 119, 123–124
character, *see integrity*
characterization 46, 49, 52, 55, 62, 65, 152, 157
   foolish ones 11, 36, 46, 46 n. 1, 48, 51, 55, 65, 73, 80, 93, 96, 116, 117, 127, 136, 141, 145 n. 20, 146, 158, 159, 161, 166, 168, 172, 172 n. 8, 173, 189

Proverbs 31 Woman 155–157, 162
   sluggard, the 14, 30, 46, 46 n. 1, 47, 55–58, 65, 133 n. 7
   Wife of Noble Character, the 46, 58, 59, 62, 62 n. 19, n. 20, 63, 65, 156, 193
   Woman (Dame) Folly 14 n. 30, 29, 46, 50–55, 65, 158, 160–161, 200
   Woman Wisdom 5 n. 8, 14 n. 30, 29, 46, 50–55, 65–66
   see also
      animals
      Kidner, Derek
      Matthews, Alice
      Newsom, Carol A.
      Waltke, Bruce
      Wolters, Al
children, *see thematic approach*
choices, *see timing*
Christ (Christological) 12, 26, 48, 51–52, 77, 88, 111, 127, 130, 140–141, 141 n. 15, 145–146, 173, 174, 186, 189–190, 191
   see also, Longman III, Tremper.
Clifford, Richard J. 118 n. 17, 136, 137
contextualize xviii, xix, xx, 9–16, 34, 61, 73, 87, 88, 98–102, 112, 116, 122, 132, 145, 148, 153, 162, 163, 193, 199, 201
   modern xviii, 3, 9, 13, 14, 33–35, 37, 37 n. 17, 46, 48, 52, 59, 62, 64, 70, 72, 75, 78–79, 81 n. 19, 82–83, 85, 93, 94, 97, 102–103, 105, 118, 132, 138–139, 142, 169
   see also
      genre
      Long, Thomas G.

contradiction(s), *see timing*
contrast   3, 7, 9, 12, 15, 32, 33, 35–38, 48, 54, 57, 63, 75, 80, 99–101, 119–120, 140 n. 15, 142
  see also, poetics
Costas, Orlando E.   129–130
Curtis, Edward M.   3 n. 5, 8 n. 21, 72, 134
Davis, Ellen F.   5, 156 n. 2
dialectical structure   101–103, 105
elaboration   7, 7 n. 18, 8, 12, 12 n. 28, 13, 119 n. 20, 120, 125
Elohim, *see God*
Escobar, Samuel E.   129–130, 172
eshet hayil   62, 62 n. 19, 156, 157–159, 161, 193, 198, 199, 201
Estes, Daniel J.   22, 113 n. 4, 128, 134 n. 9
Estienne, Robert   72
ethical dimension   118 n. 17, 136, 137, 148, 177
ethics, *see integrity*
Faro, Ingrid   60, 67, 191–202
fear of the Lord   7 n. 18, 16, 18, 20–21, 32, 61, 63–64, 95, 125, 137, 159, 167, 168, 177, 191–192, 194–201
figurative language   xix, 7, 13–15, 27–28, 41, 102 n. 10
  hyperbole   14, 56, 121
  image(ry)   xx, 6 n. 13, 7 n. 16, 8, 13–16, 25–43, 47–49, 53, 53 n. 8, 55–56, 62, 79, 82, 102 n. 10, 107–108, 111, 117, 117 n. 14, 121, 156, 167, 176, 178, 181, 182, 184–186, 199, 202
  irony   29
  metaphor   xix, 7, 14, 26–32, 42, 47, 63, 70 n. 2, 80, 82, 118, 181, 187, 196–197, 200

metonymy   29, 37, 37 n. 16
personification   5 n. 8, 14, 14 n. 30, 29, 50, 52, 54, 55, 62, 156–161
simile   xix, 7, 14, 28–30, 34, 39, 42, 47, 117
synecdoche   29
types   1, 12, 49, 55, 57
  see also
    characterization
    poetics
Weeks, Stuart
Fox, Michael V.   127, 170
Frydrych, Thomáš   118
gapping   4 n. 6, 6
genre   xviii, xix, xx, 1–23, 41, 60, 61, 93, 113, 148, 152
  form and function   1, 2, 4, 4 n. 5, 7, 7 n. 18, 8, 10, 19 n. 43, 27, 32 n. 6, 33, 37, 47, 50 n. 5, 52, 79, 82, 95, 96, 103, 108, 118, 153, 161, 162
  genre-conscious   xviii, xix, xx, 9, 16, 21, 46, 62, 65, 70, 76, 79, 84, 86, 92, 96, 102, 108, 119, 120, 121, 131, 153
  wisdom literature   2, 3, 4 n. 5
Glittering Images   107
God
  Elohim   18, 187
  Jesus   27, 48, 51–52, 75, 77–78, 85, 87–88, 114, 129, 131, 133, 141 n. 15, 148, 160, 166, 171–173, 183, 186, 188–190
  main actor   16, 17, 74
  Yahweh   18, 20 n. 45, 54
gospel   63–65, 75, 82, 116, 129, 130, 148, 172, 186
motivations   82, 100 n. 9
(The) Greatest Showman   65
Harper, Lisa Sharon   142

hayil, *see* eshet hayil
Hays, Rebecca W. Poe 60, 67, 155–163
Hernández, Dominick S. 79, 89
Holmes, Jasmine L. 114
Houston, Walter J. 133 n. 7, 135, 149
humor xx, 14, 15, 56
imagery
   controlling 13
   Dixon, W. Macneile 26, 27, 42
   marketing 25, 26
   path(way) 8, 13, 21, 31, 32 n. 6, 52, 54, 56–57, 79, 86–88, 101, 111, 113, 115, 116, 119, 125, 140, 161, 167
   sermons 13
   see also
      animals
      figurative language
      Lucas, Ernest C.
      Troeger, Thomas H.
injustice 100, 138–139, 144
integrity xx, 36, 86, 107–128, 194
   exterior life 108, 111, 118–119, 128
   inner life 109–110, 112, 114, 116, 123, 127
   see also
      Bland, Dave
      Frydrych, Thomáš
      Kidner, Derek
      Lewis, C. S.
      Longman III, Tremper
      Waltke, Bruce K.
Jeopardy 69
Jesus, *see* God
justice 18, 76, 84, 94 n. 3, 110, 122, 129–150, 160, 172
   compassion 76, 117, 131, 142, 172, 195

justicia 140
marginalized (the) 76, 138, 145, 147, 149
reaching out 171, 172
those who do justly 122, 138, 145–148
see also
   Costas, Orlando E.
   Escobar, Samuel E.
   Padilla, C. René
Karr, Mary 75
Kidner, Derek 17, 46, 80, 89, 115, 168
Kugel, James 12 n. 28
Langley, Kenneth J. xv
Langton, Stephen 72
Lausanne Covenant 129, 130, 172
lazy, *see* characterization
leadership, *see* thematic approach
legalism, *see* moralism
Lemuel, King 4, 29, 192–196, 198, 200
Lewis, C. S. 85, 118, 119, 123, 171, 187
living with "the dash" in mind 112, 123–126, 128
Long, Thomas G. xix, 2 n. 2, 8 n. 19, 9–10, 16 n. 32, 40, 152
Longman III, Tremper 2 n. 3, 4 n. 5, 5 n. 8, 7, 7 n. 18, 12, 21 n. 46, 36, 37 n. 15, 51, 54, 56, 58, 59, 62 n. 18, 62 n. 20, 70, 81 n. 19, 94 n. 3, 103, 115
Lucas, Ernest C. 4 n. 7, 6, 8 n. 21, 28, 53
lyrics, song 5, 33–34, 62, 65, 74, 104, 152
main idea (sermon) 10, 12–15, 38, 43, 145
marriage (marry) 19, 50,

53–54, 60, 73, 80–83, 121, 134, 162–163
see also, thematic approach
Mathews, Alice 64
McKenzie, Alyce M. xv, 74, 98, 104, 105 n. 12, 151–152
memorability 3, 5, 8–10, 14–16
memorization 29 n. 4, 39, 61, 71, 72, 180
misión integrál 130, 148
modern proverbs, *see proverbs*
moralism (moralistic) 12, 16 n. 32, 17, 58, 74, 111–112, 123, 140, 173, 177
Mother's Day 58, 64
music 65, 73, 95, 104, 178, 184
Newsom, Carol A. 19 n. 43, 50–51, 66, 169
obedience 18–21, 23, 77–78, 116, 134, 159–160, 192
Ogden Bellis, Alice 6 n. 13, 53, 54 n. 9, 66, 156 n. 2
opportunities, *see timing*
Padilla, C. René 129, 130, 149, 172
parenting, *see thematic approach*
path(way), *see imagery*
pedagogy (teaching) 8, 15, 19, 22, 50, 61, 72, 81, 95, 114, 166, 167
see also, memorization
Perdue, Leo G. 19, 20 n. 45, 36 n. 13
personification, *see figurative language*
poetics xix, 5–9, 10, 12–14, 15, 27, 39, 41, 47–48, 50, 56, 60–65, 131 n. 5, 161
acrostic 4, 6, 61–62, 64, 192, 196–198
antithetical parallelism 7, 7 n. 18, 12, 36, 37

parallelism xix, 6 n. 13, 7, 8, 12, 15, 28, 121
see also
Longman III, Tremper
Witherington III, Benjamin
poor, those who are, *see justice*
promise 48, 51, 73–74, 86, 116–117, 120, 121, 125, 169, 171
divine 11, 13, 116, 122, 143–148, 149, 173, 196
see also, Waltke, Bruce
prophetic preaching, *see justice*
proverbs
authorship 4 n. 7, 5, 27, 79
definition 2 n. 1, 4, 5
dimensions of 118 n. 17, 135–139, 148, 150
mashal 3, 3 n. 5, 4
modern 3, 9, 102, 103, 105
purpose 6, 17, 22, 42, 71, 77–78, 94, 109–112, 125–126, 139–143, 144 n. 18, 161–162
story of 19, 33, 38–41, 49
structure 2 n. 2, 4, 12–13, 71, 101–102, 113, 161–162
see also, Long, Thomas G.
Proverbs 31 Woman, *see characterization*
reaching out, *see justice*
relationship(s) 71, 75, 77, 68–88, 110–112, 125
with God 19, 64, 66, 74, 189
with humans 17, 19, 62 n. 20, 75–76, 78–79, 103, 119
with those who are poor 18 n. 37, 29, 59–60, 63, 98, 102, 102 n. 10, 122, 133, 145, 147, 200
religious dimension 137
restatement 11, 12
rhetorical questions 35, 97, 121
Ryken, Leland 8, 72–74

sapiential dimension 118 n. 17, 132, 136, 137
Solomon (King) 4, 4 n. 7, 5, 109, 138, 139, 161, 176
spiritual growth 82, 110–112, 116–118, 171
suffering 83, 83 n. 25, 142, 144, 186
tension in preaching 53, 95, 97, 100–102, 105, 133
thematic approach 69–90
   cautions about 73–75, 89
   children 47, 74, 75, 78–81, 113–114, 180, 201
   family 9, 19, 46 n. 1, 71, 75, 78–83, 88, 144, 151, 167
   friendship 9, 13, 73, 75–78, 84
   leadership 38–39, 49, 55, 73, 75, 86–89, 111, 135, 143, 178, 183, 195
   neighbor love 75, 83–85, 90, 153, 170, 171
   see also
      Arthurs, Jeffrey D.
      Curtis, Edward M.
      Hernández, Dominick S.
      Kidner, Derek
      Longman III, Tremper
      McKenzie, Alyce M.
      Ryken, Leland
      Wilson, Paul Scott
threefold dimension of Proverbs 118 n. 17, 136
Thurman, Howard 144
timing 41, 52, 63, 71–73, 80–81, 83, 89, 93, 109, 111, 139, 195
   choices 21, 37, 38, 46, 50, 54–55, 77, 92–93, 98–99, 101–103, 161, 177
   contradiction(s) 93–98, 101, 102, 105, 133

see also
   Arthurs, Jeffrey D.
   Estes, Daniel J.
   Longman III, Tremper
   McKenzie, Alyce M.
   Witherington III, Benjamin
   Yoder, Christine Roy
topical sermon, see thematic approach
Troeger, Thomas H. 13 n. 29, 41, 42
Waltke, Bruce K. 6 n. 13, 7 n. 16, 9, 23, 18 n. 38, 37, 37 n. 16, 37 n. 17, 48, 50 n. 5, 58, 73 n. 9, 102 n. 10, 115, 121, 143, 145 n. 20
Weeks, Stuart 30, 32 n. 6
West, Cornel 110
West, Ralph Douglas 49, 143, 176–190
Wife of Noble Character, The, see characterization
Wilson, Paul Scott 17 n. 34, 42, 74
wisdom 3–6, 8, 9, 15, 18, 21, 31, 32, 38, 39, 42, 46–48, 70, 74, 79, 83, 92, 94, 95, 97–99, 101–102, 103, 105, 108–109, 113, 116, 137, 139–141, 148, 151–152, 157–161, 167–168, 176–178, 180, 188, 191, 192, 196–199, 201 202
Wisdom Literature, see genre
Witherington III, Benjamin 4 n. 8, 29 n. 4, 36, 96
Wolters, Al 61, 66
women in Proverbs 52–53, 58–65, 81 n. 19, 155, 160, 162, 198, 201–202
   adulterous 29, 52, 53
   negative assessment of 53, 196, 197

positive assessment of 53, 53 n. 8, 63, 201

Yahweh, *see God*

Yoder, Christine Roy 19 n. 43, 66, 89, 95

young people (young men) 5, 9, 38, 39, 47, 53, 63, 66, 70, 71, 80–81, 83, 86, 91, 114, 120, 121, 134 n. 9, 140, 157, 166

CPSIA information can be obtained
at www.ICGtesting.com
Printed in the USA
LVHW030030181222
735447LV00006B/341